The
Enduring
Ghetto

David R. Goldfield
C. W. Post College of
Long Island University

James B. Lane
Indiana University

J. B. Lippincott Company
Philadelphia
New York
Toronto

The
Enduring
Ghetto

Sources and Readings

ISBN 0-397-47285-4

Printed in the United States of America

Cover design by Janice Wojcik

1 2 3 4 5 6 7 8 9

Library of Congress Cataloging in Publication Data

Goldfield, David R.   1944-   comp.
    The enduring ghetto.

    Includes bibliographical references.
    CONTENTS: Claghorn, K. H. The foreign immigrant in New
York City, 1800-1870.—Jakle, J. A. and Wheeler, J. O. The forma-
tion of Dutch ghettos in Kalamazoo, Michigan.—Murphy, R. Boston's
Chinatown. [etc.]
    1. Cities and towns—United States—Addresses, essays, lectures. 2.
Minorities—United States—Addresses, essays, lectures. 3. Slums—
United States—Addresses, essays, lectures. I. Lane, James B., 1942-
    joint comp. II. Title.
HT123.G574   301.45'1'0973   73-4833
ISBN 0-397-47285-4

To Marcia
and Toni

Preface

We want to acknowledge the professional secretarial work done by Mrs. Rosalie Zak and Mrs. Florence Crane. The efficient and courteous library staff at both Indiana University Northwest and C. W. Post College facilitated the collection of materials for this work. Mr. Conrad Schoeffling, director of interlibrary loans at Post College deserves special recognition.

We are grateful for the advice given us by Robert P. Pace of J. B. Lippincott Company and the timely suggestions of Professor Neil Betten of Florida State University and copyreader Cynthia Harris.

We are indebted to Raymond Smock, Dennis Burton, Pete Daniel, and Walker Rumble for their stimulating company during our days at the University of Maryland. Any flash of brilliance in thought or prose in our introductory essay is probably due to the careful and expert guidance of our mentors and friends Dr. George H. Callcott and Dr. Horace Samuel Merrill.

Finally, we dedicate this book with love to our wives, who share our concern for the people who inhabit America's ghettos.

DAVID R. GOLDFIELD
JAMES B. LANE

Contents

Contents

Introduction

The Ghetto:
An
American
Experience

MILLIONS OF WHITE Americans trace their New World origins to a tenement, a row house, or a shanty in a ghetto. Millions of nonwhite Americans currently reside behind invisible ghetto walls. The ghetto has transcended race, religion, and national origin to form a shared heritage between former and present residents. While the various ethnic and racial groups had unique experiences in their respective ghettos, certain features of ghetto life remained common for all. A study of the American ghetto in historical context can illuminate common bonds and perhaps suggest a means for eliminating the enduring ghetto from American life.

The formation of American ghettos resulted from a combination of coercion by established society and voluntary decision by the ghetto residents. The word "ghetto" originated with the creation of a distinct neighborhood as a means of social control over sixteenth-century Venice's Jewish population. Three centuries later the object of social control was still a prominent force in ghetto formation. For example, an American commission report in 1895 talked frankly of isolating "the undesirable classes . . . in specific neighborhoods. They can then be the more easily looked after." Investigators have commonly employed the metaphorical concept of a prison or a walled enclosure to describe the ghetto. Black sociologist Kenneth Clark, discussing Harlem, defined the ghetto as "the restriction of persons to a special area . . . on the basis of skin color."[1]

The ghetto, however, also held attractions for the potential inhabitant. It was the residence of friends and family—*paesani, landsleit,* and soul brothers and sisters. It was often the area most proximate to the available employment opportunities. Familiar institutions from native districts and states checkered the ghetto landscape. A church or synagogue, mutual aid societies, and common language and customs promised the newcomer to the American city some security and comfort. Thus the American ghetto was both a residence of minimum choice and a welcomed home.

The conflicting forces involved in residence selection underscored the paradoxical nature of American ghetto life. In the ghetto the best and worst of society vied for dominance, with the mental and physical health of the inhabitant at stake. A young citizen of Spanish Harlem summarized his feelings of repulsion and attraction toward his ghetto, or barrio: "There's a lot of pain and a lot of sorrow, but underneath there's also a lot of glory and happiness and love."[2]

The pain and sorrow engendered by the debilitating physical aspects of ghetto life, such as overcrowded housing, have been close companions to all ghetto residents. An inspector for the New York Association for the Improvement of the Condition of the Poor complained in 1881 that "there was such a demand for tenements that landlords could demand high rents without granting repairs at all." Observers recognized overcrowding "as a serious evil" as early as 1834. In early twentieth-century Philadelphia 39 percent of the rooms in three ghettos contained two or more inhabitants. High density continues to characterize the inner city today, although in many northern cities the population has begun to drop, since blacks are not moving in as fast as whites are leaving. Black rural migration is shifting slightly to such southern cities as Atlanta and New Orleans. Urban renewal, the major federal program designed, in the words of the Housing Act of 1949, to provide all Americans with homes that they can afford, has demolished far more housing units than it has constructed. Usually the victims rather than the beneficiaries of urban renewal, the poor have moved, to a large degree, to other slums and have had to pay higher rents than previously.[3]

Dilapidated housing was an inevitable consequence of overcrowding. Turn-of-the-century reformers directed their most vigorous efforts toward housing reform as the best means of eradicating vice, crime, and disease. Legislation provided only temporary salve to the decay of ghettos. The Brownsville section of Brooklyn, an enduring ghetto that has successively housed Irish, Jews, Negroes, and Puerto Ricans, resembles today the remains of a great conflagration. The center of St. Louis contains similar relics, including the ruins of a housing project just eighteen years old.[4] A 1904 report by Philadelphia housing reformer Emily Dinwiddie, taken out of its context, would be indistinguishable from current descriptions of disrepair:

> In one house the roof and ceiling over the top floor were so broken that the occupants of the rooms had a clear view to the sky. . . . [T]he floor was broken, the plaster cracked or falling, the window sashes out . . . many halls and stairs were also in bad condition . . . [and] dirt and rubbish accumulated in the cellars unchecked. . . . The lighting of halls and stairs was extremely bad in the majority of cases.[5]

The poverty of the people mirrored the squalor of the physical environment. Ghetto residents, like their accommodations, were neglected and exploited. Menial labor, low wages, underemployment, and unemployment have been common specters of ghetto life. In 1897 the Commissioner of Labor issued a report on the Italian ghetto in Chicago. More than 9 percent of the Italians of working age were unemployed, compared with 4.5 percent unemployment for the rest of the population. An additional 22 percent of the eligible Italian work force was underemployed and forced to use savings, credit, or charity to augment meager paychecks. Finally, the average yearly earning of an Italian ghetto family was $308—one-third less than the national average of $462. Current statistics on the chronic job crisis in black communities are comparable to the findings of the Labor Commissioner seventy years ago. In 1970 Harlem blacks earned an average of $6,604 a year, considerably more than the average black income, but, nevertheless, one-third less than the national average of $9,867. The unemployment rate in the black ghetto was 14.1 percent, while the national average was 6 percent.[6]

Frightful living conditions and inextricable poverty combined to crush the ghetto resident. The psychological afflictions of ghetto life—what one turn-of-the-century observer termed "tenant-house rot"—struck down the young and lingered for a lifetime. Isolation, disillusionment, and hostility were and are as ubiquitous as cracked plaster, rats, and high rents. One New Yorker viewed the human waste entombed in a nineteenth-century Irish ghetto and wrote: "so much misery, disease, and wretchedness . . . huddled together and hidden by high walls, unvisited and unthought of. . . . Alas! human faces look so hideous with hope and self-respect all gone."[7] A century later a reporter presented this view of Spanish Harlem: "Its [the ghetto's] walls are invisible; they are inside the mind. . . . Most of the young people . . . are bitter and disillusioned. They sit on the stoops because there isn't anything else most of them can do."[8] Certain individual portraits of despair stand out from the wreckage of shattered hopes: the young mother of Mulberry Street consoled by drink, as her children go hungry; and Diana Perea, a Denver Chicano, who attempted suicide at thirteen, became a prostitute at fifteen, and died from a drug overdose at nineteen.[9]

Given the psychological erosion of ghetto life, it is hardly surprising to find unusually high levels of violence and hostility within the ghetto walls. Statistics have chronicled the criminality of ghetto residents. The Irish accounted for 55 percent of the arrests made by New York City police in 1859, though they comprised one quarter of the population. Blacks and Puerto Ricans accounted for 75 percent of the arrests in New York City in 1969, while comprising less than one-third of the population. The statistics merely reported the tip of the iceberg of hostility. In fact, the selective habits of police in enforcing some laws against the dispossessed while ignoring the wrongdoings of racketeers, rent gougers, and businessmen have alienated ghetto residents to the brink of revolt.[10]

Mass violence has always lurked close to the surface of the ghetto. A half-century ago ghetto reformer Jacob A. Riis warned: "The sea of a mighty population, held in galling fetters, heaves uneasily in the tenements." Robert Williams, former NAACP official and black revolutionary in exile, issued a similar warning in more strident rhetoric, but with equally compelling logic: "When a brutally oppressed and dehumanized people are denied the peaceful channels through which to activate redress, and when their peaceful petitions are answered with ruthless violence, the only resource left to them is to meet violence with violence." The ghetto was and is an environment dangerous both to its inhabitants and to outsiders.[11]

The pathology of the ghetto has served as a continuing anomaly tarnishing the ideals of American life. Because the ghetto has symbolized poverty in a country of plenty, discrimination in a nation of equals, disease in a country of advanced technology, and crime in a society predicated on law, many Americans have preferred to ignore its existence or blame its ills on its victims. Ghetto residents have frequently been forced to suffer attacks upon the ghetto's boundaries similar to the nineteenth-century European pogroms against Jews. Nativism, anti-Catholicism, and economic competition spurred riots against Irish neighborhoods in Boston and Philadelphia during the early nineteenth century. Far more frequent were anti-Negro massacres, such as those that occurred in Cincinnati in 1829 and in the New York Draft Riot of 1863. In the 1877 San Francisco Anti-Chinese Riot and the 1909 South Omaha, Nebraska, Anti-Greek Riot, working-class ethnic groups fought each other rather than organize to meet common grievances. In fact, corporate leaders, including Pennsylvania mineowners and steel magnates in Gary, Indiana, encouraged segregated housing patterns and provoked racial antagonisms in order to frustrate unionization.[12]

The bloody race riots of 1919 were a tragic indication that race hostility among lower-class groups was a more powerful force in American cities than class solidarity. Provoked by the press and by white hostility toward the expansion of black neighborhoods, the riots were brief anarchistic expressions of long-standing white intransigence against an integrated, multiracial society. By 1919, however, urban blacks had become more militant and large enough numerically to defend themselves against white marauders.[13]

The tumultuous riots of the 1960s, stretching from Bridgeport, Connecticut, to Miami, Florida, to the Los Angeles ghetto of Watts, were different both from the one-sided massacres of the nineteenth century and the racial disorders of 1919. Similar to the spontaneous Harlem uprisings of 1935 and 1943, they were protest demonstrations against ghetto conditions. Sociologist Robert Blauner called them a "preliminary form of mass rebellion against a colonial status." He concluded:

> That motives are mixed and often unconscious, that black people want good furniture and television sets like whites is beside the point. The guiding impulse in most major outbreaks has not been integration with American society, but an attempt to stake out a sphere of control by moving against that society and destroying the symbols of its oppression.[14]

Throughout the past century and a half, reformers have attempted to alleviate the evils of the ghetto environment and to regenerate its inhabitants. The continued existence of the ghetto in all its virulent trappings suggests the ultimate failure of the good-intentioned reformer. Nevertheless, the reformer has traditionally pricked society's conscience and stirred it into fitful action to ameliorate ghetto life.

Genteel patricians dominated the movement for ghetto reform in the nineteenth century. Voluntary societies, such as the New York Association for the Improvement of the Condition of the Poor, the Baltimore Society for the Prevention of Pauperism, and the Howard Associations of the antebellum South, emphasized moral regeneration of the habits of their unfortunate charges. The managers of the Society for the Prevention of Pauperism in the City of New York lamented that immigrants were "too often led by want, by vice, and by habit, to form a phalanx of plunder." Paternalism is more evident in the following avowal of the Norfolk Association for the Improvement of the Condition of the Poor: "We will give to none who will not exhibit evidences of improvement from the aid afforded." The aim of the societies was an admirable one: to rationalize the chaos of a multitude of private charities in order to help the ghetto resident help himself. Discipline and morality, however, proved to be elusive qualities when reformers tried to instill them in understandably resentful recipients.[15]

When the voluntary associations gave way to the professional reformers, the patrician emphasis on morality and discipline remained. The *Eighth Special Report of the Commissioner of Labor* in 1895 proclaimed: "It is not a question of class, but of character. . . . [M]oral reformation is the only thing that can deal satisfactorily with the destructive class" (p. 161). The *Eighth Report* included definite ideas on the methods which should be utilized to effect moral regeneration: "Discipline, regularity, and insistence upon prompt daily payment for accommodation given, can not fail to have a reforming influence upon individual habits. . . . Tenants should be coerced into keeping themselves and their surroundings reasonably clean" (p. 441). In the brave new world of government studies, the ghetto resident was still as misunderstood as in the days of patrician paternalism.

The limited success of turn-of-the-century reformers in eradicating ghetto blight is not surprising in view of their condescending attitudes and tendency to stereotype ethnic groups. To castigate most Progressive reformers for their prejudices merely states that they were not ahead of their time. Some settlement house workers, Jane Addams and Mary White Ovington among them, transcended the racism and cultural snobbery of their era. But most Progressives epitomized the ideas and concerns of the urban professional class, and what success they had in improving the ghetto owed a great deal to their ability to articulate the acceptable rhetoric for reform. Perhaps their facile generalizations resulted from a desire to digest the voluminous statistics and facts gathered in their studies. The careful maps, the detailed building plans, and the painstakingly compiled tables suggested a genuine effort to grasp the problems of the ghetto.[16]

The Progressive reformers were realists who at least understood the breadth of the ghetto problem, if not the residents themselves. They acknowledged the ineffectuality of existing legislation, scored public apathy, attacked landlords, and advocated comprehensive measures still prominent among today's ghetto reformers. Turn-of-the-century reformers urged destruction of the physical ghetto—urban renewal. They recommended gradual removal of ghetto residents to the suburbs—scatter-site housing. Finally, Progressive reformers were unanimous in their belief in the value of education as a means of enabling the ghetto resident to improve his environment and eventually to escape from it.[17]

The optimism of the Progressive movement was shattered by the bloodbath of World War I, the Red Scare that followed like a plague in its wake, and the sterile politics of Normalcy during the 1920s. Historian Robert H. Wiebe concluded that fear of ghetto residents lay behind the conservative reaction. He wrote:

And always there was that gray amalgam of slum dwellers. Life in the tenements, predicated on poverty and chance, had little more meaning to comfortable Americans in 1919 than in 1890. Before the war the ferocious suppression of strikes in the garment, textile, and mining industries, involving many unskilled workers of new-immigrant background, had expressed that rising fear of the masses, and it was this vision of danger here that lay behind the Red Scare of 1919 and 1920. A natural extension of their earlier concern, it included wholesale arrests in the immigrant quarters, concerted strikebreaking against unskilled workers in steel and other industries, and government passivity as slum-dwelling whites beat slum-dwelling Negroes back into the ghettos they had filled during the war. When the rabble seemed quiet, the violence abated.[18]

The 1920s were a watershed for the fate of the ghetto. During that decade, so outwardly gay for the affluent and depressing for the tenement dweller, the census revealed that a majority of Americans lived in urban areas. The nation's mores and values tended to be urban, as the United States became a mass-production, consumer-oriented, Wall Street and Madison Avenue–dominated society. But ironically, less was done for the ghetto dweller than in the previous generation. Under Warren G. Harding and Calvin Coolidge, the federal government assumed that enlightened business leadership and the free-enterprise system would take care of long-term urban problems, with state and local governments and private charity providing for short-term emergencies. When taking office in 1929, Herbert Hoover believed that poverty was becoming obsolete rather than that his country was in the throes of a disastrous depression.

In 1924, when laws restricting immigration had slowed European migration to a trickle, southern blacks flocked into the cities, followed later by Latin immigrants. Misjudging the phenomena, because of their own relative prosperity, most Americans viewed Harlem, for example, as a sensuous haven of jazz and gin rather than as a squalid scene of suffering. Robert Blauner contrasted the older white ghettos with their twentieth-century nonwhite successors by terming the former temporary way stations and the latter permanent colonies. Perhaps the latter were latter-day plantations. In contrast to blacks, European groups came to America by choice, were able to gain control over their tenements, stores, and other institutions within a generation, and had a fighting chance to assimilate into the larger society.[19]

During the 1930s the Franklin D. Roosevelt administration attempted to provide a modicum of relief for ghetto residents. Roosevelt espoused goals that would have made the country an open, fluid place without ghettos. Ironically, the very programs that the New Deal inaugurated to combat poverty worked to perpetuate the ghetto. Welfare policies discouraged family unity and initiative; public housing projects too often resembled high-rise prisons. Despite the plethora of governmental programs, which seem at times to benefit bureaucrats more than the poor, ghetto residents themselves have effected the most promising ghetto reforms. Outside observers, like the Kerner Commission, which culminated twentieth-century liberal thought, have overlooked or underplayed the resilience and resource of ghetto inhabitants. This is understandable, since it is difficult to imagine creative forces emanating from such a negative environment. Nevertheless, there has been ample historical precedent to demonstrate the development of community consciousness and group solidarity among ghetto residents to enhance their life. It has been part of the paradox of the American ghetto. As Michael Harrington

observed, the ghetto was a "center of poverty out of which inhabitants [drew] strength."[20]

The strength which bound ghetto residents was often a community institution. The development of religious institutions, mutual
aid societies, and small capitalist enterprises bolstered ghetto morale
and promoted group solidarity. The creation of a self-enclosed community provided ghetto residents with shelter from a hostile world
and an opportunity to retain their culture and ease the shock of
ghetto life. The cohesion of nineteenth-century Italian communities,
for example, was well known to investigators. Emily Dinwiddie
claimed that there was not one Italian to be found outside the Italian
ghetto that she studied in Philadelphia. The unity of the Italian
community rested with its institutions. Formal clubs, informal *Paesani* groups, the extended family, and mutual aid societies spun a
web throughout the entire ghetto which drew its residents together
and attracted newcomers as well. Capitalist enterprises, such as
bakeries, restaurants, and banks, emerged from small pools of capital
and brought ghetto Italian investors some return and much hope.[21]

Other ghetto groups have duplicated the solidarity of Italian
communities. The Chinese ghettos have, historically, been almost
entirely self-contained and self-supporting; small businesses honey-
combed the Chinatowns of the country. The solidarity of Jewish
ghettos was almost legendary. Buffeted by prejudice and discrimination, Jews in America sought, like the Italians and Chinese, to
create self-sufficient communities. One student of ghetto welfare
discovered that the small antebellum Jewish ghetto in New York
boasted more than one-half of the total private welfare organizations in the city. Other immigrant groups like the Dutch and Scandinavians, though less often subjected to outside hostility, similarly
developed community institutions and group solidarity in their respective ghettos.[22]

Black and Chicano ghettos have not, until recently, followed
the patterns set by their ghetto predecessors in generating community consciousness and group solidarity. The nonwhite ghetto residents have encountered more serious obstacles in attempting to improve both themselves and their environment. The emphasis on the
goal of integration has inhibited the development of community
institutions. The reservoir for creative action existed, as demonstrated
by the popular appeal of Marcus Garvey during the 1920s. Recent
examples of resilience are such ghetto-based organizations as the
Muslims, the Panthers, and the Young Lords, whose major thrusts
have been self-regeneration, cultural pride, and group solidarity.[23]

Encouraging as the results of community cohesion have been, there is a danger that too much isolation can transform the ghetto from a cage to a cocoon. Although investigators marveled at the self-contained ethnic ghettos, most residents hoped to leave their bleak surroundings, and many did. The turnover of ethnic groups in ghetto neighborhoods proceeded rapidly. The Sixth Ward of lower Manhattan, for example, saw the Irish, the Germans, the Italians, and the Jews predominate in rapid succession from 1830 to 1900. As soon as a new immigrant group trickled in, the old immigrants quickly retreated. It was a common axiom that "the Irish build and the Italians inherit." Immigrants from southern Italy, part of the predominantly non-Protestant "new immigration" of the late nineteenth and early twentieth century, stayed in one area longer than their northern and western European predecessors. Patterns of Jewish out-migration from the ghetto differed between orthodox and secular sects. The latter were much more highly mobile within a metropolitan area. While erstwhile ghetto residents maintained ties with ghetto organizations and re-created ghetto institutions, their new surroundings confirmed their having "made it." Critic Alfred Kazin looked back with nostalgia at his boyhood days in the Brownsville ghetto of Brooklyn, yet admitted that "to leave Brownsville was the sensible ambition of every poor Jewish family." An urban safety valve operated in the ethnic ghettos in the form of the realizable promise of escape. Even such tightly knit communities as Boston's North End and the Chinatowns are increasingly losing their young people.[24]

For the nonwhite ghetto resident, there has been no safety valve, no place to go. A middle class has grown up in the ghetto—affluent, imitating the culture of white society, yet trapped by its environment. The creative ghetto did not and does not ameliorate the effects of racial segregation and discrimination. The nonwhite ghetto is threatening to engulf entire cities, while fleeing whites establish equally isolated bastions in the suburbs. Society seems to be retreating behind respective ghetto walls reminiscent of the most insecure periods of medieval Europe. Isolation, decay of institutions like the church and family, disrespect for the past and disinterest in the future, boredom, despair, resort to drugs and alcohol—the common paraphernalia of ghetto pathology—have infected the suburbs. It is clear that the enduring ghetto looms as a serious threat to American society, white and nonwhite.[25]

The white and nonwhite ghettos have had common experiences. Too often, however, the one who leaves the ghetto either wipes his past from memory or romanticizes it. The shared heritage should

enable the sons and daughters of ethnic ghettos to empathize with
the racial ghettos and, through understanding, to evolve solutions
to destroy all ghettos. Both white and nonwhite have found the
ghetto a refuge and a prison; both white and nonwhite have experienced the same broken steps, broken homes, and broken lives; both
white and nonwhite have been studied and preached to; and both
white and nonwhite have achieved uneasy equilibrium' between
themselves and their environment by promoting community pride
and group solidarity. The whites have generally been able to leave
initial ghetto residences and enter other communities—an index of
success and self-achievement; nonwhites generally have not. Living
experiences in the ghetto have been similar; leaving has not. Dispersal of the nonwhite ghetto would complete a common American
experience.

Although the ghetto has been considered an urban phenomenon, involving the isolation and exploitation of ethnic and racial
minorities, the plight of ghetto residents is similar to that of other
depressed groups in America. Rural farmers share their poverty, migrant workers their rootlessness, American Indians their anger, recent college graduates their unemployment, young dropouts their
alienation, Vietnam veterans their drug problems, homosexuals their
feelings of being scorned, and women their sense of being stereotyped. Without much exaggeration the analogy of the ghetto has
been applied to penitentiaries, public schools, and the armed forces
in descriptions of how these institutions make pawns of their isolated
wards through behavioral control. Nevertheless, the urban ghetto
generates its own unique, complex patterns of behavior, which arise
from the shared experiences of its residents in their responses to a
potentially injurious environment and a hostile outside society. Thus
Piri Thomas could refer to his barrio of Spanish Harlem in terms
of both love and hate as a place with "thousands of lights, hundreds
of millions of colors mingling with noises, swinging street sounds of
cars and curses, sounds of joy and sobs that make music." Thomas
concluded that his ghetto turf was "like a great big dirty Christmas
tree with lights but no fuckin presents."[26]

To remove the scar of the ghetto and transform America into
an integrated society, a new urban ethos and a total commitment to
pluralistic cultural values are required. The solution is not to make
it possible simply for everyone to flee the inner city—blacks, Latins,
immigrants, Appalachian whites, and the like—but to work to create
a palatable urban setting as well as an open society elsewhere. The
advice given by urban reformer Jacob A. Riis over a half-century

ago is even more relevant today. "I know of but one bridge that will carry us over safe," Riis stated, "a bridge founded upon justice and built of human hearts."[27]

Notes

1. W. E. B. Du Bois, *Dusk of Dawn* (New York, 1968), 130–31; Kenneth Clark, *Dark Ghetto: Dilemmas of Social Power* (New York: Harper and Row, 1965), 11.

2. Richard Hammer, "Report from a Spanish Harlem 'Fortress,'" *New York Times Magazine,* January 5, 1964, 32–9.

3. New York Association for the Improvement of the Condition of the Poor, *Annual Report, 1881* (New York, 1881), 16; U. S. Department of Commerce, Bureau of Census, *Employment Profiles of Selected Low-Income Areas* (Washington, D. C., 1971); Herbert Gans, "The Failure of Urban Renewal," in Alexander B. Callow, Jr., *American Urban History* (New York, 1969), 567–81.

4. Lawrence Veiller, "Settlement Contribution to Legislation," *Commons,* 5 (July, 1901), 7; *New York Times,* April 22, 1971, 1: 2; *New York Times,* December 6, 1970, 72: 1; Lee Rainwater, *Behind Ghetto Walls: Black Families in a Federal Slum* (Chicago, 1970).

5. Emily Dinwiddie, *Housing Conditions in Philadelphia* (Philadelphia, 1904), 26–7.

6. Carroll D. Wright, "The Italians in Chicago," *Ninth Special Report of the Commissioner of Labor* (Washington, D. C., 1897), 23–30; *Employment . . . of Low-Income Areas; Manhattan Borough Area II,* 4–5; *New York Times,* October 19, 1972, 30: 4.

7. *Report of the Council of Hygiene and Public Health* (1865), xv–xvi.

8. Hammer, "Spanish Harlem 'Fortress,'" 32–9.

9. Jacob A. Riis, *Out of Mulberry Street: Stories in Tenement Life in New York City* (New York, 1898), 6–8; Stan Steiner, *La Raza: The Mexican American* (New York, 1969), 231–32.

10. New York A. I. C. P., *Report, 1860,* 49; *New York Times,* January 25, 1970, 61: 4.

11. Jacob A. Riis, *How the Other Half Lives* (New York, 1919), 296; Robert F. Williams, "U.S.A.: The Potential of a Minority Revolution," *The Crusader Monthly Newsletter,* 5 (May–June, 1964).

12. Richard C. Wade, *The Urban Frontier* (Chicago, 1964), 220–29; John G. Bitzes, "The Anti-Greek Riot of 1909—South Omaha," *Nebraska History,* 51 (Summer, 1970), 199–224.

13. Arthur I. Waskow, *From Race Riot to Sit-In* (Garden City, N. Y., 1966).

14. Robert Blauner, "Internal Colonialism and Ghetto Revolt," *Social Problems,* 16 (Spring, 1969), 393–406.

15. Blanche D. Coll, "The Baltimore Society for the Prevention of Pauperism, 1820–1822," *American Historical Review,* 61 (October, 1955), 77–87; John H. Ellis, "Businessmen and Public Health in the Urban South During the Nineteenth Century: New Orleans, Memphis, and Atlanta," *Bulletin of the History of Medicine,* 44 (May–June, 1970), 197–212; Managers of the Society for the Prevention of Pauperism in the City of New York, *Second Annual Report* (New York, 1819), 6; Norfolk *Southern Argus,* November 27, 1848.

16. Roy Lubove, *The Professional Altruist: The Emergence of Social Work As a Career, 1880–1930* (Cambridge, Mass., 1965).

17. Allen F. Davis, *Spearheads for Reform: the Social Settlements and the Progressive Movement* (New York, 1967); Jane Addams, "Social Education of the Industrial Democracy," *Commons,* 5 (June, 1900), 17; Francis Lee Maxwell, "Settlement Kindergarten," *The University Settlement Studies Quarterly,* 2 (July, 1906), 79–81; Robert A. Woods, "Industrial Education from the Social Worker's Standpoint," *Charities and the Commons,* 19 (October 5, 1907), 852–55.

18. Robert H. Wiebe, *The Search for Order, 1877–1920* (New York: Hill and Wang, 1967), 290.

19. Gilbert Osofsky, *Harlem: The Making of a Ghetto* (New York, 1968), 179–87; Blauner, "Ghetto Revolt," 397–406.

20. Michael Harrington, "Slums, Old and New," *Commentary,* 30 (August, 1960), 119.

21. John S. and Leatrice D. MacDonald, "Urbanization, Ethnic Groups, and Social Segmentation," *Social Research,* 29 (Winter, 1962), 433–48.

22. Robert Lazar, "Jewish Communal Life in Fargo, North Dakota," *North Dakota History,* 36 (Fall, 1969), 346–55; Nathan Kagnoff, "Organized Jewish Welfare Activity in New York City (1848–1860)," *American Jewish Historical Quarterly,* 60 (September, 1966), 27–61; Harry H. Anderson, "Early Scandinavian Settlement in Milwaukee County," *Milwaukee County Historical Society Journal,* 26 (Fall, 1971), 2–19.

23. Theodore G. Vincent, *Black Power and the Garvey Movement* (Berkeley, Calif., 1971); Philip S. Foner, ed., *The Black Panthers Speak* (Philadelphia, 1970).

24. Clark, *Dark Ghetto,* 63–80; Alfred Kazin, "The Woman Downstairs: A Memory of Brownsville," *Commentary,* 9 (February, 1950), 163.

25. Clark, *Dark Ghetto,* 55–62; John O. Killens, *The Cotillion* (New York, 1971); see U. S. Department of Commerce, Bureau of the Census, *General Population Characteristics* (Washington, D. C., 1971).

26. Piri Thomas, *Down These Mean Streets* (New York, 1967), 9–10.

27. Riis, *How the Other Half Lives,* 297.

Section One

The Formation of the Ghetto

Ghettos, viewed as a means of isolating distinct groups of people in a particular area, are nearly as old as American history. Early European settlers often restricted the residence of Indians and religious dissenters, preventing these people from residing within their midst. Poor immigrants in colonial Philadelphia were usually forced to live in quarters on the outside of town or to cluster together in cellars and alleyways. Ethnic ghettos emerged with Irish and German immigration during the early nineteenth century and swelled with the flood tide of southern and eastern European immigration that occurred during the half-century ending in 1920. Immigrants were both coerced and drawn to the ghetto, pushed by racism and poverty, and pulled by jobs, compatriots, and a desire for security. Not surprisingly, immigrant quarters often formed around factories, and their survival depended, in part, on whether or not central business districts expanded and encroached on their territory.

The first selection, by turn-of-the-century housing reformer Kate Holladay Claghorn, describes patterns of ghetto formation in lower Manhattan, an area inhabited successively by Knickerbocker aristocrats, Irish, Germans, Jews, and Italians. In a scholarly study on the formation of the Dutch community in Kalamazoo, Michigan, historian John A. Jakle and geographer James O. Wheeler reiterate the common experience of the American ghetto as delineated by Claghorn. Drawn first by employment opportunities, Dutch immigrants flocked to Kalamazoo after the first settlers erected community institutions. Rhoads Murphey's article on Boston's Chinatown shows how the formation of this Chinese ghetto revitalized a decaying neighborhood through the establishment of small capitalist enterprises and mutual aid societies. Murphey, a geographer, discovered that group solidarity and community consciousness extended beyond the physical boundaries of Boston's Chinatown, for Chinese Americans throughout New England retained material and spiritual ties to the district.

Just as the industrial urban centers attracted foreign immigrants, a similar push-pull phenomenon worked during the great migration of black Americans to northern cities during World War I. Sociologist Emmett J. Scott, writing immediately after the war, discussed the familiar attractions of instant employment and cheap housing in the formation of black ghettos in the Middle West. Scott emphasized, though, the often violent hatred which confronted black newcomers and left them with even less of a choice of residence than immigrants. In the final selection, historians Sam Bass Warner, Jr., and Colin B. Burke warn against exaggerating the similarities between the European immigrant's experience and black ghetto formation. Most foreign immigrants never lived in ghettos, and even when they did so, their fate was not as predetermined by a closed, hostile outside society. Furthermore, class and socio-religious identifications were perhaps as important to them as racial and nationality ties. Warner and Burke conclude their essay with a reassessment of the ethnic ghetto as more of a central metropolitan base than an agent of localized acculturation.

The literature on the formation of ghettos is enormous. The following studies are a useful introduction to the subject: M. L. Hansen, *The Atlantic Migration, 1607–1860* (1940); G. M. Stephenson, *A History of American Immigration, 1820–1924* (1926); Oscar

Handlin, *Boston's Immigrants, 1790–1865* (1941); Walter I. Firey, *Land Use in Central Boston* (1947); Sam Bass Warner, Jr., *The Private City: Philadelphia in Three Periods of Its Growth* (1968); Earl F. Niehaur, *The Irish in New Orleans, 1800–1860* (1965); Robert Ernst, *Immigrant Life in New York City, 1825–1863* (1949); Gerd Korman, *Industrialization, Immigrants and Americanizers: The View from Milwaukee, 1866–1921* (1967); Maldwyn A. Jones, *American Immigration* (1960).

1 The Foreign Immigrant in New York City, 1800–1870*

Kate Holladay Claghorn

THE PROBLEMS ARISING from foreign immigration are especially and peculiarly problems of the large cities. In them the immigrants are first received; in them they settle in large proportions, for longer or shorter periods, if not permanently; and in them the pressure of great masses of population throws into situations of unusual stress and strain the incoming peoples subjected to it.

. . .

By the close of the eighteenth century the city was growing rapidly toward the north, streets were being raised and paved, and the dock frontage extended farther into the water. The docks in process of construction became gathering places of all sorts of filth, forming about the city a belt of offensiveness along the river front from which, it may be supposed, the well-to-do were ready to draw back. In the neighborhood of the docks were a large number of old

* From Kate Holladay Claghorn, "The Foreign Immigrant in New York City." *Fifteenth Annual Report of the Industrial Commission* (Washington, D.C.: Government Printing Office, 1901), 449, 451–52, 454–59.

wooden houses, many of which, built before the raising and paving of the streets, had their lower floors 2 or 3 feet below the surface of the pavements. This was particularly the case at the southern end of the island, in the First, Second, and Fourth wards; but in other quarters, too, other offensive neighborhoods had grown up.

In such neighborhoods disease flourished. The outbreak of yellow fever in 1795 "prevailed on the borders of the East River, in the low streets and what was formerly the swamp, and in the narrow alleys." And in such neighborhoods, evidently, the immigrant population found their first homes; for it will be remembered that it was in this epidemic that so large a proportion—500 out of 730—of the victims were immigrants, most of them newly arrived.

. . .

The business district was growing to the north, with Broadway as its main axis, and in the course of this growth, well-to-do residents of the neighborhoods encroached upon moved still farther to the north, leaving their substantial dwellings to be occupied by the poor, who found it desirable to remain near the business district that afforded them a livelihood, and who, to save expense, crowded themselves 4, 5, or 6 families together into a structure adapted to the uses of one family only. And "the poor," as years went on, were more and more exclusively the foreign born and their children.

By 1834 overcrowding was recognized as a serious evil. Gerrett Forbes, city inspector for that year, says that, together with intemperance, the most prominent cause of the increase of deaths over the increase of the population which he has noted is "the crowded and filthy state in which a great portion of our population live and apparently without being sensible of their condition."

Former good residence districts that were gradually being changed into crowded quarters of the poor were, notably, along the west side, up toward Greenwich Village, and in the center of the city, the old Fourth Ward, with its many fine old mansions.

North of the city hall, and to the east of Broadway, a neighborhood of evil notoriety had come into being by a somewhat different order of growth from that described above—in the famous Sixth Ward and its little less notorious neighbor on the north, the Fourteenth.

The Sixth Ward was never as good a residence district as some others in the city on account of its peculiar topography. The "Collect," a deep pond in a deep basin, covered a considerable portion of its surface, and while, in its natural state the pond added to the attractiveness of the locality, in 1800 the city began to fill it in, and from that time to 1810, when the work was finished, the spot was a center of offense and filth. The place was made a common dumping ground for garbage, dead animals, and all sorts of trash; a circumstance that would naturally hinder the development of the neighborhood as a good residence district. On the high land above this pond some good houses were probably erected; and an old print showing the "Five Points" in 1827 represents some good and substantial looking dwellings. But a large number of the houses erected in this quarter were shackling frame structures, built on made land; and the famous tenement streets about the "Five Points"—Baxter, Park, and Mulberry—were laid out over the very site of the pond, or along its edges.

By 1830 the Sixth Ward had become notorious for crime and disorder, and by 1834–35 it emerges into especial publicity as a long-settled Irish neighborhood, in the course of the Irish riots that marked those years and that had their center here.

In this ward an epidemic of "continued fever" (typhoid) broke out in 1837. A physician, describing this epidemic, said that the cases occurred in the midst of a poor population, "principally Irish and German, whose habits . . . are more or less filthy, and who lived crowded together, with a family in every room in the house, and sometimes more." All cases occurred west of the Bowery, where there was far greater crowding than to the east of that street, and all occurred in basement dwellings, or first floors with no basement or cellar beneath.

• • •

Immigration was somewhat checked during the [Civil] War, but even under those circumstances house building in the city did not keep pace with the population, and the close packing of tenants in confined quarters still brought "disease, demoralization, and death" as their consequences.

• • •

About this time it was observed not only that poor people were concentrated in certain districts, but that they were more or less segregated according to nationalities. And in 1867 it was noted that the social relations of the foreign to the native population had materially changed; that the foreigners no longer blended with the native stocks to become incorporated with them.

• • •

The inhabitants of the district were largely of foreign birth; about one-half the population were Irish, about one-fourth Germans, the remainder were Americans, Swedes, and Danes. About two-thirds of the population were laborers and mechanics with their families;

the remainder were retail shopkeepers and keepers of hotels and sailors' and immigrants' boarding houses. A large element of the population was a floating one, consisting of travelers, immigrants, sailors, and "vagabonds without a habitation and almost without a name."

. . .

From Fourteenth to Fortieth street, the foreign population is seen to have entered the district side by side with the native population in a very literal sense. Passing over Greenwich Village, they had traveled up the western edge of the district above as the native born were traveling up its eastern edge—the center of the island; and, as the foreigners were now coming into a region not already thickly built up, the brick barrack was the prevailing type of tenant house. Here then grew up the characteristic "barrack" evils and here were to be found some of the worst and most extreme types of that class of buildings.

. . .

Going still farther to the north, above Fortieth street, still another phase of foreign life in the city is seen. By this time the foreign population had fairly outrun the native population, and throughout the sparsely settled district of the upper west side, on the broadly stretching vacant lots through which the streets of a later time had not yet been cut, on the miniature crags and peaks that dotted the ground a foreign squatter population had erected its dwellings.

. . .

The Sixth Ward at this time could lay claim to the most exclusively foreign population of any district in the city. Americans constituted less than 5 per cent of the whole number. Of the foreign population, the Irish constituted 74 per cent; the remaining 26 per cent were mainly German Jews and Italians. The German Jews dealt in old clothing and made Baxter Street their headquarters; the Irish kept junk shops, liquor stores, groceries, etc.; the Italians were ragpickers, and organ grinders. By this time about one-third of the tenant houses in the ward were of the "barrack" type, containing from 10 to 50 families each. The remainder were very old wooden structures, some quite small, containing 4 to 8 families in as many rooms. Many of these houses were used as lodging houses, as many as 30 persons being packed into a single room.

. . .

The Seventh Ward, lying along the East River, and formerly a good residence neighborhood, largely settled by Quakers, was by this time changing to a tenement district. A few of the former well-to-do residents still lived in the central portion, but the population was now made up principally of mechanics, longshoremen, and sailors. In the eastern part of the ward were many crowded tenement houses of the newer type, but most of the tenement population lived in old-fashioned 2 or 3 story dwelling houses, not built for tenements. The population here was mainly Irish, with a sprinkling of other nationalities among the sailors and longshoremen.

The Tenth Ward, just to the north of the Seventh Ward, was at this time the one distinctively and exclusively German district in the city. Here this people had rushed in such numbers as to make it profitable for landlords to erect many new tenement houses, and fewer of the old, dilapidated houses were to be found here than in other quarters. The new tenant houses were said to be of pretty good character.

. . .

It will be observed from this general survey that the Irish were scattered pretty well over the city, while the Germans were largely packed into one or two crowded wards, where they formed a dense settlement of their own nationality, or were to be found in colonies among the squatter population; that in general the Irish were to be found rather more frequently on the west side, the Germans on the east.

Next to be considered are the social and moral aspects of the life of the foreign population thus widely distributed over the city. The tenement houses in which most of them found their homes were certainly little calculated to develop high social and moral types, and indeed brought to bear influences working directly the other way.

Physical devitalization led to moral degeneracy. The general lowering of vitality due to the foul air, darkness, and filth of the tenement is accompanied by a depression of spirits, a reduction of energy and ambition. The tenement dweller is not only incapacitated for work, but loses interest in it and in the progress of his family; resorts to strong drink to stimulate his system, while this in turn reduces his physical health still further and incites him directly to all kinds of vice and crime.

The state of physical and moral degradation brought about in the tenement house became so distinct a type that all observers and investigators remarked it, and some one of them in a flash of genius bestowed upon it the significant, if not elegant, name of "Tenant-house rot."

Dr. Griscom, as early as 1842, had called attention to the "depraved effects which such modes of life exert upon the moral feelings and habits;" and the city inspector in 1851 remarks that "these overpopulated houses are generally, if not always, seminaries of filthiness, indecency, and lawlessness."

. . .

For the existence of the tenement houses themselves, with all their evil influences, the immigrant, the landlord, and the city have to share the responsibility. It is plainly evident that the tenement houses were called into being by the heavy demands for housing made by the constant inpouring of great masses of immigrants, and overcrowding seemed to be an almost inevitable result of this demand, as the immigrants were very poor and land was dear in the city itself, while transportation facilities were not as yet so developed as to permit the city laborer to live in suburban districts where land was cheaper.

But the landlords were especially to blame for the ill consequences arising from the tenement houses, as they were, obviously, the ones who decided in what way and with habitations of what character the immigrants' demand for housing should be met. The immigrant himself was in no position to dictate terms. Poor, ignorant of the country, and with immediate need of shelter, he had to take what was provided for him by the landlord. And the landlord took the utmost advantage of the situation by charging the highest possible prices for the poorest possible accommodations, and disregarding every law of health and decency in erecting the big barracks meant for occupation by the poor.

Successive investigations of the housing system in New York agreed in showing the "greedy and mercenary landlord," rather than the helpless tenant, as the primary cause of tenement evils.

An inspector for the council of hygiene in 1864 thus reports the landlords' methods, with regard to repairs:

> Every expenditure of money which the law does not force them to is refused; and blinds half swung and ready to fall and crash with the first strong wind; doors long off their hinges, which open and shut by being taken up bodily and put out of or in the way; chimneys as apt to conduct the smoke into the room as out of it; stagnant, seething, overflowing privies, left uncleansed through the hot months of summer, though pestilence itself should breed from them; hydrants out of repair and flooding sink and entry; stairs which shake and quiver with every step as you ascend them; and all this day after day, month after month, year in and year out.

But the city, too, must bear a considerable share of the blame for bad tenement conditions, from its neglect to protect the community by adequate legislation against the consequences arising from the greed of landlords and the ignorance and poverty of tenants at a time when, in the first beginnings of the tenement system, legislation could easily have prevented evils which, once having come into being and become vested interests, it could not cure.

2 The Formation of Dutch Ghettos in Kalamazoo, Michigan[*]

John A. Jakle and
James O. Wheeler

IMMIGRANTS DIRECTLY FROM the Netherlands first appeared in [Kalamazoo] around 1850. Local historians eagerly recounted the arrival of one Paulus Den Bleyker and his party of twenty-eight immigrants from the Island of Texel as signaling the Dutch colony's true beginning.[1]

Intending to settle in Iowa, the party contracted cholera and stopped to rest on reaching the terminus of the Michigan Central Railroad, then located at Kalamazoo. After a prolonged stay which much reduced their numbers, the survivors elected to settle permanently in the city. Many Dutch immigrant groups came by way of this western gateway town, seeking farms not only in western Michigan but also at the Dutch settlements at Pella, Iowa, at Hollandtown and Alto, Wisconsin, and at Roseland (also called South Holland) in Illinois.

[*] Reprinted with permission from John A. Jakle and James O. Wheeler, "The Changing Residential Structure of the Dutch Population in Kalamazoo, Michigan," *Annals of the Association of American Geographers,* 59 (September, 1969), 444–48, 451–53, 456–57, 459.

Den Bleyker, wealthy beyond all local expectations, had engaged in land reclamation in his native Frisia, capitalizing several polderization projects. Carrying his fortune in gold coins literally overflowing an ancient wooden trunk, this Dutchman's impact on the specie-starved Michigan frontier favored Dutch immigration to the area for many years. Known as the "Dutch Governor" (for he purchased the estate of the then Governor of Michigan, Epaphroditus Ransom), he became overnight Kalamazoo County's largest land owner. Much of his property—poor, low-lying muck land—eventually found its way into the ownership of Dutch families destined to make Kalamazoo a market gardening center.[2]

During the 1860's and 1870's the small Dutch colony, with Den Bleyker as its nominal head, attracted an increasing number of Dutch speaking citizens each year. Most of the Dutch arrivals in Kalamazoo came directly from peasant backgrounds in the Netherlands. But this trans-Atlantic rural to urban transplantation was reinforced by a local farm to city migration, which saw both first and second generation Dutch moving from farms in Ottawa and Allegan counties to surrounding cities. Most of the immigrants professed a continuing desire to farm and, prior to the Civil War, many chose agricultural jobs in and around the city. But farm employment, beset with low wages and a degree of instability, discouraged many "thrifty Dutchmen" determined to purchase their own properties. Better the industrial job to enhance one's savings and to hasten the day of farm ownership.

Coincident with the arrival of the Dutch element in western Michigan were lumber interests: New Englanders and New Yorkers whose capital investments in manufacturing provided industrial job opportunities. For the Dutch, the paper mills of Kalamazoo and the furniture factories of Grand Rapids provided the necessary income and job security needed to establish roots in their newly adopted country and to save for the purchase of land. . . .[3]

Towns like Kalamazoo, with their established Dutch communities and job potential, proved highly attractive to Dutch immigrants during the last two decades of the nineteenth century. There the new arrival found shelter, a tie to the past, a sense of community, and of most importance the promise of a future. For most immigrants the urban way of life was satisfying, and the return to the farm was postponed indefinitely. For others the availability of cheap marshland in and around Kalamazoo proved too great an attraction and their return to the land precipitated the city's rather unique market gardening industry. . . . American farmers had little use for this poorly drained land, and thus within the immediate environs of the city sizable acreages remained idle awaiting development.

The Dutch were quick to perceive the agricultural potential of the lowland, but actual development was slow. Costs of draining the muck lands were high and, even more important, no suitable agricultural system, adjusted to local and regional market demands, immediately presented itself. Through the 1860's and 1870's, therefore, only a few market gardeners experimented with crops, perfecting drainage techniques, establishing market connections, and generally laying the basis for large-scale investment.[4] Thus the poorly drained waste lands began to produce under Dutch tutelage—not through direct transfer of old world agricultural traditions, but through cultural readjustment to the Kalamazoo physical and economic environments from a base of lowland farming heritage.

Of all the crops developed, celery was particularly suited to the needs of the Dutch farmer and thus quickly came to dominate the city's garden farms. A high value crop requiring an intensive labor input, but not a large acreage, the Dutch were able to profit from a relatively small investment in the low-cost "moss land" by utilizing family labor in all aspects of production. As with most rural immigrant groups, Dutch families were large, averaging four children; and extended families constituting a single household, were quite common.[5] A small celery plot of two or three acres was sufficient to sustain a family of eight or ten well into the twentieth century.[6] However, the income from summer celery sales was frequently supplemented by winter paper mill employment.

. . .

. . . With Dutch development of the celery industry and its stimulus to city prosperity, they won a special place in the community relative to the other less cohesive and rather anonymous immigrant elements. Yet by the 1920's their numbers had become so great that, to some, the very basis of the larger community's way of life seemed threatened. As the *Kalamazoo Telegraph* editorialized:

> The Dutchman has contributed to the business of Kalamazoo, oh yes. He has built up one of the industries of the town and extended the fame of the place to distant parts, but he has been all the time working for himself; he has kept to his own circles in the most clannish manner possible, he has learned little English, familiarized himself all too little with our local laws and public movements, and remained a Dutchman, whereas he should have become more an American.[7]

Four cross sections in time, 1873, 1910, 1939, and 1965, have been selected to portray the phases of Dutch community growth as reflected in changing Dutch residential patterns. . . .

Few in number, Kalamazoo's early Dutch population dispersed throughout the community, locating in neighborhoods fitting their general economic status. [After] two decades of Dutch occupancy, . . . there were no residential areas in the city where the Dutch were heavily clustered; neither were there sections from which the Dutch, for being Dutch, were systematically excluded. . . . In terms of size and rapidity of growth, therefore, Kalamazoo's Dutch settlement had not, by 1873, reached the threshold capable of precipitating ghetto-like development in which large numbers, shielded from the community as a whole, might attempt to maintain their former culture in the face of a new cultural environment through the medium of self-imposed residential segregation.

Yet by 1873 conditions were beginning to change in the Axtell Valley, where Dutch market gardeners had begun to give the Dutch community a separate economic base. On the agricultural plats already under Dutch ownership, extending along the valley bluffs and along arteries recently built across this lowland, gardeners were beginning to settle families, except on the Den Bleyker property still awaiting subdivision into small garden farms. Attracted by the low cost of housing inherent in the exceedingly low cost of land, these Dutch were forming the city's first ethnically defined neighborhood sustained through their unique environmental evaluation of the lowlands based on a cultural tradition brought from their native Netherlands.

By 1910 the great influx of Dutch immigrants during the late nineteenth century had fostered decided residential segregation on both the north and south sides of the city. The intensive clustering of Dutch households in the Axtell Valley was but the culmination of ghetto growth begun some twenty years earlier focussed on the garden plats which under Dutch ownership were given largely to celery production. . . .

With garden farming also established at the northern limit of the city . . . a second Dutch neighborhood developed. . . . The various Dutch Reformed and Christian Reformed churches, their related schools, as well as the numerous Dutch retail and service establishments located within the ghetto, reinforced the district. The Dutch immigrant's propensity to cling to these familiar institutions gave the community a greater sense of cohesion. By providing stronger social and economic bonds, such institutions delayed the acculturation process, since the adoption of English and other elements of American culture was no longer necessary. Thus the new immigrant found himself buffered from the Kalamazoo community at large by the Dutch subculture.

Most immigrants found their initial employment in the paper mills located within easy walking distance of the two Dutch residential districts. The Dutch immigrant found himself immediately employable without the need of learning a new language, since most paper companies employed bilingual foremen. The use of Dutch speech not only in the home, in the church, and on the street, but also at work greatly helped to maintain the aura and substance of old world ways.

The two Dutch residential concentrations represented distinct communities differentiated not only by geographical location, but by cultural differences, particularly language, reflecting immigrant provincial origins. To the north side came settlers from Frisia who spoke a dialect all but incomprehensible to the Zeelanders assembled in the Axtell Valley. Thus the general trend toward ethnic ingathering which characterized the city generally was manifest at the neighborhood level in two rather distinct Dutch subcultures. Very little mixing of the two groups occurred initially, except at the large First Christian Reformed Church and at the social clubs located in the seemingly neutral ground of the central business district. Where such intergroup contact occurred, the need for a common language was immediately felt with a resultant recourse to English on an increasing scale.

As distance from the ghettos increased, Dutch residency declined rapidly. . . . The Dutch at this time were normally forced to seek inexpensive rentals. This kept them close to the poorly drained lowlands where property values and taxes were low (but rising) or clustered along valley bluffs where opportunistic realtors invested heavily in cheap, light-frame house construction. Although the Dutch were not excluded from any residential area in 1910, relatively few lived outside the Patteson-West [north-side] and Axtell [south-side] neighborhoods. . . .

Immediately after 1910, continued migration enlarged the Dutch residential concentrations as new arrivals filled newly opened streets and inundated adjacent, formerly non-Dutch areas. . . . This growth probably reflected population increment (both through inmigration and natural increase) rather than diffusion or decentralization outward from the respective ghetto cores.

Thus the centripetal tendencies that created the two Dutch

neighborhoods continued to function after 1910; however, their strength gradually lessened with time, for after 1920 Dutch immigration to Kalamazoo declined rapidly. This decrease, coupled with an increasing standard of living among established Dutch families, encouraged acculturation; the English language and other manifestations of American society slowly displaced traditional culture forms in response to expanded economic horizons. This "Americanization" process manifested itself in a steady migration away from the two ethnically defined neighborhoods. Able to live in higher quality, less-crowded residential districts, the Dutch diffused throughout the city. Such diffusion, in turn, prompted cultural change as Dutch families became less and less distinct and increasingly "American" because of closer contact with new neighbors of varied backgrounds. Thus centrifugal forces became increasingly important.

Clearly this dispersal of Dutch households throughout the various residential areas of Kalamazoo represented the most striking residential change between 1910 and World War II. Part of this dispersal reflected changes in transportation technology, since with better urban transportation (specifically with the introduction of the automobile) it was no longer requisite for residences to be physically near employment locations. In addition, for the Dutch family establishing a home it was no longer necessary to live within a Dutch neighborhood in order to maintain social ties with family and friends. Improved mobility permitted Dutch families to break the spatial bonds of their culturally derived ghettos and retain their traditional social relationships. Yet in reality, greater urban circulation led to increased contact with non-Dutch ways of life and a general loosening of social ties.

· · ·

. . . By 1965 Dutch households were located in every residential area in the city in proportions relatively equal to the total population. . . . Acculturation is not today fully complete, as large numbers of older persons, many of whom were immigrants at the turn of the century, continue to reside in former ghettos, particularly that of the north side. Many still speak English with a decided accent and prefer to use Dutch in their homes. . . . The dominant alternative to continued expansion of the Dutch area proved to be the desire of the younger generation to move out of the area to establish itself elsewhere. No small part of this desire was the effort to avoid contact with Negroes, who were slowly encroaching on the historic Dutch residential core. . . .[8]

· · ·

. . . The Kalamazoo example shows that residential patterning is directly related to the acculturation mechanism. Where a high acculturation rate exists, the ethnic population tends toward greater dispersal in residential patterns; conversely, where the acculturation rate is low, increasing residential concentration is the rule. Large influxes of ethnic immigrants intensify the degree of ethnocentricity, reduce social interaction between the two populations, and retard the rates of acculturation. If a sufficient ethnic element is introduced, barriers may be erected by either or both populations to give more formal structure to social attitudes. One such barrier is the ethnic neighborhood, in which ethnocentricity manifests a territorial expression of place. When ethnic migration slows, acculturation becomes the dominant process and the ethnocentric neighborhood is eroded. . . .

The Kalamazoo findings suggest that ethnic group concentration is related to the rate at which new immigrants enter a community. Prior to 1870, when Dutch immigration was slow, the host society experienced little pressure in absorbing newcomers; few, if any, barriers to acculturation were erected by the community at large. By the same token, the Dutch were too few numerically to foster social and economic institutions capable of sustaining self-segregation; that Dutch acculturation into the larger society proceeded rapidly during this time is reflected in their dispersed residential patterning. However, after 1870 Dutch in-migration increased rapidly and triggered defensive mechanisms within the host society designed to prevent cultural change produced by foreign-group intrusion. At the same time, self-segregating tendencies developed among the Dutch to restrict their penetration into the dominant society. As a result, the size potential of the ethnic neighborhood grew. The development of a strong sense of ethnocentricity, manifest in institutions capable of perpetuating traditional culture traits, was therefore a prerequisite to the emergence of Dutch neighborhoods.

Important also in the growth of Kalamazoo's Dutch community was an areal focus, *i.e.*, a sense of place, translated into a territorial identity. The garden farms, the result of the Dutchmen's rather unique perception of the local physical environment and his derived resource management schemes, served as foci around which ethnic ingathering occurred. Once formed, the Dutch neighborhoods persisted not only as an ethnic expression but as a territorial expression as well.

Notes

1. W. F. Dunbar, *Kalamazoo and How It Grew* (Kalamazoo, Mich., 1959), 68.

2. Kalamazoo *Gazette*, November 18, 1928.

3. Kalamazoo *Gazette*, November 21, 1920.

4. J. E. Spencer and R. J. Horvath, "How Does an Agricultural Region Originate," *Annals*, Association of American Geographers, 53 (1963), 74–92.

5. M. H. Ayres, "A Sociological Study of the Holland Population in the City of Kalamazoo" (unpublished A. B. thesis, University of Michigan, 1928).

6. W. Walters, "The Land of Celery, Kalamazoo's Axtell Creek Valley" (unpublished manuscript, Geography Department, Western Michigan University, 1964).

7. Kalamazoo *Telegraph*, 1922.

8. *Negroes in Kalamazoo* (Lansing, Mich., 1945).

3 Boston's Chinatown*

Rhoads Murphey

BOSTON'S CHINATOWN is the fifth largest in the United States, following San Francisco, New York, Los Angeles, and Chicago. Situated in a tongue of the low-rent district and on the margins of the downtown business district, the sequent occupance of the area has included several foreign communities, of which the Chinese is the most recent. The association of low-rent areas with foreign occupance is a familiar feature of most American cities. In Boston, the case of Chinatown illustrates both this association and the particular problem of Chinese in the United States.

This is made land, reclaimed by filling a tidal flat between 1806 and 1843. It was in 1840 far enough from Boston's downtown core for residential development and near enough for convenience, a logical place for new housing in the era before automobile and railway commuter transport made settlement possible farther out. Made land in the central Boston area is usually associated with low rents

* Reprinted with permission from Rhoads Murphey, "Boston's Chinatown," *Economic Geography*, 28 (July, 1952), 244–55.

and low land values, a situation which is partly explained and partly made use of by large space–users considered "undesirable" by householders: industry, wholesaling, railways, and cheap housing. These developments required ample space, the nearer to the center of the city the better. Made land answered their needs, and their use of it tended to keep land values and housing rents there low.

Railway connections were completed from Boston to New York by the late 1840's, with the Boston terminus at South Station, which was also used as a terminus by the main line west to Albany. During the next 20 years the expansion of yard and terminal space erected a barrier to further growth of the new residential area eastward and southward, and in addition acted to depress land values in the sector already occupied by housing. The presence of the railway after 1850, and the low value of the made land, attracted the leather industry into the three blocks between South Station and the present Chinatown, where it had easy access to transport for hides from New England and the West, and by sea. This solid industrial and wholesaling development filled in the last gap in the barrier to the east.

After 1860, the garment industry, displaced from the growing retail district along Washington Street and from the older center of the city by rising land values, began to encroach onto the made land from the west and north. The building of an elevated railway in 1899 through the northern part of the present Chinatown depressed rents and land values to a new low, and stimulated further invasion by the garment industry. The garment industry has continued to spread into the Chinatown area through the 1930's and 1940's, almost completely replacing the original residential development in its northernmost block (north of Beach Street), and sending fingers into most of the remaining housing area, including a wall of fifteen-story textile wholesaling and manufacturing buildings erected during the 1920's and 1930's along the major east-west artery of Kneeland Street, which bisects Chinatown.

The original housing in this area has been most seriously cut into, however, by the demolition of tenements to save taxes following the universal drop in land values after 1928 unaccompanied by a decline in assessments. By 1950 total housing space in Chinatown had been reduced by more than one-third as compared with 1925. The neighborhood is within easy walking distance of Boston's major commercial center along Washington Street, with its subway junction and large department stores. There is thus a ready use, as parking lots, for land cleared by demolition, and parking lot signboards give prominent notice that they are "only five minutes' walk from Filene's."

With encirclement by incompatible land uses virtually complete, the original residential neighborhood remained as a low-rent housing pocket, connected with the poor-quality housing area of the South End only tenuously across the railway tracks. . . . In approximately 120 years, the physical character of the area has thus shown a continuous decline. This pattern is logically reflected in the occupance of the area by successive groups of foreign immigrants, each inheriting a neighborhood increasingly deteriorated, and each replacing in turn an earlier group which had moved out as it had moved up economically and socially.

The original inhabitants of the new housing built between 1835 and 1850 were middle-income native Americans. . . . The arrival of the railway on the area's eastern borders and the subsequent development of the leather industry articulated with it coincided with the beginning of mass Irish immigration to Boston. . . . It seems likely that the advent of the railway and the industrial growth around the borders of the area had combined by the 1850's to lower rents and land values sufficiently to open the neighborhood to immigrant Irish settlement. At the same time, new and more desirable residential areas were being developed farther out from the center of the city, made accessible by the new railway connections, and to these native families tended to move.

The Irish remained the major occupants until the 1880's. The tenements were now 30 or 40 years older than when the Irish first came, and the physical character of the neighborhood had continued to decline, especially with the encroachments of the garment industry. This meant not only less pleasant, but cheaper living. Like their native predecessors, the Irish began to move out to more attractive neighborhoods, now made more accessible by horse cars and the first electric cars in addition to the railways. As an established American group and a notable feature of Boston life by the end of the nineteenth century, many of the Irish were able to rise into higher income brackets and to graduate into appropriate surroundings to which access was also possible socially. Their places were gradually taken by new immigrant groups, who inherited a neighborhood which had already declined far below its original income and social level, as well as in its physical character. Immigration in the 1880's and 1890's was however far more heterogenous in nationality than in the heyday of the Irish invasion, and the new groups tended to overlap each other in their occupance of this by now traditional first stop on the road to Americanization.

The Irish were superseded in this area by Central European Jews and by Italians, part of the later wave of nineteenth century immigration, whose arrival followed on the intensified invasion by industry and the railway yards. The Jews and Italians never spread over the entire neighborhood, and were apparently there only briefly, since by 1900 it was predominantly Syrian. . . .

It is in keeping with the record of decline in the physical character of the area that, following the original native inhabitants, succeeding immigrant waves have had a lower and lower status in American eyes and have been progressively more foreign: from Ireland across Europe through Jewry and Italy to Syria, and finally to China. . . . The outstanding attraction of this neighborhood for the Chinese was clearly its low rents, which had gradually fallen as successive immigrant waves passed through it, each group leaving the tenements shabbier and each year seeing the deteriorating effect of the railway yards and encroaching industry gathering force. In addition, it was the nearest low-rent housing area to the railway station. As the Chinese themselves explain, their first settlements in most cities tend to be near the railway station as their first point of entry into a strange place where the language and ethnic barriers restrict their range and encourage them to keep in close contact with transport to friends and relatives in other cities. This seems to have been the case in Chicago, Pittsburgh, Los Angeles, and St. Louis. In New York and San Francisco, where the majority of the Chinese arrived by ship, the Chinatowns are more closely articulated with the harbors. As a general principle, American Chinatowns are closely oriented to transport terminals.

Some of the older residents of Chinatown suggest that the first Chinese to come to Boston were runaway crews from ships in the harbor, but this does not seem as likely a source as California. Chinese immigration into California began in force about 1852, and averaged nearly 30,000 a year through the 1860's. Their labor was important in the building of the transcontinental railways, but with the completion of the Central Pacific in 1869 feeling began to turn against them, and in 1871 the anti-Chinese movement began with a series of race riots in which several Chinese were killed. Chinese migration from California to east coast cities began at about that time, and the total Chinese population of California continued to fall until the present, when New York's Chinatown is only slightly smaller than San Francisco's.

The appearance of the first Chinese in Boston was delayed as late as 1869 or 1870, and was apparently in no way connected with Boston's earlier prominence in the China trade. . . .

. . . Boston's Chinese population seems to have arrived almost entirely overland.

. . .

Chinese are the ultimate foreigners in the United States. The majority of those who live and carry on their business in Boston's Chinatown do so because race prejudice makes living and business difficult or impossible elsewhere. American laws until recently denied citizenship to all Asians, and they are in this country only on sufferance. The first Chinese came to the United States as coolies for manual labor under an infamous contracting system, and they have remained in the eyes of the American community social outcasts, obliged to live in ghettos in their own way.

Nearly every new immigrant group in American cities has for at least a generation tended to stick together in one area of the city, by choice, and usually also because, for this first generation, livelihood tends to center around particular national skills or trades which are most profitably carried on in the same area. With the second generation, largely educated in American public schools, this areal exclusiveness has usually broken down and the majority of each original immigrant group has dispersed over the city as a whole. The Chinese however have constituted a distinct community in Boston for over 60 years. Choice and economic advantage have certainly been factors in maintaining this exclusiveness, but the uniquely foreign character of the Chinese in American eyes has perhaps been even more important. Americanization of the Chinese has also been retarded by the fact that until recently their community has been predominantly composed of adult males so that few Chinese went through the public schools to learn American ways and language. . . .

In such a situation, it is natural that Boston's Chinatown should have become a distinct and close-knit community with special functions as a central place for all the Chinese in New England, who are excluded from most aspects of the general American community. . . . Chinatown comes to life on Friday night and until late Sunday is a hive of activity for Chinese laundrymen and restaurateurs from as far away as Springfield, Mass., and Portland, Maine. They come to see friends and relatives, to speak their own language and live in their own customs, and to find recreation in Chinese opera or gambling, which is unfortunately a major vehicle of organized social activity for at least the older generation.

...

Despite its poverty, Boston's Chinatown, like other American Chinatowns, has the lowest crime rate of any area in the city. . . . In Boston, as in other American cities, the Chinese have moved into a blighted low-rent area and transformed it into an attractive restaurant and art shop neighborhood whose inhabitants stick zealously to business. Chinatown does not in any significant sense belong to Boston's South End, a rooming-house area which leads the city in crime and juvenile delinquency rates. Property values in Chinatown, in contrast with the Syrian area or with the South End as a whole, did not share the catastrophic downfall of real estate after 1928. Values did drop to be sure, but relatively little, and they have since recovered and exceeded the earlier levels.

In this recovery Chinatown has been materially aided by a *deus ex machina* when the Elevated was torn down for scrap in 1941. Earlier it was said that the Chinese lived there because no one else would, but in 1941 they found themselves on potentially very valuable property. Their area was just behind Washington Street (with its theater district) and convenient to the center of the city or to the Back Bay, an ideal location for restaurants. The war gave Chinatown a further boost as part of the general acceleration of economic activity, and since 1942 nearly a dozen new restaurants have been built or remodelled, complete with modern architecture and neon signs to attract the non-Chinese trade, replacing or overshadowing the former dingy eating places beside the Elevated. Restaurateurs estimate that before this development three quarters of their business came from their own people, whereas at present the balance is exactly reversed in favor of the non-Chinese Americans.

...

The Chinese are still obliged to earn their living primarily on the basis of their nationality and within a separate community. . . .

The Chinese have selected the means of livelihood in which they could best compete in an unfriendly foreign community. A laundry may be started by an illiterate with no knowledge of English and with a very small amount of capital, and its major requirement is hard work for long hours, a sphere in which the Chinese need fear little competition. The restaurants serve partly a central place function for all the New England Chinese, and more recently are being supported largely by the non-Chinese trade. The grocery stores, also part of Chinatown's central place function, are parasitic on the local and New England Chinese communities, and sell special Chinese food, both imported and raised locally, to restaurants and to Chinese families. The trading companies do some importing of Chinese goods for large American retail stores, but their empty windows and dark interiors indicate that their most important function is as fronts for "clubs."

The Chinese are acutely conscious of the limited employment opportunities open to them. A few fortunate individuals have gone from Chinatown to American universities, and have been able to establish themselves in professions or in business. On the other hand, many of the Chinatown boys who have graduated from American universities in the last few years have been unable to find jobs in their fields and are now working as waiters in Chinatown restaurants. . . . Perhaps because they are relatively more recent arrivals, the Boston Chinese seem to have found fewer economic opportunities outside their own community than the Chinese in New York or San Francisco. . . . It has remained for the women in Boston's Chinatown to enter non-Chinese industry. Nearly all of the women residents, despite the fact that nearly all of them are married, are employed in the local garment factories, but almost none of the men. They are hired even though they are Chinese because they are willing to work for low wages on menial jobs. Businessmen among the Chinese would like to buy an interest in the garment industry as the clearest first step toward branching out into the general economic life of the city, but so far this has been limited to the Chinese ownership of a small company wholesaling textile machinery.

The most obvious landmark in Chinatown has just been completed: a large six-story building in "modern Chinese" architectural style erected on the northeast corner of Hudson and Kneeland Streets by the Consolidated Chinese Merchants and Benevolent Association of New England. This imposing building is to be used primarily as a recreation center, and also to house the offices of the Association. The need for such a center is clear, especially given the particular social problem of the Chinese in the general American community, and the overcrowded depressed area in which they live, but so much Chinese capital available for apparently non-profit investment seems to require an explanation. One answer may be found in the increasing difficulty of remitting money to China. The overseas Chinese in all areas habitually send large proportions of their earnings, however small, back to their relatives in China, or for investment in land there. Political developments in China since 1948 have greatly reduced the volume of this flow, especially from the United States, and may thus have made capital available locally. In this case it is being used for the assistance of local Chinese instead of for those at home, since the Association, as its name implies, acts as a semi-official welfare organization for all Chinese in New England, and is primarily responsible for the fact that no Chinese in this area has yet appeared on federal or state relief rolls.

4 The Growth of Black Ghettos in the Midwest During World War I*

Emmett J. Scott

IT WILL BE BOTH interesting and profitable to follow [the black] migrants into their new homes in the North. Among the most interesting of these communities is the black colony in St. Louis. St. Louis is one of the first cities of the border states, a city first in the memory of the unsettled migrant when the North was mentioned. During a long period thousands had gone there, settled down for a while and moved on, largely to Illinois, a sort of promised land. Conservative estimates place the number of Negro migrants who have remained there at 10,000. The number of migrants passing through this city, its reception of them, the living conditions provided and the community interest displayed in grappling with the problem are facts extremely necessary to an understanding of the readjustment of the migrants in the North.

The composition of the city's population is significant. It has a large foreign element. Of the foreign population Germans predominate, probably because of the brewery industry of the Amer-

* From Emmett J. Scott, *Negro Migration During the War* (New York: Oxford University Press, 1920), 95–105.

ican white population. The southern whites are of longest residence and dominate the sentiment. The large industrial growth of the town, however, has brought great numbers of northern whites. The result is a sort of mixture of traditions. The apparent results of this mixture may be observed in these inconsistencies: separate schools, but common transportation facilities; separate playgrounds, but common bath houses; separate theaters and restaurants with the color line drawn as strictly as in the South. There has been considerable migration of whites to this city from Kentucky, Tennessee, Alabama and Mississippi.

. . .

How St. Louis secured her migrants makes an interesting story. The difficulty of apprehending labor agents can be appreciated when it is recalled that the most zealous efforts of authority in the majority of cases failed to find more than a trace of where they had been operating. It was asserted by many of the migrants to this city, however, that they had been approached at some time by agents. Large industrial plants located in the satellite city of St. Louis sent men to Cairo, a junction point, to meet incoming trains and make offers. There developed a competition for men. They were first induced to accept jobs in smaller towns, but lack of recreational facilities and amusements and the monotony of life attracted them to the bright lights of St. Louis. The large alien population of this city at the beginning of the war made some employers anxious about the safety of their plants. The brick yards had been employing foreigners exclusively. When war began so many left that it was felt that their business was in danger. They advertised for 3,000 Negroes, promising them $2.35 per day. The railroad construction companies sent out men to attract Negroes to the city. They assert, however, that their agents solicited men only after they had started for the North.

The industries of St. Louis had much to do with the migration. In this city there are more than twenty breweries. None of these employ Negroes. St. Louis also has a large shoe industry. In this line no Negroes are employed. A short while ago a large steel plant employing foreigners in large numbers had a strike. The strike was settled but the management took precautions against its repetition. For each white person employed a Negro was placed on a corresponding job. This parallel extended from unskilled work to the highest skilled pursuits. The assumption was that a strike, should it recur, could not cripple their industry entirely. About 80 per cent of the employes of the brick yards, 50 per cent of the employes of the packing houses, 50 per cent of the employes of the American Car and Foundry Company are Negroes. The terra cotta works, electrical plants, united railways and a number of other foundries employ Negroes in large numbers.

The range of wages for unskilled work is $2.25 to $3.35 per day, with an average wage of about $2.75. For some skilled work Negroes receive from 35 cents to 50 cents an hour. Wages differ even between St. Louis and East St. Louis, because of a difference in the types of industries in the two cities. Domestic service has been literally drained, and wages here have been forced upwards to approximate in some measure the increase in other lines.

The housing facilities for Negroes, though not the best, are superior to such accommodations in most southern cities. There are about six communities in which the Negroes are in the majority. Houses here are as a rule old, having been occupied by whites before they were turned over to Negroes. Before the migration to the city, property owners reported that they could not keep their houses rented half of the year. According to the statements of real estate men, entire blocks stood vacant, and many vacant houses, after windows had been broken and plumbing stolen, were wrecked to avoid paying taxes on them. Up to the period of the riot in East St. Louis, houses were easily available. The only congestion experienced at all followed the overnight increase of 7,000 Negroes from East St. Louis, after the riot. Rents then jumped 25 per cent, but normal conditions soon prevailed. Sanitation is poor, but the women coming from the South, in the opinion of a reputable physician of the city, are good housewives. New blacks have been added to all of the Negro residential blocks. In the tenement district there have been no changes. The select Negro residential section is the abandoned residential district of the whites. Few new houses have been built. An increase of rent from $5 to $10 per month is usually the sequel of the turning over of a house to Negroes.

. . .

East St. Louis, another attractive center for the migrants, is unique among northern industrial cities. It is an industrial offshoot of St. Louis, which has outstripped its parent in expansion. Its geographical advantage has made it a formidable rival even with its less developed civic institutions. Perched on the banks of the Mississippi River, with twenty-seven railroads radiating from it, within easy reach of the coal mines, there has been made possible a rapid and uneven growth. It has doubled its population for three successive decades. Revolving around this overgrown center are a number of small towns: Brooklyn, Lovejoy, Belleville, Venice, Granite City and Madison. Its plant owners live in St. Louis and other cities, and consequently have little civic interest in East St. Louis. Land is cheaper, taxes are low. In fact, some of the largest concerns have been accused of evading them entirely. It has been artificially fed and, in process of growth, there have been irregularities in the structure of the community which eventually culminated in the greatest disgrace of the North, the massacre of about one hundred Negroes.

Fifty years ago before the river dividing St. Louis from East St. Louis was bridged, men rowed over from St. Louis for their cock fights, dog fights and prize fights. Escaped prisoners found a haven there. The town was called "The Bloody Isle." The older population is made up of whites from West Tennessee, Mississippi, Kentucky and Georgia. The men who have risen to political prominence in the city are for the most part saloon keepers. As many as 100 saloons flourished in the town before the riot. The city government has always been bad. The attitude of the citizenry appeared to be that of passive acceptance of conditions which must not be interfered with. As an example of the state of mind, much surprise was manifested when an investigation of the rioting was begun. Criminals have been known to buy immunity. The mayor was assassinated some time ago and little or no effort was made to punish his murderers.

Long before an influx was felt, it had been foreseen and mentioned by several men, most notably, Mr. Charles Nagel, Secretary of Commerce and Labor under President Taft. The East St. Louis plants had been going to Ellis Island for laborers. When this supply was checked, steps were taken to secure Negroes. Agents were sent to Cairo to get men en route further North. One advertisement which appeared in a Texas paper promised Negroes $3.05 a day and houses. It is estimated that as a result of this beckoning the increase in population due to the migration was 5,000. A number of other Negro migrants, however, work in East St. Louis and live in St. Louis, Lovejoy and Brooklyn, a Negro town. The school registration of the city showed that the largest numbers of these blacks came from Mississippi and West Tennessee. Despite the advertisement for men in Texas newspapers, few came to this city from that State.

The industries requiring the labor of these Negroes were numerous. The packing plants of Swift, Armour, Nelson and Morris employ large numbers of Negroes. In some of the unskilled departments fifty per cent of the employes are black. The Aluminum Ore Works employs about 600 blacks and 1,000 whites. This is the plant in which occurred the strike which in a measure precipitated the riot.

The Missouri Malleable Iron Works makes it a policy to keep three classes of men at work and as nearly equal numerically as possible. The usual division is one-third foreign whites, one-third American whites and one-third blacks. The theory is that these three elements will not unite to strike. Negroes are also employed in the glass works, cotton presses and transfer yards. Their wages for unskilled work range from $2.75 to $3.75 generally for eight hours a day. Semiskilled work pays from 35 cents to 50 cents an hour.

The housing of the Negro migrants was one of the most perplexing problems in East St. Louis. The type of houses available for Negroes, before being burned during the riot, were small dilapidated cottages. Congestion, of course, was a problem which accompanied the influx of Negroes. The incoming population, consisting largely of lodgers, was a misfit in the small cottages designed for families, and they were generally neglected by the tenant and by the local authorities. The segregated vice district was located in the Negro locality. The crowding which followed the influx forced some few Negroes into the white localities. Against this invasion there was strong opposition which culminated in trouble.

The roots of the fateful horror that made East St. Louis notorious, however, are to be found largely in a no less notorious civic structure. Politics of a shady nature was the handmaiden of the local administration. The human fabric of the town was made up of sad types of rough, questionable characters, drawn to the town by its industries and the money that flowed from them. There was a large criminal element. These lived in a little corner of the town, where was located also the segregated vice district. Negroes were interested in politics. In fact, they were a considerable factor and succeeded in placing in office several black men of their choice.

Trouble started at the Aluminum Ore Works which employed a large number of whites and blacks. In February of 1917 the men struck while working on government contracts. Immediately, it is claimed, Negroes were sought for in other states to take their places. An adjustment was made, but it lasted only a short while. Then followed a second strike at which the employers balked. In this they felt reasonably secure for Negroes were then pouring into the city from the South during the spring exodus. There followed numerous evidences of brooding conflict such as insults on the street cars, comments and excitement over the daily arrival of large numbers from the South. On one day three hundred are said to have arrived. Standing on the streets, waiting for cars, lost in wandering about the streets searching for homes, the Negroes presented a helpless group.

The search for homes carried them into the most undesirable sections. Here the scraggy edges of society met. The traditional attitude of unionists toward Negroes began to assert itself. Fear that such large numbers would weaken present and subsequent demands aroused considerable opposition to their presence. Meetings were held, exciting speeches were made and street fights became common. The East St. Louis *Journal* is said to have printed a series of articles under the caption, "Make East St. Louis a Lily White Town." It was a simple matter of touching off the smoldering tinder. In the riot that followed over a hundred Negroes were killed. These, for the most part, lived away from the places of the most violent disturbances, and were returning home, unconscious of the fate that awaited them. The riot has recently been subject to a congressional investigation, but few convictions resulted and those whites convicted escaped serious punishment.

Chicago, the metropolis of the West, remembered in the South since the World's Fair as a far-away city of hope from which come all great things, unceasingly advertised through its tremendous mail order and clothing houses, schools and industries until it became a synonym for the "North," was the mouth of the stream of Negroes from the South. It attracted all types of men, brought them in, encouraged them and cared for them because it needed them. It is estimated that within the period of eighteen months beginning January, 1916, more than fifty thousand Negroes entered the city. This estimate was based on averages taken from actual count of daily arrivals.

There were at work in this city a number of agencies which served to stimulate the movement. The stock yards were sorely in need of men. It was reported that they had emissaries in the South. Whether it is true or not, it is a fact that it was most widely advertised throughout the States of Mississippi and Louisiana that employment could easily be secured in the Chicago stock yards district. The report was circulated that fifty thousand men were needed, and the packers were providing houses for migrants and caring for them until they had established themselves. The Illinois Central Railroad brought hundreds on free transportation with the understanding that the men would enter the employ of the company. The radical Negro newspapers published here urged Negroes to leave the South and promised employment and protection. It is indeed little wonder that Chicago received so great a number.

The most favorable aspect of their condition in their new home is their opportunity to earn money. Coming from the South, where they were accustomed to work for a few cents a day or a few dollars a week, to an industrial center where they can now earn as much in an hour or a day, they have the feeling that this city is really the land overflowing with milk and honey. In the occupations in which they are now employed, many of them are engaged at skilled labor, receiving the same and, in some cases, greater compensation than was paid white men in such positions prior to the outbreak of the war. Talking with a number of them the investigator obtained such information as, that men were working at the Wilson Packing House and receiving $3 a day; at the Marks Manufacturing Company for $3.75; as lumber stackers at $4 a day, at one of the rolling mills for $25 a week, and on the railroads at $125 a month. The large majority of these migrants are engaged in the packing houses of Chicago where they are employed to do all sorts of skilled and unskilled labor with the corresponding compensation.

. . .

The great majority of Negroes in Chicago live in a limited area known as the South Side. State Street is the thoroughfare. It is the black belt of the city. This segregation is aided on one hand by the difficulty of securing houses in other sections of the city, and on the other, by the desire of Negroes to live where they have greatest political strength. Previous to the migration, hundreds of houses stood vacant in the sections of the district west of State Street from which they had moved only a few years before, when it was found that better homes were available. The presence of Negroes in an exclusively white locality usually brought forth loud protests and frequently ended in the abandonment of the block by whites. The old district lying west of State Street held the worst type of houses. It was also in disrepute because of its proximity to the old segregated vice area. The newcomers, unacquainted with its reputation, found no hesitancy in moving in until better homes could be secured.

Congestion has been a serious problem only during short periods when the influx was greater than the city's immediate capacity for distributing them. During the summer of 1917 this was the situation. A canvass of real estate dealers supplying houses for Negroes conducted by the Chicago Urban League revealed the fact that on a single day there were 664 Negro applicants for houses, and only 50 supplied, while there were 97 houses advertised for rent. In some instances as many as ten persons were listed for a single house. This condition did not continue long. There were counted thirty-six new localities opening up to Negroes within three months. These localities were formerly white.

5 Cultural Change and the Ghetto*

Sam Bass Warner, Jr., and Colin B. Burke

GHETTO LITERATURE, the product of intense feeling and dramatic experience, has always been the most readable material of American urban history, indeed the only books which could command a wide audience.[1] Today inter-racial conflict and the segregated pattern of Negro housing in our cities encourage urbanists to seek analogies between the urbanization of European peasants in American cities and the urbanization of the formerly rural American Negro.[2]

Both literary tradition and current interest create a severe historical distortion. The first tells of the integration of American society through the diffusion of immigrants and their descendants from a first settlement in tight urban clusters to a later suburban inter-mixture. Although such a process of cultural change did take place on a massive scale in many cities, assimilation by way of a ghetto has always been a limited case in American urban history, limited both

* Reprinted with permission from Sam Bass Warner, Jr., and Colin B. Burke, "Cultural Change and the Ghetto," *Journal of Contemporary History*, 4 (October, 1969), 173–188. By permission of Sage Publications Ltd.

in time span and in membership. Most foreign immigrants to American cities never lived in ghettos, and most immigrant ghettos that did exist were the product of the largest cities and the eastern and southern European immigrants of 1880–1940. Moreover, if a ghetto be defined as a place inhabited almost exclusively by one ethnic group, then only the caste-isolated northern Negro has an extended tradition of ghetto living. Only the northern Negro has had a heavy preponderance of his group confined to a segregated quarter of a city.[3]

If historians are to explain the process of cultural change which accompanied American urbanization and immigration, they must advance a new hypothesis to supplement the well-established ghetto one, one designed to interpret the majority of cases and to cover the entire period of immigration and ethnic acculturation. The new hypothesis will have to seek out cities other than the literary centres of New York, Chicago, and Boston, periods other than 1880–1940, and immigrants other than those who lived in the most crowded central wards.

Until after the Second World War, urban literature dealt in cultural dichotomies: immigrants vs. the rest of the city, or an immigrant group (Jews, Irish, Bohemians, Italians, or whoever) vs. the rest of the city. The dichotomy always implied a social geography of acculturation. There was an inner city ghetto, or port of entry, where the immigrant arrived and learned some American ways from his neighbours who were also immigrants. When in the course of time he prospered, he either stayed within the ghetto or he or his children moved to the outer city where well-established Americans lived according to a changeless culture.[4] It is obvious from today's historical vantage point that at least since 1800 the social geography and the culture of immigrants, descendants of recent immigrants, and Americans of long standing, have all been changing rapidly.

Theory, however, cannot be blamed for the inadequacies of the ghetto concept. The idea matured from direct and practical experience. The idea of a ghetto, or more modestly of "our neighbourhood," seen in contradistinction to a uniform outer world of America, came naturally to immigrants both because of the strangeness of American life and because they were poor and their poverty distinguished them from those they hoped to imitate. The settlement workers and sociologists, too, who first sought to understand immigrant life, began their studies in the poorest, most crowded, and most problem-beset quarters of the city, where conditions in the early twentieth century, and the arrival of the largest wave of Jewish immigrants, combined to suggest the aptness of the term "ghetto" for the American immigrant slum.* Reinforcing this from the other side, nativism, fear of foreigners, Americanization campaigns, and the hasty writings of journalists and politicians have all left a thick historical deposit of two-culture thinking about urban America.

In complete contrast to this line of thinking, the best descriptions of American urban culture today portray a complicated structure of variations by class and by socio-religious identification. According to current analysis, the attitude and presumably the behaviour of almost all urban Americans can be located on a matrix of four classes (upper class, middle class, working class, and lower class) and four socio-religious identifications—white Protestant, white Catholic, white Jewish, and Negro Protestant. These latter four are considered by all authorities to be the direct outcome of the process of the American urbanization of immigrants, and it will be useful to consider the dimensions of cultural change as dependent variables, and economic class structure as the independent variables.[5]

It seems reasonable to suppose that these four socio-religious groupings are the latest chapter in the history of America's fast-changing culture. The suggestion for such a cultural classification was first put forward in 1944 by Ruby Jo Kennedy on the basis of her studies of Protestant, Catholic, and Jewish marriage patterns in New Haven, Connecticut, for the years 1870–1940. Will Herberg then offered a general essay on religious history in 1955, and the full construct was tested and confirmed by Gerhard Lenski's 1958 survey of metropolitan Detroit. This showed that in respect to attitudes towards social mobility, education, family relations, manners, interracial housing, and politics, city dwellers divided as sharply by their socio-religious identification as they did by class. In short, for all those issues that can be considered ingredients of culture, from what one hopes for one's children to one's attitude toward science, Protestant, Catholic, Jewish, and Negro Protestant loyalties were major unities of modern American urban life. In 1961 Oscar Handlin, who had previously written two classics of the ghetto interpretation of urban history, adopted the four socio-religious categories as the latest product of American cultural change. A few years later, Glazer and

---

* Statistics may also bedevil urban studies and have persuaded students of cities that ghettos existed when they did not. Statistics that show 70 per cent of the Italian foreign-born living in 15 per cent of a city's wards cannot by themselves be taken as indicating a ghetto; a strong cluster of a group in a limited number of wards may or may not indicate a ghetto depending on whether or not these wards are shared with others.

Moynihan published their popular study of ethnicity in New York City and predicted the same cultural outcome for people in the municipal core of that giant metropolis. The consequence of this postwar writing has been to harness the former literature of the ghetto process of cultural change to the explanation of the history of the four-part socio-religious culture of today's metropolis.

Since this ghetto hypothesis is the most popular and fully formulated construct of urban cultural change, and since it does describe accurately an important number of cases, it is worth considering how this interpretation might be applied to a longer time span, an exercise which will demonstrate both its validity and its limitations. The exercise might go as follows:

In the early nineteenth century, during the first years of rapid urbanization, white Protestant culture dominated the cities. It derived largely from rural America, but included some of the traditions of the old Atlantic seaboard towns. Protestantism in 1800 or 1820 was not a homogeneous culture. It was divided by strong denominational loyalties and long traditions of conflict among Anglicans, Quakers, Presbyterians, Congregationalists, Baptists, Methodists, and pietists of several varieties. A general wave of evangelism, beginning with the revivals of 1795, if not earlier, was, however, steadily eroding denominational differences. By 1850, most Protestant Americans were agreed that the essence of religion lay in belief in immortality, faith in the theory of rewards and punishments, and confidence that the individual was the leading actor in religion.[6]

During these early nineteenth-century decades, waves of poor Irish and German immigrants poured into New York, Boston, Philadelphia, Pittsburgh, Cincinnati, St. Louis, and New Orleans. Being poor, many of them had to crowd together in the old houses of the city, thus forming immigrant slums near the waterfront where the largest concentration of decayed houses existed. In this manner ghettos (or immigrant quarters) first appeared in the nation's port and river cities. But as the immigrants prospered, or as their children mastered American ways and prospered, the successful began to move out of the ghetto into the newer sections of the city. Their patterns of settlement changed as they moved; they began to live like other Americans in mixed neighbourhoods, and over the years became more and more diffused throughout the metropolis.[7] The ghetto became the historical agent of ethnic culture, the place where old ways were first blended with some American ways to make the first hyphenated cultures. The suburb, in turn, became the site of the new, fully American, socio-religious cultures.

No matter who lived where, some compelling features of American life bore upon immigrant and native alike. Rapid change in methods of business and manufacture altered the traditions of native artisans and shopkeepers and forced new habits upon immigrants. Extreme geographical mobility, the response partly to the opening up of new land in the west, and partly to the fluid state of the economy which encouraged men to move from shop to shop and from town to town seeking work, wore down traditional local loyalties and identifications. As native Americans were more and more swept up in the fast pace of money-making in the Jacksonian era, and as the immigrant became more and more American, both sought more universally acceptable and more generalized identifications than either denomination or birthplace. Finally, the continuing conflicts between native Protestants and immigrant Catholics over schools, temperance, sabbath observance, abolition, and nativism forced all city dwellers to think of themselves either as Protestants or Catholics, not as Connecticut Congregationalists or County Cork Irishmen. Under such pressures the large body of English, Canadian, and German Protestant immigrants merged with the native Protestant mass, while the Irish Catholic church was forced to accommodate earlier French groups and the German Catholics.

Stimulated by political needs as well as by visible cultural contrasts, this process of cultural change—first set in motion by native American denominationalists and Irish and German immigrants in the decades before 1850—continued througout the next hundred years, during which the basic forces of evangelism, immigration, urbanization, and industrialization made their powerful impact on the country's history. As new immigrant groups succeeded the old, as Italians, Poles, Rumanians, Russians, and Mexicans took the place of English, Irish, and Germans, the pattern of the earlier years was repeated over and over again.

This view of cultural change has the merit of encompassing all the major forces of the past 150 years while at the same time reconciling our abundant ghetto literature with the concept of the four-part metropolitan culture. But however reasonable and inclusive this interpretation of urban cultural change may be, it suffers from two fatal weaknesses. First, most urban immigrants never lived in ghettos; second, such ghettos as did exist were probably not the uniform environments that the interpretation implies.

Although not enough research has been done to warrant new hypotheses to supplement the ghetto one, some illustrative material exists which helps to define the boundaries of the ghetto interpretation. Statistical fragments from the years before the Civil War, as well as studies of sixteen major cities for the years 1910 and 1950, suggest that among the "old immigration," the Canadians, Irish, and British never had ghettos except in an occasional city for a brief period. For example, the mid-nineteenth-century Boston and Philadelphia statistics on the distribution of the Irish show that during the first era of immigration and urbanization newcomers were not highly segregated. There were strong concentrations at a few points in the city, but these places were shared with others, native and foreign alike, and many immigrants were scattered throughout all the city wards.

. . . The degree of concentration of groups [is measured] by an Index of Dissimilarity. This index states the degree to which those of a given group reside in some districts of a city in proportions different from their proportion of the total city population. For example: if the foreign-born Irish were 30 per cent of the population of a city, and if they made up 30 per cent of the population of every ward in the city, then the Index of Dissimilarity would be zero. If, on the other hand, all the Irish lived in one ward, then the Index of Dissimilarity would stand at 100. This index has been widely used for comparisons of Negro segregation in American cities, and in a thorough statistical study of the foreign-born in ten cities. They show that values of about 25 mark the boundary between weak and strong residential clustering. Values below 25 indicate that most members of a group live scattered through the city, without a large concentrated district of their own. Values above 25 indicate the presence of one or more large clusters where members of the group in question live in substantially greater proportion than their share of the city's total population.[8]

. . . The Irish figures for 1855 [in Boston, with an Index of Dissimilarity of 8.0] and 1860 [in Philadelphia, with an Index of Dissimilarity of 19.8] show a remarkable residential diffusion. The Irish, who formed so large a part of Boston's population (28.6 per cent in 1855), and who were so much the object of popular prejudice, settled in a scattered pattern, living in about the same proportions in all twelve wards. To be sure there were in Boston crowded wards of poverty, but these the Irish shared with native poor and immigrants from other nations. The Irish of Philadelphia (16.9 per cent of the 1860 population) clustered more than they did in Boston, but considering the violent riots and strong prejudice against them in that city, they were quite evenly settled in every ward.

The Germans, on the other hand, a group noted for its assimilation into the general culture, appear to have had some strong residential clusters even from the earliest times. Those persons with German patronyms in Philadelphia in 1774, German foreign-born in Philadelphia in 1860, and German and Dutch foreign-born in Boston in 1855 all show some evidence of strong clustering. Indeed their index values [33.8 in Boston and 34.1 in Philadelphia] approach those of the caste-isolated Negroes of Manhattan and Brooklyn and of Philadelphia.

In sum, our statistical fragments suggest that late eighteenth-century and mid-nineteenth-century American urban settlement patterns were of two types. The largest immigrant group, the Irish, was scattered throughout the city; the Germans were both scattered and had a strong cluster or clusters in each large city. If these figures are representative, they hardly support a ghetto interpretation of urban cultural change.

Two historical conditions account for the diffusion of pre-Civil War immigrants in American cities. First, and most important, no large stock of old housing existed to quarter the new immigrants. No matter how the poor might crowd together, and the contemporary accounts report intolerably crowded conditions in cellars, attics, alley shacks, converted warehouses, and made-over churches,[9] there were not enough old buildings in the early nineteenth-century American city to make a large ghetto. Like many native Americans, many immigrants in these booming cities had to find quarters in new buildings, in the cheapest of row houses, in tiny cottages, or in scattered shanties on the vacant lots on the edge of town. The ubiquity of cheap new structures in those days before the introduction of fire, sanitary, and zoning codes, encouraged the scattering of native and immigrant poor. By the end of the nineteenth century, however, many American cities had been large enough for long enough to have a big stock of cheap housing, and it was here that the immigrant ghettos, or ports of entry, were located.

Second, the small scale of most urban economic activity, especially during the early years of the nineteenth century, encouraged the diffusion of trades through every neighbourhood and worked directly against the creation of purely residential, or purely business districts. The large all-residential neighbourhoods of the late nineteenth century and subsequent years were new and important places of strict income-grading in housing and strong ethnic clustering. In the late nineteenth century, large-scale manufacturing, retailing, and commercial organizations created distinct business quarters in cities: mixed retail, office, and manufacturing downtowns, wholesaling and manufacturing districts, satellite heavy manufacturing districts, and their opposites, working-class and middle-class residential suburbs.

It was these new suburbs which played so important a part in determining the later urban patterns of housing selection and segregation, and in the 1920s these same twentieth-century business and housing dispositions received legal sanction when American cities adopted zoning ordinances to maintain uniform tracts of land use and structure type. Immigrant ghetto literature flourished within this 1880–1940 pattern of urban social geography.

From this brief review of urban development and segregation we can estimate that of the "old immigration," the Canadians, the Irish, and the British never sustained ghettos except in an occasional city for a brief period. The Germans, the other major old immigration group, presumably always had a strong concentration of settlement which could be called a ghetto in each of the sixteen cities so far studied, and these concentrations persisted from the early nineteenth century until the Second World War. At all times, however, very heavy proportions of Germans lived scattered through the city. The "new immigration" of East Europeans and Italians was drawn into ghettos, and Stanley Lieberson and others have demonstrated that these groups followed the concentrated-diffused sequence of residence of the ghetto interpretation of history.[10] So far there have not been enough Mexican and Puerto Rican studies to make intercity comparisons possible. To sum up, we can say that both in respect to the proportions of immigrants of all nations in the twentieth century (the old immigration plus the non-ghetto new immigration), and in respect to the period 1770–1950, the majority of American immigrant city dwellers achieved assimilation outside ghettos.

Differences among cities suggest that the ghetto hypothesis may be limited not only to specific periods and nationalities, but also in its applicability to the largest American cities. First and foremost, cities vary in size.[11] Ranking cities by the size of their population in 1910 and 1950, it can be seen that the largest among them tended to be the most heavily immigrant, and that this relationship grew more pronounced as the century advanced. The larger the city, the more powerful its attraction for immigrants. Chicago and New York ghetto literature should be read as pertaining to the special cases of the nation's largest and heaviest immigrant cities, not merely as large-scale versions of a common state of affairs.

When one seeks to generalize about the sort of social geography immigrants experienced in American cities in the twentieth century, the reasonably smooth relationships and possible explanatory power of city size disappear. Instead one confronts a pattern of great diversity, indeed rising diversity between 1910 and 1950.* Measuring the degree of concentration of immigrants by the Index of Dissimilarity, Baltimore for its size seems inexplicably highly segregated in 1910; Boston and Pittsburgh are likewise abnormally highly segregated in 1950. On the other hand, Los Angeles and San Francisco, the one a new city, the other old, are surprisingly less segregated than all others on the list except the two old Ohio River cities of Louisville and Cincinnati. By 1950, all four displayed patterns similar to others on the list.

Common sense suggests that the variations in the levels of segregation might well stem from differences in the origins of the immigrants. A predominantly German-Irish-Russian city might be different from a Polish-Russian-Canadian-Mexican one. It is well

Eleven Cities Ranked by Size Giving Index of Dissimilarity for Foreign-born and Negro Population 1910, 1950

	Foreign-born 1910	Negro 1910
Manhattan–Brooklyn	23.4	32.2
Chicago	20.2	68.2
Boston	16.1	50.9
St. Louis	19.5	53.4
San Francisco–Oakland	15.4	42.0
Baltimore	29.7	40.3
Pittsburgh	19.1	42.9
Cincinnati	13.4	46.6
Los Angeles	7.0	27.7
Kansas City	19.3	34.0
Louisville	7.8	18.9

	Foreign-born 1950	Negro 1950
Manhattan–Brooklyn	25.8	83.3
Los Angeles	20.3	83.6
Chicago	21.5	90.8
Boston	54.9	77.8
San Francisco–Oakland	19.8	67.7
Pittsburgh	47.9	69.1
St. Louis	21.4	84.0
Baltimore	31.1	74.6
Cincinnati	26.5	78.5
Kansas City	26.7	76.0
Louisville	21.9	72.0

Source: Data taken or calculated from the U.S. Census.

* In the spring of 1967 a group of students in the Washington University urban history seminar calculated Index of Dissimilarity values for 1910 and 1950 for eleven cities in respect to Negroes, all foreign-born, the three largest ethnic groups of each city, and one working-class income category.

known that just as the Germans lived more clustered together in nineteenth-century cities than the Irish, so in the twentieth century Italian, Polish, and Russian immigrants formed strong residential clusters. These are the historian's common distinction between the "old immigration" from Ireland, Britain and Germany, and the "new immigration" of eastern and southern Europeans. Thus, in 1910, the Manhattan-Brooklyn sector of metropolitan New York (with its leading immigrant groups of Russians, Italians, and Irish) quite logically showed a more segregated pattern of housing for foreign-born than Los Angeles with its Germans, Canadians, and Orientals. Nevertheless, these variations in the mixture of leading immigrant groups do not seem an adequate explanation of the variations in the Index of Dissimilarity values. Chicago maintained a steady housing pattern although its leading foreign population groups shifted between 1910 and 1950 from Germans, Austrians, and Russians, to Poles, Germans, and Italians. Boston's markedly diffused 1910 pattern was the outcome of a mix of Irish, Canadians, and Russians. It became highly segregated when Canadians, Italians, and Irish became its three largest immigrant groups, a development which can hardly account for a radical change in housing patterns.

Clearly, forces other than city size and ethnic mix have been at work in each city to produce considerable variations in [its] residential patterns. There is no comparative historical literature dealing with the variations in immigrant experience from city to city, but some guesses may be hazarded. Differences in the rate of growth of cities probably created different degrees of residential segregation. For example, boom times would promote rapid class turnover in old central city housing and large-scale migration to new working class and middle-class suburbs. On the other hand, slow growth, as in Boston or St. Louis during the years 1910–50, may have meant both slow shifts towards the outer suburbs and slow rates of social mobility as well. In slack times immigrants may well have been held both to old neighbourhoods and to low-paying jobs longer than their counterparts living in prosperous regions. Finally, differing rates of arrival of Negro migrants who would be competitors for cheap housing may also help to explain variations among the dispersal of foreign-born. Whatever the source or sources of differences among American cities in respect to immigrant housing patterns, the subject is one for serious study by historians.

If this brief survey of urban residential characteristics reveals great diversity, how should our ghetto literature be interpreted? What information may the specialist rely on until further studies of acculturation are done, and how should the non-specialist read this literature?

First, ghettos of foreign-born from eastern and southern Europe did exist in American cities, perhaps in every major city since 1880, and such concentrations persisted at least until the Second World War. Orientals, Scandinavians, and other foreign-language groups, too, have lived in ghettos in some cities for varying lengths of time. These particular environments are the limited cases which the ghetto literature documents so well.

Second, one should not reason from this immigrant literature to the ecology of the northern urban Negro. If the high Index of Dissimilarity values are evidence of national trends, then the Negro as a member of a disfavoured group has, at least since 1830, maintained highly segregated ghettos in nothern cities. In the twentieth century, when large numbers of Negroes moved into northern citi₃s, the vast majority of them lived in almost all-black areas.

Third, the immigrant ports of entry were dense concentrations of poverty, or slums, in the same sense as the Negro ghettos, but the white immigrant shared his quarter with other poor immigrants and the native American poor as well.

Fourth, at all times large numbers of immigrants settled outside the ghettos. Irish, Canadian, Japanese, and Germans have customarily scattered more than Italians, Russians, Poles, Chinese, and Mexicans, but all groups have had many of their members scattered all over the city. These "outsiders" accomplished their Americanization without the immediate benefit or hindrance of a neighbourhood crowded with their fellow countrymen.

The possibility of supplementing our history of urban cultural change with accounts of the alternative paths of the "outsiders" is intriguing. Such an account would stress the preparedness of many immigrants for America. Cultural affinities and similarities would be sought for on both sides of the Atlantic as a means of explaining the relative ease of adjustment of so many newcomers. Class variations and variations in skills among immigrants at the time of landing would be stressed.

The position of "outsiders" may also account in part for the development of the four-part socio-religious culture of urban America; those living dispersed amongst natives would make alliances with co-religionists in order to build parish churches in these outer neighbourhoods. It is tempting also to see these outsiders as the families who experienced the buffeting of the competitive world in the same way as native families, and, like the natives, sought the communal neighbourhood church as a refuge sooner than those living amongst fellow nationals.

This view of the ghetto as a limited case also changes one's view of the ghetto itself. The ghetto becomes more than an agent of localized acculturation; its metropolitan functions grow in importance. The ghetto has long been stressed as the home of the first generation of immigrants, the place to which the children of immigrants returned for special foods, or for the foreign-language theatre, or the national church. If one conceives of the ghetto providing such functions from the years of its first formation for a majority of people who live outside it, then it becomes a special kind of metropolitan central place. Given the enlarged functions of catering to many "outsiders," the proximity and persistence of ghettos next to the metropolitan downtown ceases to be an historical accident. Ghettos were so located not only because of cheap slum housing, but because they, like the downtown stores, had to be central for a metropolitan clientele. Like the downtown, too, ghettos probably had a high concentration of retailers and small manufacturers who supplied a regional, sometimes even a national, ethnic market. Finally, the need to be located in such central places meant that ghettos occupied very expensive land and hence rents had to be high and crowding intense. Thus the American ghetto should be considered as a special element in the metropolitan economy of American cities before the Second World War, as well as a special event in the history of urban cultural change.

Notes

1. Some of the best works are Jacob A. Riis, *How the Other Half Lives* (1890); Jane Addams, *Twenty Years at Hull House* (1910); Robert A. Woods, *Americans in Process* (1903); Louis Wirth, *The Ghetto* (1928); Edith Abbott and Sophonisba Breckinridge, *The Tenements of Chicago 1908–1935* (1936); and such novels as Abraham Cahan, *The Rise of David Levinsky* (1917); James T. Farrell, *Studs Lonigan* (1935); Meyer Levin, *The Old Bunch* (1937). This literature has been summarized in Oscar Handlin's poetical *The Uprooted* (1951).

2. Daniel P. Moynihan has suggested that the analogue to the social pathology of the urban Negro family is to be found in the condition of the Irish family in the mid-nineteenth-century American slums. Hearings before the Senate Committee on Government operations on S–843, "Full Opportunity and Social Accounting Act of 1967," July 27, 1967, 90th Congress, 1st Session. See also N. Glazer and D. P. Moynihan, *Beyond the*

Melting Pot (Cambridge, Mass., 1963), 238–50; L. Rainwater and W. L. Yancey, eds., *The Moynihan Report and the Politics of Controversy* (Cambridge, Mass., 1967).

3. See K. E. and A. F. Taeuber, *Negroes in Cities* (Chicago, 1965), 52–5.

4. Cf. Oscar Handlin, *Boston's Immigrants, A Study in Acculturation* (rev. ed., Cambridge, Mass., 1959), 91–9.

5. Cf. R. J. R. Kennedy, "Single or Triple Melting Pot? Intermarriage Trends in New Haven 1870–1940," *American Journal of Sociology* (January, 1944); Will Herberg, *Protestant, Catholic, Jew* (New York, 1955); Gerhard Lenski, *The Religious Factor: A Sociological Study of Religion's Impact on Politics, Economics and Family Life* (New York, 1961); Oscar Handlin, "Historical Perspectives on the American Ethnic Group," *Daedalus* (Spring, 1961); M. M. Gordon, *Assimilation in American Life* (New York, 1964); A. M. Greeley, *Religion and Career, A Study of College Graduates* (New York, 1963). See also essays by M. A. Fried, L. Rainwater, and B. Berger, in Sam Bass Warner, Jr., ed., *Planning for a Nation of Cities* (Cambridge, Mass., 1966).

6. Sidney E. Mead, *The Lively Experiment; The Shaping of Christianity in America* (New York, 1963), Ch. 7.

7. This model of dispersal and integration of ethnic groups, developed by the Chicago school of sociologists, was first given systematic shape by Paul Cressey, "The Succession of Cultural Groups in the City of Chicago" (Ph.D. thesis, University of Chicago, 1930). It has been subjected to detailed and more sophisticated statistical analysis in Stanley Lieberson, *Ethnic Patterns in American Cities* (New York, 1963).

8. There is an extended discussion of the Index of Dissimilarity and the problems of measuring segregation in Taeuber and Taeuber, *Negroes in Cities*, 43–62, 197–242.

9. Matthew Carey, *A Plea for the Poor* (Philadelphia, 1837); J. H. Griscom, *The Sanitary Condition of the Laboring Population of New York* (New York, 1845); *Transactions of the American Medical Association*, 2 (1849); Citizens' Association of New York, *Report of the Council of Hygiene and Public Health upon the Sanitary Condition of the City* (New York, 1865).

10. Lieberson, *Ethnic Patterns*, 44–91; J. M. Beshers, E. O. Laumann, and B. S. Bradshaw, "Ethnic Congregation-Segregation, Assimilation, and Stratification," *Social Forces* (May, 1964).

11. The age of cities is another powerful variable in differing patterns of settlement. See the analysis of 76 southern cities in 1960, using the Index of Dissimilarity, by L. F. Schnore and P. C. Evenson, "Segregation in Southern Cities," *American Journal of Sociology* (July, 1966).

Section Two

The Ecology of the Ghetto

Haunting the ghetto resident are physical and psychological depredations, or what Kenneth Clark has called the "objective and subjective dimensions of the American urban ghetto." Most tangible are the physical signs of squalor and suffering—the dilapidated housing, overcrowding, decaying business establishments, high crime and drug rates, soaring rent and mortality rates, and the prevalence of disease. A century ago the New York Council of Hygiene and Public Health described the condition of Irish immigrants in lower Manhattan in this manner:

The high brick blocks and closely-packed houses . . . seemed to be literally *hives of sickness and vice*. It was wonderful to see, and difficult to believe, that so much misery, disease, and wretchedness can be huddled together and hidden by high walls, unvisited and unthought of, so near our own abodes. . . . Alas! human faces look so hideous with hope and self-respect all gone!

Less measurable are the psychological scars of ghetto life, which surface in antisocial behavior, fatalism, hopelessness, suspicion, hostility, and self-hatred. Amid the frenetic activity of the city, boredom and frustration gnaw at the ghetto resident.

Experts differ on the question of whether or not the ghetto produces a distinct life-style and on the extent to which Old World folkways and values remain influential in their new setting. Anthropologist Oscar Lewis, author of *La Vida: A Puerto Rican Family in the Culture of Poverty—San Juan and New York* (1965), argued that there is a common culture of poverty among all oppressed groups. Many ethnic and black nationalists claim that their heritage makes their situation unique. In the essay "Fifth Avenue, Uptown," novelist James Baldwin takes a middle position but concludes that ghetto culture transcends race and class and that ghetto residents share common effects from discrimination. In "Report from a Spanish Harlem 'Fortress,'" which appeared in the *New York Times Magazine* on January 5, 1964, Richard Hammer describes life for Puerto Rican newcomers:

> The people will tell you that this block is a fortress. Its walls are invisible; they are inside the mind, built by the people who live on the block and by society outside. But the walls are as real as if they were made of mortar and stone; they keep 3,000 people locked-up inside, afraid, and they keep most outsiders away, afraid. . . . Most of the young people . . . are bitter and disillusioned. They sit on the stoops because there isn't anything else most of them can do.

In the first two selections in this section, John H. Griscom, an antebellum New York physician, and Emily Dinwiddie, a Philadelphia housing reformer, examine the mean environment of working-class ghetto residents in New York and Philadelphia in two different periods, covering a time span of more than half a century. Their reports are remarkably similar to each other and to those of present conditions. Psychological effects of ghetto life are also similar regardless of locale or ethnic group. The selection by Stan Steiner chronicles the loss of identity in Chicano barrios of western cities. Steiner also sees a possibility of redemption from cultural genocide through group pride and solidarity. Historian Rudolph J. Vecoli's article on south Italians in Chicago emphasizes the danger of making sweeping generalizations about the universality of ghetto traits. Vecoli takes issue with Oscar Handlin's *The Uprooted* (1951), a poetic synthesis of the European immigrant's experience. Vecoli questions Handlin's model of the alienated newcomer, who emigrated from a homogeneous peasant village to an atavistic urban environment which threatens the formerly tight-knit institutional bonds of religion and community. Vecoli focuses on the continuity of many traditions, values, and customs in the New World, at least in the case of south Italian peasants. In the final two selections psychologist Robert Coles and essayist James Baldwin describe the caged and demoralizing living patterns of black residents in Boston and Harlem respectively.

For further reading see Louis Wirth, *The Ghetto* (1928); Donald B. Cole, *Immigrant City: Lawrence, Massachusetts, 1845–1921* (1949); Gordon Atkins, *Health, Housing, and Poverty in New York City, 1865–1898* (1947); Robert Woods and Albert J. Kennedy, *The Zone of Emergence* (1914); Allan H. Spear, *Black Chicago: The Making of a Negro Ghetto, 1890–1920* (1967); Oscar Lewis, "The Culture of Poverty," *Scientific American* (1966); Charles A. Valentine, *Culture and Poverty* (1968); William F. Whyte, *Street Corner Society* (1943); Kenneth Clark, *Dark Ghetto* (1966); Karl E. and Alma T. Taeuber, *Negroes in Cities: Residential Segregation and Neighborhood Change* (1965); David R. Hunter, *The Slums: Challenge and Response;* Mitchell Gordon, *Sick Cities: Psychology and Pathology of American Urban Life* (1965); Robert E. Forman, *Black Ghettos, White Ghettos and Slums* (1971).

6 Old New York's Working-Class Ghetto*

John H. Griscom

. . .

THE SYSTEM OF TENANTAGE to which large numbers of the poor are subject, I think, must be regarded as one of the principal causes of the helpless and noisome manner in which they live. The basis of these evils is the subjection of the tenantry to the merciless inflictions and extortions of the *sub-landlord*. A house, or a row, or court of houses, is hired by some person of the owner, on a lease of several years, for a sum which will yield a fair interest on the cost. The *owner* is thus relieved of the great trouble incident to the changes of tenants and the collection of rents. His income is sure from one individual and obtained without annoyance or oppression on his part. It then becomes the object of the lessee to make and save as much as possible with his adventure, sufficient sometimes to enable him to purchase the property in a short time.

The tenements, in order to admit a greater number of families, are divided into small apartments, as numerous as decency will admit. Regard to comfort, convenience, and health is the last mo-

* From John H. Griscom, *Sanitary Condition of the Labouring Population of New York* (New York, 1845), 6–10.

tive; indeed, the great ignorance of this class of speculators (who are very frequently foreigners and keep a grog shop on the premises) would prevent a proper observance of these, had they the desire. These closets, for they deserve no other name, are then rented to the poor from week to week, or month to month, the rent being almost invariably required in advance, at least for the first few terms. The families moving in first after the house is built find it clean, but the lessee has no supervision over their habits, and however filthy the tenement may become, he cares not, so that he receives his rent. He and his family are often found steeped as low in depravity and discomforts as any of his tenants, being above them only in the possession of money, and doubtless often beneath them in moral worth and sensibility.

It is very frequently the case that families, after occupying rooms a few weeks, will change their location, leaving behind them all the dirt which their residence has occasioned. Upon this the next comers will sit down, being so much occupied with the hurry of moving, and with the necessity of placing their furniture immediately in order, that attention to cleansing the apartment is out of the question until they are "settled," and then, if done at all, it is in the most careless and inefficient manner. Very often, perhaps in a majority of the cases in the class of which I now speak, no cleaning other than washing the floor is ever attempted, and that but seldom. Whitewashing, cleaning of furniture, of bedding, or persons, in many cases is *never* attempted. Some have old pieces of carpet which are never shaken (they would not bear it) and are used to hide the filth on the floor. Every corner of the room, of the cupboards, of the entries and stairways, is piled up with dirt. The walls and ceilings, with the plaster broken off in many places, exposing the lath and beams and leaving openings for the escape from within of the effluvia of vermin, dead and alive, are smeared with the blood of unmentionable insects and dirt of all indescribable colours. The low rooms are diminished in their areas by the necessary encroachments of the roof or the stairs leading to the rooms above; and behind and under them is a hole into which the light of day never enters, and where a small bed is often pushed in, upon which the luckless and degraded tenants pass their nights, weary and comfortless.

In these places the filth is allowed to accumulate to an extent almost incredible. Hiring their rooms for short periods only, it is very common to find the poor tenants moving from place to place every few weeks. By this practice they avoid the trouble of cleansing their rooms, as they can leave behind them the dirt which they have made.

The same room being occupied in rapid succession by tenant after tenant, it will easily be seen how the walls and windows will become broken, the doors and floors become injured, the chimneys filled with soot, the whole premises populated thickly with vermin, the stairways, the common passage of several families, the receptacle for all things noxious, and whatever of self-respect the family might have had be crushed under the pressure of the degrading circumstances by which they are surrounded.

Another very important particular in the arrangements of these tenements must here be noticed. By the mode in which the rooms are planned, *ventilation is entirely prevented*. It would seem as if most of these places were built expressly for this purpose. They have one or two windows and a door at one side of the room but no opening anywhere else. A draught of air *through* is therefore an utter impossibility. The confined position of the dwelling itself, generally, prevents the access of the external currents of air, even to the outside, to any considerable extent. The window sashes, in addition, perhaps are so arranged that the upper one (if there are two) cannot be let down, being permanently fastened up; hence the external air, poor as it is, cannot visit the upper section of the room unless by opening the door, by which the interior of the room is exposed to view. If there is a sleeping apartment, it is placed at the extremity of the room farthest from the windows, is generally but little larger than sufficient to hold a bedstead, and its area is reduced . . . by the bed furniture, trunks, boxes, &c. and having no windows, fresh air and sun light are entire strangers to its walls. In this dark hole there is, of course, a concentrated accumulation of the effluvia of the bodies and breaths of the persons sleeping in it, (frequently the whole family, several in number), and this accumulation goes on from night to night, without relief, until it can easily be believed the smell becomes intolerable and its atmosphere productive of the most offensive and malignant diseases. There is no exaggeration in this description. I cannot too highly color the picture if I would. What, then, will be thought of the condition of thousands of our fellow-citizens in the *winter season*, when every crevice is closed to keep out the cold air, and when I state that what I have described I have repeatedly seen and felt in the *summer*, when the windows and doors are opened to the fullest extent, day and night, admitting all the ventilation possible, small as it is.

I have had recent occasion to visit several of these pestiferous places, and I pen these paragraphs in the month of August, with their sight and smell fresh upon my senses.

The almost entire absence of household conveniences contributes much to the prostration of comfort and self-respect of these wretched people. The deficiency of water and the want of a convenient place for washing, with no other place for drying clothes than the common sitting and bed room, are very serious impediments in the way of their improvement. Without any convenient or safe place to deposit wood, or coal, or food in large quantities, all their purchases are by "the small," from the neighboring grocer (who is perhaps the landlord), at prices from 10 to 50 per cent above the rates at which they might be obtained under better circumstances.

But the most offensive of all places for residence are the *cellars*. It is almost impossible, when contemplating the circumstances and condition of the poor beings who inhabit these holes, to maintain the proper degree of calmness requisite for a thorough inspection and the exercise of a sound judgment respecting them. You must descend to them; you must feel the blast of foul air as it meets your face on opening the door; you must grope in the dark or hesitate until your eye becomes accustomed to the gloomy place to enable you to find your way through the entry, over a broken floor, the boards of which are protected from your tread by a half inch of hard dirt; you must inhale the suffocating vapor of the sitting and sleeping rooms; and in the dark, damp recess endeavor to find the inmates by the sound of their voices, or chance to see their figures moving between you and the flickering blaze of a shaving burning on the hearth, or the misty light of a window coated with dirt and festooned with cobwebs—or if in search of an invalid, take care that you do not fall full length upon the bed with her by stumbling against the bundle of rags and straw dignified by that name, lying on the floor under the window, if window there is;—all this, and much more, beyond the reach of my pen, must be felt and seen ere you can appreciate in its full force the mournful and disgusting condition in which many thousands of the subjects of our government pass their lives.

> There vapors, with malignant breath
> Rise thick, and scatter midnight death.

There are two features of a cellar residence which more especially render them objectionable; 1st, the dampness, and 2d, the more incomplete ventilation. In *any* cellar the impossibility of access for the heat of the sun to the parts of the soil adjacent to the floor and walls, and the absence of currents of air through the room, keep it much more damp than rooms above ground, where the heat and air have freer access. This is emphatically the case with *inhabited* cellars, inasmuch as the inmates are careful to exclude the external air by closing all the avenues of its approach in order to preserve the temperature high in winter and low in summer. The moisture, whose escape is thus prevented, is in itself a very prolific source of disease, and combined with the darkness and impure air of these places, is actually productive of a great amount of sickness. Could the sun and air be made to reach them, and were it possible to establish a sufficient ventilation through them, much of their noxiousness would be relieved; but under no circumstances can they be made fit for the residence of *living* beings; they are properly adapted only as receptacles for the dead.

In addition to these impediments to the drying of these places, they are very often so situated that the surface water finds its way into them at every rain storm. It may be remembered that in the summer of 1843 all the underground apartments in many sections of the city were completely flooded by a deluge of rain. In the eastern part of the city, in Delancy, Rivington, Stanton, and many other of the neighbouring streets, almost every cellar (and great numbers of them are inhabited) were half filled with water. This evil will not recur to so great an extent in the neighborhood alluded to, sewers having been built in some of the streets. But in other sections, indeed in every section where the position of the basement is unaltered and sewers are not constructed, the nuisance must be suffered at every rain storm. In some courts to which I can point, *the surface is below the level of the street,* and at every rain, the water being unable to run off into the street, is all discharged down into the adjacent areas and cellars, keeping them almost constantly wet. It was but a short time ago I met with the case of a woman, the wife of a tailor living in a noted court in Walker-street, and occupying partly a basement, in which she was compelled to pass much of her time. She has lived there six months, four of which she has been sick with rheumatism, and on that account unable to work. Otherwise she would be able to earn considerable by assisting her husband. They have four children depending upon them and are obliged to seek assistance from the public in consequence of this sickness. She attributes her disease to the water in the cellar, which runs in and obliges her to bale out and wipe up at every storm. The money expended upon them in charity would have rectified all this difficulty, have preserved the health and strength of the family, and saved all parties much trouble and suffering.

Another case is that of a woman with two children—her husband a labourer—living in a cellar in Lewis-street, two months. Before moving to this place, she lived in an upper room in Spring-street and was there always well, *but has been sick ever since she went to live in the cellar.*

Another applied for medical aid who lives in a cellar *immediately adjoining which is the vault of a church-yard, the moisture from which comes through into the apartment, to such an extent as obliged them to move the bed away from the wall.*

It is not a difficult matter for the Dispensary Physician, while receiving applications for medical aid at the office, to distinguish, in a majority of cases, the cellar residents from all others without asking a question. If the whitened and cadaverous countenance should be an insufficient guide, *the odor of the person* will remove all doubt; a musty smell, which a damp cellar only can impart, pervades every article of dress, the woolens more particularly, as well as the hair and skin.

At No. 50 Pike-street is a cellar about ten feet square and seven feet high, having only one very small window and the old fashioned, inclined cellar door. In this small place were lately residing *two families consisting of ten persons* of all ages. . . . The general arrangement of the cells in the City Prison is but little if any better.

7 Housing Conditions in Philadelphia's Ghettos*

Emily Dinwiddie

THE SELFISHNESS which refuses to be its brother's keeper brings its punishment with especial swiftness in such a city as Philadelphia, where wretched, unhealthful alleys are found near the business streets or just back of handsome residences, as well as in the so-called slums. The points of contact are many—the man or woman who jostles one in the street car may have come straight from the tenement or alley house concerning the disease-breeding condition of which the polite world prefers to be ignorant. Mere enlightened self-interest should furnish sufficient motive for effort to maintain in all parts of the city conditions required for decency and health. The contagion of disease and vice fostered in the neglected districts spreads to the remotest sections.

The city prides itself upon the rows of workingmen's cottages, the absence of the "dumbbell" tenement house, the low buildings, the consequent small density of the population per acre, and the

* From Emily Dinwiddie, *Housing Conditions in Philadelphia* (Philadelphia, 1904), 1–4, 6–7, 10, 13–14, 19–20, 22.

comparative freedom from evils of insufficient light and ventilation. These points of superiority are not to be under-rated, yet they do not furnish a ground for the comfortable feeling that all is thoroughly healthful and satisfactory and that there is nothing to be done. A community may be free from the special evils of other cities and yet have a housing problem of great seriousness. London, for example, is supposed to have the worst conditions in Europe, yet it is without a tenement house problem in the sense in which New York knows it, the situation there being in many ways strikingly similar to that in Philadelphia.

The complacency which prevails here is dangerous; and the conditions are generally unknown. Those who discuss Philadelphia's housing problems are often met by the surprised exclamation, "I thought Philadelphia had no bad conditions; that it was a city of homes." Yet the intricate network of courts and alleys with which the interior of the blocks are covered is a conspicuous feature, and also the crowding together of the houses so closely that a large proportion have no open space at the rear or side, all light and air coming from the front windows opening on the narrow court, so that ventilation through the house is impossible. In many of the courts there is only surface drainage, slops are thrown out into a gutter, and if the alley is not properly paved and graded, as is frequently the case, the foul water remains in stagnant pools before the houses. Often there are stables among the dwellings and the tenants must go over or around the manure pits into which the refuse from these is thrown. There are a few large tenements, nearly all of which were built before the passage of the Tenement House Act of 1895, and are of bad types, but far more important are the numbers of smaller houses, not built for tenements, and not containing accommodations adequate for more than one family, which are occupied by three, four, five, six or more separate households.

• • •

The first district investigated was in the heart of the Italian quarter, where the black-eyed children, rolling and tumbling together, the gaily colored dresses of the women and the crowds of street venders, all give the neighborhood a wholly foreign appearance. Goats wandering the streets are a conspicuous feature, and rag pickers may be seen at their work in many of the alleys. In this block also is the Italian marionette theatre, which is attended nightly by crowds of the men and boys of Little Italy.

• • •

The second district is tenanted by a mixed population of Russian and Austro-Hungarian Jews and Christians, Germans, Poles, Irish and Americans. Huge breweries and stables stand out conspicuously. There are some fairly large tenement houses, but the greater number of buildings are small alley dwellings, many very old and some in so dilapidated a condition as to be unfit for habitation.

The third district lies in the colored neighborhood. This section has greatly changed in character within the past seven years. The preponderance of colored over white has increased in marked degree since 1897 and 1898 when the material for the "Philadelphia Negro" was gathered. It is evident that the colored people are being crowded westward by the influx of Russian Jews on their eastern boundary.

. . .

In one sense it is true that Philadelphia has no tenement house problem, since very few of the houses were originally built for tenements. This does not mean, however, that a large number are not so occupied, most of which, unfortunately, are totally unsuited to the purpose. Over 4,000 buildings in Philadelphia, according to the last census report, are tenanted by three or more families each. Of the houses visited in the present investigation nearly 12 per cent were tenements, which means of course that very considerably more than 12 per cent of the families were tenement dwellers, for houses of this sort may be occupied by a large number of families. The largest inspected contained thirty families. Rear or alley houses are of even greater importance, being equally bad and found in much larger numbers. Such buildings do not face upon the street, but stand in a yard, alley or court back of another house. It is difficult to obtain statistics as to the exact number of these buildings throughout the city, but it is very large, and the alleys are widely distributed. Of the houses visited in the three main districts inspected, 42 per cent were alley dwellings. In the second district the rear houses numbered nearly twice as many as the front dwellings.

Most of the rear houses in Philadelphia are one-family buildings, but we can hardly doubt that a rear single-family house bears the same relation of increased unhealthfulness to a front building of this kind as a rear three-family house to one facing on the street.

The type of court common in Philadelphia has been characterized as the horizontal tenement. The name is not a bad one. The tenants of little alley houses live together on much the same terms as those of a large tenement house. They share the use of courts and passageways, and usually of water supply fixtures and toilet accommodations as well. The same conditions of dirt and neglect are apt to result in both cases from the divided responsibility. What is everybody's business is commonly found to be nobody's business. In only two tenements was there found to be a janitor; in the courts, of course, there was no provision of a caretaker. In tenements and alleys all the worst conditions of inadequacy of water supply and sanitary accommodations are found. The lack of light and ventilation is frequently similar in the two types. Yard space is often sacrificed in order to crowd the largest possible number of families upon a lot. A large proportion of alley houses have no yards; where they are found they are generally so small as not to deserve the name. Half of the rear houses in the first block inspected, had no open space at the back or side, and no through circulation of air. The blank wall at the back sometimes faced on a neighboring lot, the yard of which adjoined this wall, but there was no possibility of a circulation through. In other cases the houses were built up on three sides; these were the back-to-back dwellings so long denounced abroad, where a number of investigations made showed a terrible increase in mortality among the tenants of buildings of this type in excess of the death rate among the general population.

• • •

One tenement visited was a three story house, without fire-escapes, containing a grocery store, a fish stand and a meat shop on the first floor. Above in the seventeen living rooms of all kinds—kitchens, bed-rooms and dining-rooms—were eight families, consisting of thirty-three persons. A goat was kept in the room back of the grocery and three dogs upstairs. The second story hall was filthy and strewn with accumulations of garbage and ashes. Two long hopper water closets in the hall were the toilet accommodations for the eight families, an outdoor privy compartment serving for the stores. The closets and also the privy were extremely foul and in bad repair. The privy vault was in an archway under the upper part of the building and was the common well over which sixteen toilet rooms were built, one for the tenement, the others for the rows of rear houses beyond. The vault was also used as a cesspool, receiving the discharge from some of the waste pipes of the house. There was leakage into the cellar, which was damp, foul and full of rubbish. The yard, a tiny passageway, extending from the grocery store to the toilet room, was in a filthy condition, being covered with fish, refuse and foul water from the first and third story sinks, which discharged on the surface of the ground. The waste pipe from the sink back of the grocery was a rubber hose. In the second story hall one trap served for the two closets and a sink. The odors in the building were very offensive.

• • •

In the yards such refuse as old mattresses, bed springs, the blood and feathers of slaughtered fowls, garbage, and rags of all kinds were to be seen. Owing to the very small size of the yards, these accumulations were usually directly under the windows of the living rooms. Where the drainage was inadequate, pools of stagnant water added to the general insanitary condition. Only a little over half of the yards had entire sewer drainage.

Many of the cellars were in such a state as to endanger the health of the occupants of the houses. One had a stream of considerable size flowing through it from a broken flush pipe in the yard; it had worn a fairly deep channel, and the tenants stated that this had been the condition for more than a month. In a row of rear houses the water supply consisted of hydrants in the cellars, without sinks or drains, the water discharging on the earth floors on which the tenants threw their garbage and slops. The odors were overpowering. Five houses on one court, of which four were occupied, had cellars flooded with sewage from a leaking soil pipe, the foul water standing about a foot deep in all but one of the buildings. One does not wonder that there was sickness in each of the families tenanting the houses. Many other instances might be quoted of cellars wet from leaky vaults and broken pipes or from surface drainage percolating through. A large proportion were filled with junk and rubbish of every sort. Beds and bedding, said to have been cast aside because someone had died upon them, and it was "bad luck" to use them again, were not infrequently found in cellars. No less than 43.73 per cent of the cellars, or nearly one-half, were noticeably damp, wet, or covered with standing water. Often the walls were overgrown with mould from the moisture, as well as tapestried with cobwebs and thick with dust and dirt. In more than half of the cellars the walls had at one time been whitewashed over their entire extent, but in only two or three cases did it appear that this had been done within the year. Usually barely enough remained beneath the dirt to show that there had once been a coat of wash. The majority of the ceilings had never been whitewashed. Frequently whitewash had been put on only beside the stairs and on the floor beams, the rest being untouched.

. . .

The toilet accommodations for the houses investigated were totally inadequate in number as well as defective in kind. Many instances might be quoted: For example, six houses were visited having only one foul privy compartment for the whole number. A tenement was seen in which the sole toilet for five families and the employees in a store was one yard privy, of which the seat had fallen into the vault and the floor was broken. The filth of this toilet room and the yard outside was indescribable. In the Italian district alone, 48 families, over 13 per cent of the total number, had only one toilet for each six families, and over 65 per cent of the families here shared the use of a toilet compartment with from one to five others. In the second and third districts, the conditions were but slightly less serious. In the three districts there were 622 toilet rooms for 843 families and 149 stores and places of business.

Health and decency are surely sacrificed under such conditions, and cleanly tenants suffer unjustly from the filthy habits of others. Every facility also is given to the spread of disease, for the toilets used by several families can almost never be kept locked, and thus are open to the public.

Of all the toilet rooms seen, 92.60 per cent were in the yards or courts, most of which were so small that the vaults or closets were within a few feet of the windows of the houses, if not directly against the walls of the building. Not infrequently the compartments were found in dark archways under the second story living rooms. Probably the most common complaint which meets the investigator is that offensive odors from vaults render kitchens or bedrooms almost unendurable.

. . .

In spite of the rows of one-family houses, overcrowding of living rooms exists to a startling extent in certain sections of the city. In the Italian district more than one family in every four, almost one in three, had but one room for kitchen, dining-room and bedroom. One hundred and four single room "housekeeping apartments" were found in this one block. In the other districts they were found in smaller numbers. Of all the families, 137, or about one-sixth, lived in one-room apartments. Five instances were met in which as many as seven persons of all ages and both sexes slept in one room, which served as kitchen as well; in six other one-room apartments there were six occupants each; in thirteen, five each, and in twenty-seven, four each. It is difficult to imagine what this means without having seen life under such conditions. Except in freezing weather the members of the family who are able to do so, stay out of doors because the rooms are unendurable. Cleanliness is impossible and decency is utterly disregarded, while contagious diseases spread with frightful rapidity. There is no home life and no privacy anywhere; to call such a habitation a home is but mockery. Moral and physical evils of every kind result. Under vitalization and nervous tension are common.

. . .

In spite of crowded conditions and inadequacy of water supply, the great majority of rooms investigated were clean, a fact which may surprise those not familiar with the sections of the city inspected. One room in eighty-four was in a state which could only be described as filthy; one in seven was dirty, but the rest were all clean or fairly clean. Not infrequently the scrubbed and shining floors of tiny rear houses would put some large and pretentious dwellings to shame. Unquestionably there are many conditions of dirt and neglect in the houses and yards for which the tenants are responsible, but the cleanliness of the living rooms is a matter which they feel more vitally concerns their self-respect and their standing with their neighbors.

8 The Chicanos*

Stan Steiner

. . . THE BARRIOS of the Chicanos are not like the gray tenement tombs of the ghetto. The barrios sprawl over the hills and into the arroyos and valleys, amid the weeds and flowers, like wandering Indian villages. They are a paradox that defies easy comparisons.

Ghettos are the refuse dumps of the industrial city.

"Who creates the ghetto?" asks Eliezer Risco, the editor of *La Raza,* the newspaper of the barrios of East Los Angeles.

The ghetto is where you are forced to live by housing discrimination. But La Raza has been living in the barrios for hundreds of years. No one has forced us. The barrios are not ghettos, although we do have ghettos in the barrios. There are suburbs and there are skidrows; there are ghettos of the poor and there are neighborhoods of the rich. We have everything here that you have in the larger city, but one thing—you, in the larger

* Abridged from pp. 142–43, 230–36, 240–41 in *La Raza: The Mexican Americans* by Stan Steiner. Copyright © 1969, 1970 by Stan Steiner. By permission of Harper & Row, Publishers, Inc.

city, govern us. We do not run our own lives because you do
not let us. You run the barrios and you don't know how.

"Barrio" is a Spanish word that simply means "neighborhood."
In the colonial era of Mexico the Spanish rulers subtly changed the
meaning by using barrio to designate the "native quarter," where the
Indians lived. It was a word of contempt. The word barrio, as it is
used in the United States to designate the Mexican or "Spanish"
neighborhood, is a modern version of that colonial term; except that
today the Chicanos have once more changed the demeaning meaning
of the old colonial word to one of pride.

It is a city within a city within a city. Wherever the outsider
sees one barrio, there are not one but many barrios within the boundaries of family ties, origins in Mexico, or simply street-map geography. Each barrio has its own loyalties, churches, local shrines, shopkeepers, gangs of boys, customs, history, and old village patriarchs.

"Urban villages" may be a better definition of "barrios." In these
communities the Chicanos try to live in the best of both worlds: those
of the village and those of the city.

• • •

The girl was thirteen when she tried to kill herself. She was
"tired of working." But she was too inexperienced with death to die,
and she lived through her death. To escape her loneliness she married, at fifteen. Her child was born that year, but her husband was
sent to prison. "I got a car. The car broke down. I couldn't pay for it.
They wanted to sue me. So I forged a check." In the barrios of Denver to be left with a baby, without a husband, at fifteen, was to be
lonelier than death. She became a prostitute.

"I worked the town. They call it hustling. I wouldn't go for less
than thirty dollars. Because I needed the money. I got it too. All you
have to do is be nice," the young girl said. "But to go out and hustle
I had to be under the influence of narcotics."

Diana Perea told her own life story to the National Conference
on Poverty in the Southwest, held in January, 1965, to launch the
War on Poverty. In the winter sun of Tucson, Arizona, the nearly two
hundred delegates who had gathered under the auspices of the
Choate Foundation, to hear Vice President Hubert Humphrey, were
as overwhelmed by the frail and frightened girl as she was by the
presidential emissary. "Go back and tell them [your people] that the
war against unemployment, discrimination, disease, and ignorance
has begun. Tell them to get out and fight!" the Vice President said.
"The wonderful thing about the War on Poverty is that we have the

means to win it. We cannot fail." He reminded his listeners, "Fifteen minutes from where we sit tonight there is abject poverty."

In the audience was Diana Perea. A few weeks later she succeeded in killing herself.

Her death was due to an overdose of narcotics, the autopsy report declared. There were some nonmedical causes. On the frontispiece of the Summary Report of the National Conference on Poverty in the Southwest there was a black border of mourning around these simple words:

DIANA PEREA

1946–1965

VICTIM OF POVERTY

Death is an ordinary thing. No one would have heard of the young girl from the streets of Denver's barrio if she had not happened to share a microphone with the Vice President of the United States.

In the streets misery is said to be so common no one notices. Life in the barrios is cruel—to outsiders, for the sons and daughters of the poor, it is said, are too hardened and brutalized to be able to do anything but fight to survive.

A young girl cries of a brown child dying of hunger in the barrios of San Antonio:

> In the land of the free
>   and the home of the brave,
> He is dying of hunger,
>   he cannot be saved;
> Come brothers and sisters
>   and weep by his grave.
> This is our child—

The ordeal of these youths is bemoaned by sympathetic writers. Not by the youth. Diana Perea did not weep. The Chicana was matter of fact: this is the way it is. Life in the barrio streets is just a way of life—happy, unhappy, ordinary, exciting, boring, deadly. The streets are not dangerous, they are only treacherous. It doesn't frighten youth. Seldom do they curse the barrio. They curse themselves for their inability to survive. It is not the barrio that the Chicano fears, but the lonely and hostile world outside.

Loneliness, the coldness of urban life, is what depresses the Chicano. In his family there is a warmth and gregarious love voiced with passion, uninhibited honesty, and gusto. The city frustrates and mutes this love. Faced with a society that he feels is hostile, the barrio youth becomes lost. He tries to defend himself by forming a gang, not just to fight for his manhood, his *macho,* but for his right to be a Chicano.

"The most brutal method of birth control is the one we practice on ourselves," a young man writes in *La Raza.*

To *La Raza Chicana,* a young girl writes a bitter note:

I wish to compliment brother Perfecto Vallego and his friends for doing with Caterino B. Heredia. Keep up the good work, Baby, you and the cops [can] get together on the Chicano Annual Shoot. Your game is as bad as the racist cop who goes after Chicano's who fail to halt. You dudes don't have to kill your brothers; Uncle Sam is doing that for you in Viet Nam. You are shooting the wrong guy. *No sean tan pendejos.* If you have enough *huevos* [testicles] to shoot your brother you should be able to take on a racist cop.

The street gangs of the barrios are different from those in most ghettos. In a sense they are born not solely of poverty, but also of cultural pride. Like street-corner chambers of commerce the gangs of barrio youth defend the spirit of La Raza with bravado and youthful boisterousness.

Of the many barrio gangs the oldest and best known is that of the legendary Pachucos, who have become a heroic myth. They were born in blood that was real enough, and they not only are remembered but are imitated with awe. They began on a day in August, 1942. In the tensions of World War II, the racial hatreds of Los Angeles were about to erupt in what was to be known as the "Zoot Suit Riots." Two groups of Chicanos had a boyish fight over a pretty girl and hurt pride, in a gravel pit on the outskirts of the city. In the morning the body of young José Díaz was found on a dirt road nearby, dead. Bored newspapermen, seeking local color, dubbed the gravel pit the "Sleepy Lagoon" (it had a mud puddle in it), and an orgy of sensational headlines celebrated the boy's death.

Not one but twenty-four Mexican boys were arrested; nine were convicted of second-degree murder. All were freed later, two years later, when the Court of Appeals reversed the sentences unanimously for "lack of evidence."

The "Sleepy Lagoon" case is still remembered bitterly in the barrios, much as the Dreyfus case in France, or that of the Scottsboro Boys in the Deep South.

Amid headlines of hysteria—"Zoot Suit Hoodlums" and "Pachuco Gangsters"—the Los Angeles police raided the barrios, blockaded the main streets, searched every passing car and passer-by. Six hundred Chicanos were taken into custody in a two-day sweep that Police Captain Joseph Reed called "a drive on Mexican gangs." The Los Angeles sheriff's "Bureau of *Foreign* Relations" justified the dragnet by officially philosophizing that the Chicanos' "desire to kill, or at least let blood" was an "inborn characteristic."

The next summer the tensions exploded. When a fist fight broke out on a downtown street between a gang of Chicano boys and U.S. Navy men in June, 1943, fourteen off-duty policemen led by a lieutenant of the Detective Squad set up an impromptu group of vigilantes they named the "Vengeance Squad" and set out "to clean up" the Mexicans.

Night after night hundreds of restless and beached sailors of the U.S. Navy, bored and frustrated by their inaction in the war against Japan, seized upon the nearest available dark-skinned enemies—the young Chicanos—and beat them up. The white rioters toured the barrios in convoys of taxi cabs, attacking every brown boy they found on the streets, in bars and restaurants and movie houses, by the dozens, by the hundreds, while the Los Angeles police looked the other way. No sailor was arrested. Inspired by the inflammatory news stories about "zoot suit roughnecks," the white rioters sought out these most of all—zoot suits were an early Humphrey Bogart style Mexicanized by Chicano boys and lately revived in its classic form by *Bonnie and Clyde.*

It was a long, hot summer week. When the white rioters exhausted their racial fervor, the riots—known not as the "U.S. Navy Riots" but oddly as the "Zoot Suit Riots"—had left hundreds of injured and a residue of race hatred in Los Angeles.

The zoot-suit boys were Pachucos. Where the name came from is vague, but it may have been taken from the city of Pachuco in Mexico, known for its brilliantly hued costumes. In the riots, these gangs of Pachucos were not the aggressors but the defenders of the barrios. They were an early self-defense group. Youths who never knew the Pachucos remember them not as victims but as resistance fighters of the streets, the Minutemen of *machismo,* who fought to defend the reputation of La Raza. Wherever the barrio youth organize, the spirit of the Pachucos is evoked and revived.

"I hope you tell the story of the Pachucos," a Brown Beret says to me. "We have to learn about our heroes."

One of many Pachuco-type gangs is the Vatos. It is a fictitious name of a small gang in the San Fernando Valley of Los Angeles whose "territory" ranges from Laurel Canyon Boulevard to O'Melveny Street. The Vatos hang out mostly in the dark alleys near Acala Avenue, a poorly lit thoroughfare.

A member of the Vatos talks of his gang:

"This is the story of life in a Mexican barrio. The barrio is called 'San Fer.' The kids, so-called Pachucos, run this barrio. Life in this barrio is rough, harsh. The boys learned early to carry can openers and knives. As soon as they got a little older they graduated to switchblades, lengths of chain, and guns, if they could get hold of them.

"Boys joined together to form street gangs, and some of them sported the Pachuco brand between the thumb and forefinger of their left hand," the Vato says. "This gang is the stuff of life, as the Pachuco knows it."

The gang member has to prove his manhood and his ability to survive. "He will undertake the most fantastic stunts to prove a great deal. He will risk his life and his freedom to maintain his growing reputation as a tough fighter, a rugged guy." These rituals are not merely rites of initiation, or idle bravado. The gang youth has to demonstrate not only that he can fight in the streets, but that he has the strength to withstand the hostility of society, to stand up to the *placa*, the police, and if he is courageous enough, to become visible to the outsider, by wearing a Brown Beret. "That is real *macho*," a Los Angeles community leader says.

It is a new kind of political and urban *pachuquismo*. The society outside the barrio is defied by the gang. Consciously the rituals of brotherhood enforce the laws and culture of the barrio. Inside the gang the Chicano is insulated from his own conflicts. The Chicanos "find conflicts so perplexing and so full of both cultures—that of their parents and that of America—that [they] create their own world of *pachuquismo*," says the Vato.

The Vato goes on: "The Vatos have created their own language, Pachucano, their own style of dress, their own folklore, and their own behavior patterns. The Vatos have developed a barrio group spirit. The Vatos in this area are better organized and a little tighter, due to the fact that it is a smaller group; and therefore all the Vatos participate in the activities planned by them.

"They formed a closely knit group that regarded the Anglos as their natural enemies."

In every barrio the social clubs and folk religious societies have always existed in semisecrecy, with their own rules and symbols, hidden from the world outside. Chicano gangs are the progeny of that invisible heritage—to outsiders—by which the barrio has protected itself. They re-create in their own youthful way, the society and culture of their forefathers; yet they are urban.

Eliezer Risco, the editor of *La Raza,* describes these methods of barrio organizations as "our own survival techniques. It is difficult for the culture of a minority to survive in the larger society. If we can utilize them for social action, now that we are stronger, we will surprise the country," he says. "The country won't know where our strength is coming from or how we organize."

In the dark alleyways and gregarious streets, the Brown Berets began. They have developed a political *pachuquismo.* A generation ago they would have been a street gang, nothing more. Less obvious are the barrio origins of the youthful leaders of the La Raza movements that have gained national prominence and importance. Cesar Chavez, Rodolfo "Corky" Gonzales, Reies Tijerina: these men learned their organizing techniques on the back streets of the barrio.

"They say the La Raza movements come from the universities. I disagree," says "José," the "Field Marshal" of the Brown Berets. "I say they come from the streets."

So few youths in the barrios graduated from high school in the past, or entered college, that those who achieved that miraculous feat feared to look down from their pinnacle of anxiety. If they did, the barrios beneath them seemed a bottomless arroyo. And yet, in the wholly anglicized realms of higher education they were also strangers.

"You see a Chicano [university] student is alienated from his language; he is de-culturized and finally dehumanized so as to be able to function in a white, middle class, protestant bag," the *Chicano Student News* reports. "It is damn obvious to the Chicano in college that education means one of two things: either accept the system—study, receive a diploma, accept the cubicle and the IBM machine in some lousy bank or factory, and move out of the barrio—or reject the system. . . ."

Youths who made it to the university clung to their privileged and precarious achievements: non-Mexican name and anglicized accent, an Ivy League suit, a blond wife, and a disdain for the "dumb Mexicans" left behind. "THE PURPLE TIO TOMAS" (Uncle Tom), *El Gallo* has dubbed these high achievers. "This is the middle class Tomás. He isn't a Tomás because he lives on the other side of town, but because the Purple Tomás believes he is better than other Chicanos. Purple is the Royal Color!" The would-be intellectual *patróns* —"the new conservatives," Corky Gonzales calls them.

Now the university students have begun the climb down from their lonely success to the streets of the barrios and the fields of the campesinos. They come as on a pilgrimage, seeking an identity. Los Angeles community leader Eduardo Pérez says, "I find that many Mexicans-turned-Spanish are coming back into the fold and are being identified for what they are: Mexicans." They have a "pride in being Mexican."

. . .

"I stand naked in the world, lost in angry solitude," the Chicano poet Benjamin Luna writes in *La Raza*. The loneliness of the urban society—impersonal, cold, efficient, foreign to his heart—evokes the feeling of a hostile world. The futility the Chicano feels is not fatalism, but a rage of frustration.

> *Soy Indio con alma hambrienta,*
> *traigo en la sangre coraje,*
> *rojo coraje en la sangre.*

> I am Indian with a hungry soul,
> tragic in the passionate blood,
> red passion in the blood.

> I stand naked in the world,
> hungry
> homeless
> despised. . . .

In the barrios, brotherhood is in the blood, the blood of La Raza. "One boy will bring beer, while others will bring *rifa;* still others bring money for the use of activities, or gas in a member's car. This is a thing that goes on every night with something different every night that can be called a 'dead kick.'" At best, their inner brotherhood is limited by the outer world of their "natural enemy," and at worst is defined by it.

A Brown Beret laments, "We are not what we were when we started out. All those TV cameras and news reporters took over our image and changed us into their image of us."

"Who am I?" asks a young woman in a suburban church of Los Angeles. "I have been afraid to speak up for my rights. Rights? What rights do we have? So many of our youth plead guilty in court when they know they are not guilty of anything. Anything but being a Mexican."

9 Contadini in Chicago: A Critique of The Uprooted*

Rudolph J. Vecoli

IN *THE UPROOTED*[1] Oscar Handlin attempted an overarching interpretation of European peasant society and of the adjustment of emigrants from that society to the American environment. This interpretation is open to criticism on the grounds that it fails to respect the unique cultural attributes of the many and varied ethnic groups which sent immigrants to the United States. Through an examination of the south Italians, both in their Old World setting and in Chicago, this article will indicate how Handlin's portrayal of the peasant as immigrant does violence to the character of the *contadini* (peasants) of the Mezzogiorno.[†]

The idealized peasant village which Handlin depicts in *The Uprooted* did not exist in the southern Italy of the late nineteenth

---

* Reprinted with permission from Rudolph J. Vecoli, "*Contadini* in Chicago: A Critique of *The Uprooted*," *Journal of American History*, 51 (December, 1964), 404–417.

† The Mezzogiorno of Italy includes the southern part of continental Italy, i.e., the regions of Abruzzi e Molise, Campania, Puglia, Basilicata, Calabria, and the island of Sicily.

century. Handlin's village was an harmonious social entity in which the individual derived his identity and being from the community as a whole; the ethos of his village was one of solidarity, communality, and neighborliness.[2] The typical south Italian peasant, however, did not live in a small village, but in a "rural city" with a population of thousands or even tens of thousands.[3] Seeking refuge from brigands and malaria, the *contadini* huddled together in these hill towns, living in stone dwellings under the most primitive conditions and each day descending the slopes to work in the fields below.

Nor were these towns simple communities of agriculturists, for their social structure included the gentry and middle class as well as the peasants. Feudalism died slowly in southern Italy, and vestiges of this archaic social order were still visible in the attitudes and customs of the various classes. While the great landowners had taken up residence in the capital cities, the lesser gentry constituted the social elite of the towns. Beneath it in the social hierarchy were the professional men, officials, merchants, and artisans; at the base were the *contadini* who comprised almost a distinct caste. The upper classes lorded over and exploited the peasants whom they regarded as less than human. Toward the upper classes, the *contadini* nourished a hatred which was veiled by the traditional forms of deference.[*]

This is not to say that the south Italian peasants enjoyed a sense of solidarity either as a community or as a social class. Rather it was the family which provided the basis of peasant solidarity. Indeed, so exclusive was the demand of the family for the loyalty of its members that it precluded allegiance to other social institutions. This explains the paucity of voluntary associations among the peasantry. Each member of the family was expected to advance its welfare and to defend its honor, regardless of the consequences for outsiders. This single-minded attention to the interests of the family led one student of south Italian society to describe its ethos as one of "amoral familism."[4]

While the strongest ties were within the nuclear unit, there existed among the members of the extended family a degree of trust, intimacy, and interdependence denied to all others. Only through the ritual kinship of *comparaggio* (godparenthood) could non-relatives gain admittance to the family circle. The south Italian family was

---

[*] The following thought, which Handlin attributes to the immigrant in America, would hardly have occurred to the oppressed *contadino:* "Could he here, as at home, expect the relationship of reciprocal goodness between master and men, between just employer and true employee?" *Uprooted,* 80.

"father-dominated but mother-centered." The father as the head of the family enjoyed unquestioned authority over the household, but the mother provided the emotional focus for family life.

Among the various families of the *paese* (town), there were usually jealousies and feuds which frequently resulted in bloodshed. This atmosphere of hostility was revealed in the game of *passatella,* which Carlo Levi has described as "a peasant tournament of oratory, where interminable speeches reveal in veiled terms a vast amount of repressed rancor, hate, and rivalry."[5] The sexual code of the Mezzogiorno was also expressive of the family pride of the south Italians. When violations occurred, family honor required that the seducer be punished. The south Italian was also bound by the tradition of personal vengeance, as in the Sicilian code of *omertà.* These cultural traits secured for southern Italy the distinction of having the highest rate of homicides in all of Europe at the turn of the century.[6] Such antisocial behavior, however, has no place in Handlin's scheme of the peasant community.

If the south Italian peasant regarded his fellow townsman with less than brotherly feeling, he viewed with even greater suspicion the stranger—which included anyone not native to the town. The peasants knew nothing of patriotism for the Kingdom of Italy, or of class solidarity with other tillers of the soil; their sense of affinity did not extend beyond town boundaries. This attachment to their native village was termed *campanilismo,* a figure of speech suggesting that the world of the *contadini* was confined within the shadow cast by his town campanile.[7] While this parochial attitude did not manifest itself in community spirit or activities, the sentiment of *campanilismo* did exert a powerful influence on the emigrants from southern Italy.

During the late nineteenth century, increasing population, agricultural depression, and oppressive taxes, combined with poor land to make life ever more difficult for the peasantry. Still, misery does not provide an adequate explanation of the great emigration which followed. For, while the peasants were equally impoverished, the rate of emigration varied widely from province to province. J. S. McDonald has suggested that the key to these differential rates lies in the differing systems of land tenure and in the contrasting sentiments of "individualism" and "solidarity" which they produced among the peasants.[8] From Apulia and the interior of Sicily where large-scale agriculture prevailed and cultivators' associations were formed, there was little emigration. Elsewhere in the South, where the peasants as small proprietors and tenants competed with one another, emigration soared. Rather than practicing communal agriculture as did Handlin's peasants, these *contadini,* both as cultivators and emigrants, acted on the principle of economic individualism, pursuing family and self-interest.

Handlin's peasants have other characteristics which do not hold true for those of southern Italy. In the Mezzogiorno, manual labor—and especially tilling the soil—was considered degrading. There the peasants did not share the reverence of Handlin's peasants for the land; rather they were "accustomed to look with distrust and hate at the soil."[9] No sentimental ties to the land deterred the south Italian peasants from becoming artisans, shopkeepers, or priests, if the opportunities presented themselves. Contrary to Handlin's peasants who meekly accepted their lowly status, the *contadini* were ambitious to advance the material and social position of their families. Emigration was one way of doing so. For the peasants in *The Uprooted* emigration was a desperate flight from disaster, but the south Italians viewed a sojourn in America as a means to acquire capital with which to purchase land, provide dowries for their daughters, and assist their sons to enter business or the professions.

If the design of peasant society described in *The Uprooted* is not adequate for southern Italy, neither is Handlin's description of the process of immigrant adjustment an accurate rendering of the experience of the *contadini.* For Handlin, "the history of immigration is a history of alienation and its consequences."[10] In line with this theme, he emphasizes the isolation and loneliness of the immigrant, "the broken homes, interruptions of a familiar life, separation from known surroundings, the becoming a foreigner and ceasing to belong." While there is no desire here to belittle the hardships, fears, and anxieties to which the immigrant was subject, there are good reasons for contending that Handlin overstates the disorganizing effects of emigration and underestimates the tenacity with which the south Italian peasants at least clung to their traditional social forms and values.

Handlin, for example, dramatically pictures the immigrant ceasing to be a member of a solidary community and being cast upon his own resources as an individual.[11] But this description does not apply to the *contadini* who customarily emigrated as a group from a particular town, and, once in America, stuck together "like a swarm of bees from the same hive."[12] After working a while, and having decided to remain in America, they would send for their wives, children, and other relatives. In this fashion, chains of emigration were established between certain towns of southern Italy and Chicago.[13]

From 1880 on, the tide of emigration ran strongly from Italy to this midwestern metropolis where by 1920 the Italian population reached approximately 60,000.[14] Of these, the *contadini* of the Mezzogiorno formed the preponderant element. Because of the sentiment of *campanilismo*, there emerged not one "Little Italy" but some seventeen larger and smaller colonies scattered about the city. Each group of townsmen clustered by itself, seeking, as Jane Addams observed, to fill "an entire tenement house with the people from one village."[15] Within these settlements, the town groups maintained their distinct identities, practiced endogamy, and preserved their traditional folkways. Contrary to Handlin's dictum that the common experience of the immigrants was their inability to transplant the European village,[16] one is struck by the degree to which the *contadini* succeeded in reconstructing their native towns in the heart of industrial Chicago. As an Italian journalist commented:

> Emigrating, the Italian working class brings away with it from the mother country all the little world in which they were accustomed to live; a world of traditions, of beliefs, of customs, of ideals of their own. There is no reason to marvel then that in this great center of manufacturing and commercial activity of North America our colonies, though acclimating themselves in certain ways, conserve the customs of their *paesi* of origin.[17]

If the south Italian immigrant retained a sense of belongingness with his fellow townsmen, the family continued to be the focus of his most intense loyalties. Among the male emigrants there were some who abandoned their families in Italy, but the many underwent harsh privations so that they might send money to their parents or wives. Reunited in Chicago the peasant family functioned much as it had at home; there appears to have been little of that confusion of roles depicted in *The Uprooted*. The husband's authority was not diminished, while the wife's subordinate position was not questioned. If dissension arose, it was when the children became somewhat "Americanized"; yet there are good reasons for believing that Handlin exaggerates the estrangement of the second generation from its immigrant parentage. Nor did the extended family disintegrate upon emigration as is contended. An observation made with respect to the Sicilians in Chicago was generally true for the south Italians: "Intense family pride . . . is the outstanding characteristic, and as the family unit not only includes those related by blood, but those related by ritual bonds as well (the *commare* and *compare*), and as intermarriage in the village groups is a common practice, this family pride becomes really a clan pride."[18] The alliance of families of the town through intermarriage and godparenthood perpetuated a social organization based upon large kinship groups.

The south Italian peasants also brought with them to Chicago some of their less attractive customs. Many a new chapter of an ancient vendetta of Calabria or Sicily was written on the streets of this American city. The zealous protection of the family honor was often a cause of bloodshed. Emigration had not abrogated the duty of the south Italian to guard the chastity of his women. Without the mitigating quality of these "crimes of passion" were the depredations of the "Black Hand." After 1900 the practice of extorting money under threat of death became so common as to constitute a reign of terror in the Sicilian settlements. Both the Black Handers and their victims were with few exceptions from the province of Palermo where the criminal element known collectively as the *mafia* had thrived for decades. The propensity for violence of the south Italians was not a symptom of social disorganization caused by emigration but a characteristic of their Old World culture.[19] Here too the generalizations that the immigrant feared to have recourse to the peasant crimes of revenge, and that the immigrant was rarely involved in crime for profit,[20] do not apply to the south Italians.

To speak of alienation as the essence of the immigrant experience is to ignore the persistence of traditional forms of group life. For the *contadino,* his family and his townsmen continued to provide a sense of belonging and to sanction his customary world-view and life-ways. Living "in," but not "of," the sprawling, dynamic city of Chicago, the south Italian was sheltered within his ethnic colony from the confusing complexity of American society.

While the acquisition of land was a significant motive for emigration, the south Italian peasants were not ones to dream, as did Handlin's, of possessing "endless acres" in America.[21] Their goal was a small plot of ground in their native towns. If they failed to reach the American soil, it was not because, as Handlin puts it, "the town had somehow trapped them,"[22] but because they sought work which would pay ready wages. These peasants had no romantic illusions about farming; and despite urgings by railroad and land companies, reformers, and philanthropists to form agricultural colonies, the south Italians preferred to remain in the city.[23]

Although Chicago experienced an extraordinary growth of manufacturing during the period of their emigration, few south Italians found employment in the city's industries. Great numbers of other recent immigrants worked in meat-packing and steelmaking, but it was uncommon to find an Italian name on the payroll of these enterprises.[24] The absence of the *contadini* from these basic industries was due both to their aversion to this type of factory work and to discrimination against them by employers. For the great majority of the south Italian peasants "the stifling, brazen factories and the dark, stony pits" did not supplant "the warm living earth as the source of their daily bread."[25] Diggers in the earth they had been and diggers in the earth they remained; only in America they dug with the pick and shovel rather than the mattock. In Chicago the Italian laborers quickly displaced the Irish in excavation and street work, as they did on railroad construction jobs throughout the West.[26]

The lot of the railroad workers was hard. Arriving at an unknown destination, they were sometimes attacked as "scabs," they found the wages and conditions of labor quite different from those promised, or it happened that they were put to work under armed guard and kept in a state of peonage. For twelve hours a day in all kinds of weather, the laborers dug and picked, lifted ties and rails, swung sledge hammers, under the constant goading of tyrannical foremen. Housed in filthy boxcars, eating wretched food, they endured this miserable existence for a wage which seldom exceeded $1.50 a day. Usually they suffered in silence, and by the most stern abstinence were able to save the greater part of their meager earnings. Yet it happened that conditions became intolerable, and the *paesani* (gangs were commonly composed of men from the same town) would resist the exactions of the "boss." These uprisings were more in the nature of peasants' revolts than of industrial strikes, and they generally ended badly for the *contadini*.[27]

With the approach of winter the men returned to Chicago. While some continued on to Italy, the majority wintered in the city. Those with families in Chicago had households to return to; the others formed cooperative living groups. Thus they passed the winter months in idleness, much as they had in Italy. Railroad work was cyclical as well as seasonal. In times of depression emigration from Italy declined sharply; many of the Italian workers returned to their native towns to await the return of American prosperity. Those who remained were faced with long periods of unemployment; it was at these times, such as the decade of the 1890s, that the spectre of starvation stalked through the Italian quarters of Chicago.[28]

Because the *contadini* were engaged in gang labor of a seasonal nature there developed an institution which was thought most typical of the Italian immigration: the padrone system.[29] Bewildered by the tumult of the city, the newcomers sought out a townsman who could guide them in the ways of this strange land. Thus was created the padrone who made a business out of the ignorance and necessities of his countrymen. To the laborers, the padrone was banker, saloonkeeper, grocer, steamship agent, lodging-house keeper, and politician. But his most important function was that of employment agent.

While there were honest padrones, most appeared unable to resist the opportunities for graft. Although Handlin states that "the padrone had the virtue of shielding the laborer against the excesses of employers,"[30] the Italian padrones usually operated in collusion with the contractors. Often the padrones were shrewd, enterprising men who had risen from the ranks of the unskilled; many of them, however, were members of the gentry who sought to make an easy living by exploiting their peasant compatriots in America as they had in Italy. The padrone system should not be interpreted as evidence "that a leader in America was not bound by patterns of obligation that were sacred in the Old World"; rather, it was a logical outcome of the economic individualism and "amoral familism" of south Italian society.

In their associational life the *contadini* also contradicted Handlin's assertion that the social patterns of the Old Country could not survive the ocean voyage.[31] The marked incapacity of the south Italians for organizational activity was itself a result of the divisive attitudes which they had brought with them to America. Almost the only form of association among these immigrants was the mutual aid society. Since such societies were common in Italy by the 1870s,[32] they can hardly be regarded as "spontaneously generated" by American conditions. Instead, the mutual aid society was a transplanted institution which was found to have especial utility for the immigrants. An Italian journalist observed: "If associations have been found useful in the *patria,* how much more they are in a strange land, where it is so much more necessary for the Italians to gather together, to fraternize, to help one another."[33] Nowhere, however, was the spirit of *campanilismo* more in evidence than in these societies. An exasperated Italian patriot wrote: "Here the majority of the Italian societies are formed of individuals from the same town and more often from the same parish, others are not admitted. But are you or are you not Italians? And if you are, why do you exclude your brother who is born a few miles from your town?"[34] As the number of these small societies multiplied (by 1912 there were some

400 of them in Chicago),[35] various attempts were made to form them into a federation. Only the Sicilians, however, were able to achieve a degree of unity through two federations which enrolled several thousand members.

The sentiment of regionalism was also a major obstacle to the organizational unity of the Italians in Chicago. Rather than being allayed by emigration, this regional pride and jealousy was accentuated by the proximity of Abruzzese, Calabrians, Genoese, Sicilians, and other groups in the city. Each regional group regarded those from other regions with their strange dialects and customs not as fellow Italians, but as distinct and inferior ethnic types. Any proposal for cooperation among the Italians was sure to arouse these regional antipathies and to end in bitter recriminations.[36] The experience of emigration did not create a sense of nationality among the Italians strong enough to submerge their parochialism. Unlike Handlin's immigrants who acquired "new modes of fellowship to replace the old ones destroyed by emigration,"[37] the south Italians confined themselves largely to the traditional ones of family and townsmen.

The quality of leadership of the mutual aid societies also prevented them from becoming agencies for the betterment of the *contadini*. These organizations, it was said, were often controlled by the "very worse [sic] element in the Italian colony,"[38] arrogant, selfish men, who founded societies not out of a sense of fraternity but to satisfy their ambition and vanity. The scope of their leadership was restricted to presiding despotically over the meetings, marching in full regalia at the head of the society, and gaining economic and political advantage through their influence over the members. If such a one were frustrated in his attempt to control a society, he would secede with his followers and found a new one. Thus even the townsmen were divided into opposing factions.[39]

The function of the typical mutual aid society was as limited as was its sphere of membership. The member received relief in case of illness, an indemnity for his family in case of death, and a funeral celebrated with pomp and pageantry. The societies also sponsored an annual ball and picnic, and, most important of all, the feast of the local patron saint. This was the extent of society activities; any attempt to enlist support for philanthropic or civic projects was doomed to failure.[40]

Since there was a surplus of doctors, lawyers, teachers, musicians, and classical scholars in southern Italy, an "intellectual proletariat" accompanied the peasants to America in search of fortune.[41]

Often, however, these educated immigrants found that America had no use for their talents, and to their chagrin they were reduced to performing manual labor. Their only hope of success was to gain the patronage of their lowly countrymen, but the sphere of colonial enterprise was very restricted. The sharp competition among the Italian bankers, doctors, journalists, and others engendered jealousies and rivalries. Thus this intelligentsia which might have been expected to provide tutelage and leadership to the humbler elements was itself rent by internecine conflict and expended its energies in polemics.

For the most part the upper-class immigrants generally regarded the peasants here as in Italy as boors and either exploited them or remained indifferent to their plight. These "respectable" Italians, however, were concerned with the growing prejudice against their nationality and wished to elevate its prestige among the Americans and other ethnic groups. As one means of doing this, they formed an association to suppress scavenging, organ-grinding, and begging as disgraceful to the Italian reputation. They simultaneously urged the workers to adopt American ways and to become patriotic Italians; but to these exhortations, the *contadino* replied: "It does not give me any bread whether the Italians have a good name in America or not. I am going back soon."[42]

Well-to-do Italians were more liberal with advice than with good works. Compared with other nationalities in Chicago, the Italians were distinguished by their lack of philanthropic institutions. There was a substantial number of men of wealth among them, but as an Italian reformer commented: "It is strange that when a work depends exclusively on the wealthy of the colony, one can not hope for success. Evidently philanthropy is not the favored attribute of our rich."[43] Indeed, there was no tradition of philanthropy among the gentry of southern Italy, and the "self-made" men did not recognize any responsibility outside the family. Projects were launched for an Italian hospital, an Italian school, an Italian charity society, an Italian institute to curb the padrone evil, and a White Hand Society to combat the Black Hand, but they all floundered in this morass of discord and disinterest. Clearly Handlin does not have the Italians in mind when he describes a growing spirit of benevolence as a product of immigrant life.[44]

If there is one particular in which the *contadini* most strikingly refute Handlin's conception of the peasant it is in the place of religion in their lives. Handlin emphasizes the influence of Christian doctrine on the psychology of the peasantry,[45] but throughout the

Mezzogiorno, Christianity was only a thin veneer.[46] Magic, not religion, pervaded their everyday existence; through the use of rituals, symbols, and charms, they sought to ward off evil spirits and to gain the favor of powerful deities. To the peasants, God was a distant, unapproachable being, like the King, but the local saints and Madonnas were real personages whose power had been attested to by innumerable miracles. But in the devotions to their patron saints, the attitude of the peasants was less one of piety than of bargaining, making vows if certain requests were granted. For the Church, which they had known as an oppressive landlord, they had little reverence; and for the clergy, whom they knew to be immoral and greedy, they had little respect. They knew little of and cared less for the doctrines of the Church.

Nor was the influence of established religion on the south Italian peasants strengthened by emigration as Handlin asserts.[47] American priests were scandalized by the indifference of the Italians to the Church.[48] Even when Italian churches were provided by the Catholic hierarchy, the *contadini* seldom displayed any religious enthusiasm. As one missionary was told upon his arrival in an Italian colony: "We have no need of priests here, it would be better if you returned from whence you came."[49] As in their native towns, the south Italian peasants for the most part went to church "to be christened, married or buried and that is about all."[50]

Because they were said to be drifting into infidelity, the south Italians were also the object of much of the home mission work of the Protestant churches of Chicago. Drawing their ministry from Italian converts and Waldensians, these missions carried the Gospel to the *contadini*, who, however, revealed little inclination to become "true Christians." After several decades of missionary effort, the half dozen Italian Protestant churches counted their membership in the few hundreds.[51] The suggestion that Italians were especially vulnerable to Protestant proselyting was not borne out in Chicago. For the *contadini*, neither Catholicism nor Protestantism became "paramount as a way of life."[52]

According to Handlin, the immigrants found it "hard to believe that the whole world of spirits and demons had abandoned their familiar homes and come also across the Atlantic,"[53] but the *contadino* in America who carried a *corno* (a goat's horn of coral) to protect him from the evil eye harbored no such doubts. The grip of the supernatural on the minds of the peasants was not diminished by their ocean crossing. In the Italian settlements, sorcerers plied their magical trades on behalf of the ill, the lovelorn, the bewitched.

As Alice Hamilton noted: "Without the help of these mysterious and powerful magicians they [the *contadini*] believe that they would be defenseless before terrors that the police and the doctor and even the priest cannot cope with."[54] For this peasant folk, in Chicago as in Campania, the logic of medicine, law, or theology had no meaning; only magic provided an explanation of, and power over, the vagaries of life.

The persistence of Old World customs among the south Italians was perhaps best exemplified by the *feste* which were held in great number in Chicago. The cults of the saints and Madonnas had also survived the crossing, and the fellow townsmen had no doubt that their local divinities could perform miracles in Chicago as well as in the Old Country. Feast day celebrations were inspired not only by devotion to the saints and Madonnas; they were also an expression of nostalgia for the life left behind. The procession, the street fair, the crowds of townsmen, created the illusion of being once more back home; as one writer commented of a *festa:* "There in the midst of these Italians, with almost no Americans, it seemed to be truly a village of southern Italy."[55] Despite efforts by "respectable" Italians and the Catholic clergy to discourage these colorful but unruly celebrations, the *contadini* would have their *feste*. After the prohibition of a *festa* by the Church was defied, a priest explained: "The feast is a custom of Sicily and survives despite denunciations from the altar. Wherever there is a colony of these people they have the festival, remaining deaf to the requests of the clergy."[56] The south Italian peasants remained deaf to the entreaties of reformers and radicals as well as priests, for above all they wished to continue in the ways of their *paesi*.

The *contadini* of the Mezzogiorno thus came to terms with life in Chicago within the framework of their traditional pattern of thought and behavior. The social character of the south Italian peasant did not undergo a sea change, and the very nature of their adjustments to American society was dictated by their "Old World traits," which were not so much ballast to be jettisoned once they set foot on American soil. These traits and customs were the very bone and sinew of the south Italian character which proved very resistant to change even under the stress of emigration. Because it overemphasizes the power of environment and underestimates the toughness of cultural heritage, Handlin's thesis does not comprehend the experience of the immigrants from southern Italy. The basic error of this thesis is that it subordinates historical complexity to the symmetrical pattern of a sociological theory. Rather than constructing ideal types of "the peasant" or "the immigrant," the historian of immigration must study the distinctive cultural character of each ethnic group and the manner in which this influenced its adjustments in the New World.

Notes

1. Oscar Handlin, *The Uprooted* (Boston, 1951).
2. Ibid., 7–12.
3. On south Italian society see Edward C. Banfield, *The Moral Basis of a Backward Society* (Glencoe, Ill., 1958); Robert F. Foerster, *The Italian Emigration of Our Times* (Cambridge, Mass., 1919), 51–105; Leopoldo Franchetti and Sidney Sonnino, *La Sicilia nel 1876* (2 vols., Florence, 1925); Carlo Levi, *Christ Stopped at Eboli* (New York, 1947); Leonard W. Moss and Stephen C. Cappannari, "A Sociological and Anthropological Investigation of an Italian Rural Community" (mimeographed, Detroit, 1959); Luigi Villari, *Italian Life in Town and Country* (New York, 1902); Arrigo Serpieri, *La Guerra e le Classi Rurali Italiane* (Bari, 1930), 1–21; Friedrich Vöchting, *La Questione Meridionale* (Naples, 1955); Phyllis H. Williams, *South Italian Folkways in Europe and America* (New Haven, 1938); Rocco Scotellaro, *Contadini del Sud* (Bari, 1955).
4. Banfield, *Moral Basis of a Backward Society*, 10. In his study of a town in Basilicata, Banfield found that both gentry and peasants were unable to act "for any end transcending the immediate, material interest of the nuclear family." On the south Italian family see also Leonard W. Moss and Stephen C. Cappannari, "Patterns of Kinship, Comparaggio and Community in a South Italian Village," *Anthropological Quarterly*, 33 (January, 1960), 24–32; Leonard W. Moss and Walter H. Thomson, "The South Italian Family: Literature and Observations," *Human Organization*, 18 (Spring, 1959), 35–41.
5. Levi, *Christ Stopped*, 179.
6. Napoleone Colajanni, "Homicide and the Italians," *Forum*, 31 (March, 1901), 63–66.
7. Richard Bagot, *The Italians of Today* (Chicago, 1913), 87.
8. J. S. McDonald, "Italy's Rural Social Structure and Emigration," *Occidente*, 12 (September–October, 1956), 437–55. McDonald concludes that where the peasantry's "aspirations for material betterment were expressed in broad associative behavior, there was little emigration. Where economic aspirations were integrated only with the welfare of the individual's nuclear family, emigration rates were high." Ibid., 454.
9. Kate H. Claghorn, "The Agricultural Distribution of Immigrants," in U. S. Industrial Commission, *Reports* (19 vols., Washington, 1900–1902), 15: 496; Banfield, *Moral Basis of a Backward Society*, 37, 50, 69.

10. Handlin, *Uprooted*, 4.

11. Ibid., 38.

12. Pascal D'Angelo, *Son of Italy* (New York, 1924), 54.

13. These chains of emigration are traced in Rudolph J. Vecoli, "Chicago's Italians Prior to World War I: A Study of Their Social and Economic Adjustments" (doctoral dissertation, University of Wisconsin, 1963), 71–234.

14. On the Italians in Chicago see Vecoli, "Chicago's Italians"; U. S. Commissioner of Labor, *Ninth Special Report: The Italians in Chicago* (Washington, 1897); Frank O. Beck, "The Italian in Chicago," *Bulletin of the Chicago Department of Public Welfare*, 2 (February, 1919); Jane Addams, *Twenty Years at Hull House* (New York, 1910); Giuseppe Giacosa, "Chicago e la sua colonia Italiana," *Nuova Antologia di Scienze, Lettere ed Arti*, Third Series, 128 (March 1, 1893), 15–33; Giovanni E. Schiavo, *The Italians in Chicago* (Chicago, 1928); Alessandro Mastro-Valerio, "Remarks upon the Italian Colony in Chicago," in *Hull House Maps and Papers* (New York, 1895), 131–42; Harvey Warren Zorbaugh, *The Gold Coast and the Slum* (Chicago, 1929), 159–81; I. W. Howerth, "Are the Italians a Dangerous Class?" *Charities Review*, 4 (November, 1894), 17–40.

15. Jane Addams, *Newer Ideals of Peace* (New York, 1907), 67.

16. Handlin, *Uprooted*, 144.

17. Chicago, *L'Italia*, August 3, 1901. See also Anna Zaloha, "A Study of the Persistence of Italian Customs Among 143 Families of Italian Descent" (master's thesis, Northwestern University, 1937).

18. Zorbaugh, *Gold Coast*, 166–67. *Commare* and *compare* are godmother and godfather. See also Zaloha, "Persistence of Italian Customs," 103–05, 143–48.

19. *The Italian "White Hand" Society in Chicago, Illinois, Studies, Actions and Results* (Chicago, 1906); Illinois Association for Criminal Justice, *Illinois Crime Survey* (Chicago, 1929), 845–62, 935–54; Vecoli, "Chicago's Italians," 393–460.

20. Handlin, *Uprooted*, 163.

21. Ibid., 82.

22. Ibid., 64.

23. Vecoli, "Chicago's Italians," 184–234; Luigi Villari, *Gli Stati Uniti d'America e l'Emigrazione Italiana* (Milan, 1912), 256. Villari observed that even Italian immigrants who worked as gardeners in the suburbs of Boston preferred to live with their countrymen in the center of the city, commuting to their work in the country. Ibid., 224.

24. In 1901, for example, of over 6,000 employees at the Illinois Steel works only two were Italian. John M. Gillette, "The Culture Agencies of a Typical Manufacturing Group: South Chicago," *American Journal of Sociology*, 7 (July, 1901), 93–112. In 1915 the Armour packing company reported that there was not one Italian among its 8,000 workers in Chicago.

U. S. Commission on Industrial Relations, *Final Report and Testimony* (11 vols., Washington, 1916), 4: 3530.

25. Handlin, *Uprooted*, 73.

26. Chicago *Tribune*, March 20, 1891; Frank J. Sheridan, "Italian, Slavic and Hungarian Unskilled Laborers in the United States," U. S. Bureau of Labor, *Bulletin*, 15 (September, 1907), 445–68; Vecoli, "Chicago's Italians," 279–337.

27. D'Angelo, *Son of Italy*, 85–119; Dominic T. Ciolli, "The 'Wop' in the Track Gang," *Immigrants in America Review*, 2 (July, 1916), 61–64; Gino C. Speranza, "Forced Labor in West Virginia," *Outlook*, 74 (June 13, 1903), 407–10.

28. U. S. Commissioner of Labor, *Italians in Chicago*, 29, 44; Rosa Cassettari, "The Story of an Italian Neighbor (as told to Marie Hall Ets)," 342–50, ms., on loan to the author; Mayor's Commission on Unemployment (Chicago), *Report* (Chicago, 1914); Vecoli, "Chicago's Italians," 279–337.

29. On the padrone system see Grace Abbott, "The Chicago Employment Agency and the Immigrant Worker," *American Journal of Sociology*, 14 (November, 1908), 289–305; John Koren, "The Padrone System and the Padrone Banks," U. S. Bureau of Labor, *Bulletin*, 2 (March, 1897), 113–29; S. Merlino, "Italian Immigrants and Their Enslavement," *Forum*, 15 (April, 1893), 183–90; Gino C. Speranza, "The Italian Foreman As a Social Agent," *Charities*, 11 (July 4, 1903), 26–28; Vecoli, "Chicago's Italians," 235–278; Giovanni Ermengildo Schiavo, *Italian-American History* (2 vols., New York, 1947–1949), 1: 538–40.

30. Handlin, *Uprooted*, 69–70.

31. Ibid., 170–71.

32. Franchetti and Sonnino, *La Sicilia*, 2: 335.

33. Chicago, *L'Unione Italiana*, March 18, 1868.

34. *L'Italia*, October 23–24, 1897.

35. Schiavo, *Italians in Chicago*, 57.

36. Giacosa, "Chicago," 31–33; Comitato Locale di Chicago, *Primo Congresso degli Italiani all'estero sotto l'atto patronato di S. M. Vittorio Emanuelle III* (Chicago, 1908).

37. Handlin, *Uprooted*, 189.

38. Edmund M. Dunne, *Memoirs of "Zi Pre"* (St. Louis, 1914), 18. Father Dunne was the first pastor of the Italian Church of the Guardian Angel on Chicago's West Side.

39. Comitato Locale di Chicago, *Primo Congresso*; *L'Italia*, February 18, 1888, October 21, 1899.

40. Beck, "The Italian in Chicago," 23; Comitato Locale di Chicago, *Primo Congresso*; *L'Italia*, August 24, 1889, April 28, 1906.

41. Amy A. Bernardy, *Italia randagia attraverso gli Stati Uniti* (Turin, 1913), 293; Giacosa, "Chicago," 31; *L'Italia*, January 19, 1889.

42. Robert E. Park and Herbert A. Miller, *Old World Traits Trans-*

planted (New York, 1921), 104; Mastro-Valerio, "Remarks upon the Italian Colony," 131–32; *L'Italia*, August 6, 1887, April 5, 1890.

43. *L'Italia*, August 24–25, 1895; Luigi Carnovale, *Il Giornalismo degli Emigrati Italiani nel Nord America* (Chicago, 1909), 67; Comitato Locale di Chicago, *Primo Congresso*.

44. Handlin, *Uprooted*, 175–76.

45. Ibid., 102–03.

46. Levi, *Christ Stopped*, 116–18; Leonard W. Moss and Stephen C. Cappannari, "Folklore and Medicine in an Italian Village," *Journal of American Folklore*, 73 (April, 1960), 85–102; Banfield, *Moral Basis of a Backward Society*, 17–18, 129–32.

47. Handlin, *Uprooted*, 117.

48. On the religious condition of the Italian immigrants, see the discussions in *America*, 12 (October 17, 31, November 7, 14, 21, 28, December 5, 12, 19, 1914), 6–7, 66, 93, 121, 144–45, 168–69, 193–96, 221, 243–46.

49. G. Sofia, ed., *Missioni Scalabriniane in America, estratto da "Le Missioni Scalabriniane tra gli Italiani"* (Rome, 1939), 122.

50. "Church Census of the 17th Ward, 1909," Chicago Commons, 1904–1910, Graham Taylor Papers, Newberry Library.

51. Palmerio Chessa, "A Survey Study of the Evangelical Work Among Italians in Chicago" (bachelor of divinity thesis, Presbyterian Theological Seminary, Chicago, 1934); Jane K. Hackett, "A Survey of Presbyterian Work with Italians in the Presbytery of Chicago" (master's thesis, Presbyterian College of Christian Education, Chicago, 1943).

52. Handlin, *Uprooted*, 117, 136.

53. Ibid., 110.

54. Alice Hamilton, "Witchcraft in West Polk Street," *American Mercury*, 10 (January, 1927), 71; Chicago *Tribune*, January 19, 1900; *L'Italia*, October 3, 1903. See also Zaloha, "Persistence of Italian Customs," 158–63.

55. *L'Italia*, July 28–29, 1894; Cassettari, "Story of an Italian Neighbor," 419. See also Zaloha, "Persistence of Italian Customs," 90–100.

56. Chicago *Tribune*, August 14, 1903.

10 Like It Is in the Alley*

Robert Coles

"IN THE ALLEY it's mostly dark, even if the sun is out. But if you look around, you can find things. I know how to get into every building, except that it's like night once you're inside them, because they don't have lights. So, I stay here. You're better off. It's no good on the street. You can get hurt all the time, one way or the other. And in buildings, like I told you, it's bad in them, too. But here it's o.k. You can find your own corner, and if someone tries to move in you fight him off. We meet here all the time, and figure out what we'll do next. It might be a game, or over for some pool, or a Coke or something. You need to have a place to start out from, and that's like it is in the alley; you can always know your buddy will be there, provided it's the right time. So you go there, and you're on your way, man."

Like all children of nine, Peter is always on his way—to a person, a place, a "thing" he wants to do. "There's this here thing we thought we'd try tomorrow," he'll say; and eventually I'll find out that

* Reprinted from Robert Coles, "Like It Is in the Alley," by permission of *Daedalus*, Journal of the American Academy of Arts and Sciences, Boston, Mass., vol. 97, Fall 1968, *The Conscience of the City*, pp. 1315-30.

he means there's to be a race. He and his friends will compete
with another gang to see who can wash a car faster and better. The
cars belong to four youths who make their money taking bets, and
selling liquor that I don't believe was ever purchased, and pushing
a few of those pills that "go classy with beer." I am not completely
sure, but I think they also have something to do with other drugs;
and again, I can't quite be sure what their connection is with a "residence" I've seen not too far from the alley Peter describes so posses-
sively. The women come and go—from that residence and along the
street Peter's alley leaves.

Peter lives in the heart of what we in contemporary America
have chosen (ironically, so far as history goes) to call an "urban
ghetto." The area was a slum before it became a ghetto, and there
still are some very poor white people on its edges and increasing
numbers of Puerto Ricans in several of its blocks. Peter was not
born in the ghetto, nor was his family told to go there. They are
Americans and have been here "since way back before anyone can
remember." That is the way Peter's mother talks about Alabama,
about the length of time she and her ancestors have lived there. She
and Peter's father came north "for freedom." They did not seek out
a ghetto, an old quarter of Boston where they were expected to live
and where they would be confined, yet at least some of the time
solidly at rest, with kin, and reasonably safe.

No, they sought freedom. Americans, they moved on when the
going got "real bad," and Americans, they expected something better
someplace, some other place. They left Alabama on impulse. They
found Peter's alley by accident. And they do not fear pogroms. They
are Americans, and in Peter's words: "There's likely to be another
riot here soon. That's what I heard today. You hear it a lot, but one
day you know it'll happen."

Peter's mother fears riots too—among other things. The Jews of
Eastern Europe huddled together in their ghettos, afraid of the bar-
barians, afraid of the *Goyim,* but always sure of one thing, their God-
given destiny. Peter's mother has no such faith. She believes that
"something will work out one of these days." She believes that "you
have to keep on going, and things can get better, but don't ask me
how." She believes that "God wants us to have a bad spell here, and
so maybe it'll get better the next time—you know in Heaven, and I
hope that's where we'll be going." Peter's mother, in other words, is
a pragmatist, an optimist, and a Christian. Above all she is American:
"Yes, I hear them talk about Africa, but it don't mean anything to
us. All I know is Alabama and now it's in Massachusetts that we are.

It was a long trip coming up here, and sometimes I wish we were back there, and sometimes I'd just as soon be here, for all that's no good about it. But I'm not going to take any more trips, no sir. And like Peter said, this is the only country we've got. If you come from a country, you come from it, and we're from it, I'd say, and there isn't much we can do but try to live as best we can. I mean, live here."

What is "life" like for her over there, where she lives, in the neighborhood she refers to as "here"? A question like that cannot be answered by the likes of me, and even her answer provides only the beginning of a reply: "Well, we does o.k., I guess. Peter here, he has it better than I did, or his daddy. I can say that. I tell myself that a lot. He can turn on the faucet over there, and a lot of the time, he just gets the water, right away. And when I tell him what it was like for us, to go fetch that water—we'd walk three miles, yes sir, and we'd be lucky it wasn't ten—well, Peter, it doesn't register on him. He thinks I'm trying to fool him, and the more serious I get, the more he laughs, so I've stopped.

"Of course it's not all so good, I have to admit. We're still where we were, so far as knowing where your next meal is coming from. When I go to bed at night I tell myself I've done good, to stay alive and keep the kids alive, and if they'll just wake up in the morning, and me too, well then, we can worry about that, all the rest, come tomorrow. So there you go. We do our best, and that's all you can do."

She may sound fatalistic, but she appears to be a nervous, hardworking, even hard-driven woman—thin, short, constantly on the move. I may not know what she "really" thinks and believes, because like the rest of us she has her contradictions and her mixed feelings. I think it is fair to say that there are some things that she can't say to me—or to herself. She is a Negro, and I am white. She is poor, and I am fairly well off. She is very near to illiterate, and I put in a lot of time worrying about how to say things. But she and I are both human beings, and we both have trouble—to use that word— "communicating," not only with each other, but with ourselves. Sometimes she doesn't tell me something she really wants me to know. She has forgotten, pure and simple. More is on her mind than information I might want. And sometimes I forget too: "Remember you asked the other day about Peter, if he was ever real sick. And I told you he was a weak child, and I feared for his life, and I've lost five children, three that was born and two that wasn't. Well, I forgot to tell you that he got real sick up here, just after we came. He was three, and I didn't know what to do. You see, I didn't have my mother to help out. She always knew what to do. She could hold a child and get him to stop crying, no matter how sick he was, and no matter how much he wanted food, and we didn't have it. But she was gone —and that's when we left to come up here, and I never would have left her, not for anything in the world. But suddenly she took a seizure of something and went in a half hour, I'd say. And Peter, he was so hot and sick, I thought he had the same thing his grandmother did and he was going to die. I thought maybe she's calling him. She always liked Peter. She helped him be born, she and my cousin, they did."

. . .

. . . I cannot think of a better way to begin knowing what life is like for Peter and his mother than to hear the following and hear it again and think about its implications: "No sir, Peter has never been to a doctor, not unless you count the one at school, and she's a nurse I believe. He was his sickest back home before we came here, and you know there was no doctor for us in the county. In Alabama you have to pay a white doctor first, before he'll go near you. And we don't have but a few colored ones. (I've never seen a one.) There was this woman we'd go to, and she had gotten some nursing education in Mobile. (No, I don't know if she was a nurse or not, or a helper to the nurses, maybe.) Well, she would come to help us. With the convulsions, she'd show you how to hold the child, and make sure he doesn't hurt himself. They can bite their tongues real, real bad.

"Here, I don't know what to do. There's the city hospital, but it's no good for us. I went there with my husband, no sooner than a month or so after we came up here. We waited and waited, and finally the day was almost over. We left the kids with a neighbor, and we barely knew her. I said it would take the morning, but I never thought we'd get home near suppertime. And they wanted us to come back and come back, because it was something they couldn't do all at once—though for most of the time we just sat there and did nothing. And my husband, he said his stomach was the worse for going there, and he'd take care of himself from now on, rather than go there.

"Maybe they could have saved him. But they're far away, and I didn't have money to get a cab, even if there was one around here, and I thought to myself it'll make him worse, to take him there.

"My kids, they get sick. The welfare worker, she sends a nurse here, and she tells me we should be on vitamins and the kids need all kinds of check-ups. Once she took my daughter and told her she had to have her teeth looked at, and the same with Peter. So, I went with my daughter, and they didn't see me that day, but said they could in a couple of weeks. And I had to pay the woman next door to mind the little ones, and there was the carfare, and we sat and sat, like before. So, I figured, it would take more than we've got to see that dentist. And when the nurse told us we'd have to come back a few times—that's how many, a few—I thought that no one ever looked at my teeth, and they're not good, I'll admit, but you can't have everything, that's what I say, and that's what my kids have to know, I guess."

What *does* she have? And what belongs to Peter? For one thing, there is the apartment, three rooms for six people, a mother and five children. Peter is a middle child with two older girls on one side and a younger sister and still younger brother on the other side. The smallest child was born in Boston: "It's the only time I ever spent time in a hospital. He's the only one to be born there. My neighbor got the police. I was in the hall, crying I guess. We almost didn't make it. They told me I had bad blood pressure, and I should have been on pills, and I should come back, but I didn't. It was the worst time I've ever had, because I was alone. My husband had to stay with the kids, and no one was there to visit me."

Peter sleeps with his brother in one bedroom. The three girls sleep in the living room, which is a bedroom. And, of course, there is a small kitchen. There is not very much furniture about. The kitchen has a table with four chairs, only two of which are sturdy. The girls sleep in one big bed. Peter shares his bed with his brother. The mother sleeps on a couch. There is one more chair and a table in the living room. Jesus looks down from the living room wall, and an undertaker's calendar hangs on the kitchen wall. The apartment has no books, no records. There is a television set in the living room, and I have never seen it off.

Peter in many respects is his father's successor. His mother talks things over with him. She even defers to him at times. She will say something; he will disagree; she will nod and let him have the last word. He knows the city. She still feels a stranger to the city. "If you want to know about anything around here, just ask Peter," she once said to me. That was three years ago, when Peter was six. Peter continues to do very poorly at school, but I find him a very good teacher. He notices a lot, makes a lot of sense when he talks, and has a shrewd eye for the ironic detail. He is very intelligent, for all the trouble he gives his teachers. He recently summed up a lot of American history for me: "I wasn't made for that school, and that school wasn't made for me." It is an old school, filled with memories. The name of the school evokes Boston's Puritan past. Pictures and statues adorn the corridors—reminders of the soldiers and statesmen and writers who made New England so influential in the nineteenth century. And naturally one finds slogans on the walls, about freedom and democracy and the rights of the people. Peter can be surly and cynical when he points all that out to the visitor. If he is asked what kind of school he would *like*, he laughs incredulously. "Are you kidding? No school would be my first choice. They should leave us alone, and let us help out at home, and maybe let some of our own people teach us. The other day the teacher admitted she was no good. She said maybe a Negro should come in and give us the discipline, because she was scared. She said all she wanted from us was that we keep quiet and stop wearing her nerves down, and she'd be grateful, because she would retire soon. She said we were becoming too much for her, and she didn't understand why. But when one kid wanted to say something, tell her why, she told us to keep still, and write something. You know what? She whipped out a book and told us to copy a whole page from it, so we'd learn it. A stupid waste of time. I didn't even try; and she didn't care. She just wanted an excuse not to talk with us. They're all alike."

Actually, they're all *not* alike, and Peter knows it. He has met up with two fine teachers, and in mellow moments he can say so: "They're trying hard, but me and my friends, I don't think we're cut out for school. To tell the truth, that's what I think. My mother says we should try, anyway, but it doesn't seem to help, trying. The teacher can't understand a lot of us, but he does all these new things, and you can see he's excited. Some kids are really with him, and I am, too. But I can't take all his stuff very serious. He's a nice man, and he says he wants to come and visit every one of our homes; but my mother says no, she wouldn't know what to do with him, when he came here. We'd just stand and have nothing to talk about. So she said tell him not to come; and I don't think he will, anyway. I think he's getting to know."

. . .

Peter sees rats all the time. He has been bitten by them. He has a big stick by his bed to use against them. They also claim the alley, even in the daytime. They are not large enough to be compared with cats, as some observers have insisted; they are simply large, confident, well-fed, unafraid rats. The garbage is theirs; the land is theirs; the tenement is theirs; human flesh is theirs. When I first started visiting Peter's family, I wondered why they didn't do something to rid themselves of those rats, and the cockroaches, and the mosquitoes, and the flies, and the maggots, and the ants, and especially the garbage in the alley which attracts so much of all that "lower life." Eventually I began to see some of the reasons why. A large apartment building with many families has exactly two barrels in its basement. The halls of the building go unlighted. Many windows have no screens, and some windows are broken and boarded up. The stairs are dangerous, some of them have missing timber. ("We just jump over them," says Peter cheerfully.) And the landowner is no one in particular. Rent is collected by an agent, in the name of a "realty trust." Somewhere in City Hall there is a bureaucrat who unquestionably might be persuaded to prod someone in the "trust"; and one day I went with three of the tenants, including Peter's mother, to try that "approach." We waited and waited at City Hall. (I drove us there, clear across town, naturally.) Finally we met up with a man, a not very encouraging or inspiring or generous or friendly man. He told us we would have to try yet another department and swear out a complaint; and that the "case" would have to be "studied," and that we would then be "notified of a decision." We went to the department down the hall, and waited some more, another hour and ten minutes. By then it was three o'clock, and the mothers wanted to go home. They weren't thinking of rats anymore, or poorly heated apartments, or garbage that had nowhere to go and often went uncollected for two weeks, not one. They were thinking of their children, who would be home from school and, in the case of two women, their husbands who would also soon be home. "Maybe we should come back some other day," Peter's mother said. I noted she didn't say *tomorrow*, and I realized that I had read someplace that people like her aren't precisely "future-oriented."

Actually, both Peter and his mother have a very clear idea of what is ahead. For the mother it is "more of the same." One evening she was tired but unusually talkative, perhaps because a daughter of hers was sick: "I'm glad to be speaking about all these things tonight. My little girl has a bad fever. I've been trying to cool her off all day. Maybe if there was a place near here, that we could go to, maybe I would have gone. But like it is, I have to do the best I can and pray she'll be o.k."

I asked whether she thought her children would find things different, and that's when she said it would be "more of the same" for them. Then she added a long afterthought: "Maybe it'll be a little better for them. A mother has to have hope for her children, I guess.

But I'm not too sure, I'll admit. Up here you know there's a lot more jobs around than in Alabama. We don't get them, but you know they're someplace near, and they tell you that if you go train for them, then you'll be eligible. So maybe Peter might someday have some real good steady work, and that would be something, yes sir it would. I keep telling him he should pay more attention to school, and put more of himself into the lessons they give there. But he says no, it's no good; it's a waste of time; they don't care what happens there, only if the kids don't keep quiet and mind themselves. Well, Peter has got to learn to mind himself and not be fresh. He speaks back to me, these days. There'll be a time he won't even speak to me at all, I suppose. I used to blame it all on the city up here, city living. Back home we were always together, and there wasn't no place you could go, unless to Birmingham, and you couldn't do much for yourself there, we all knew. Of course, my momma, she knew how to make us behave. But I was thinking the other night, it wasn't so good back there either. Colored people, they'd beat on one another, and we had lot of people that liquor was eating away at them; they'd use wine by the gallon. All they'd do was work on the land, and then go back and kill themselves with wine. And then there'd be the next day—until they'd one evening go to sleep and never wake up. And we'd get the Bossman and he'd see to it they got buried.

"Up here I think it's better, but don't ask me to tell you why. There's the welfare, that's for sure. And we get our water and if there isn't good heat, at least there's some. Yes, it's cold up here, but we had cold down there, too, only then we didn't have any heat, and we'd just die, some of us would, every winter with one of those freezing spells.

"And I do believe things are changing. On the television they talk to you, the colored man and all the others who aren't doing so good. My boy Peter, he says they're putting you on. That's all he sees, people 'putting on' other people. But I think they all mean it, the white people. I never see them, except on television, when they say the white man wants good for the colored people. I think Peter could go and do better for himself later on, when he gets older, except for the fact that he just doesn't *believe*. He don't believe what they say, the teacher, or the man who says it's getting better for us —on television. I guess it's my fault. I never taught my children, any of them, to believe that kind of thing, because I never thought we'd ever have it any different, not in this life. So maybe I've failed Peter. I told him the other day, he should work hard, because of all the 'opportunity' they say is coming for us, and he said I was talking good, but where was my proof. So I went next door with him, to my neighbor's, and we asked her husband, and you know he sided with Peter. He said they were taking in a few here and a few there, and putting them in the front windows of all the big companies, but that all you have to do is look around at our block and you'd see all the young men, and they just haven't got a thing to do. Nothing."

Her son also looks to the future. Sometimes he talks—in his own words—"big." He'll one day be a bombardier or "something like that." At other times he is less sure of things: "I don't know what I'll be. Maybe nothing. I see the men sitting around, hiding from the welfare lady. They fool her. Maybe I'll fool her, too. I don't know what you can do. The teacher the other day said that if just one of us turned out o.k. she'd congratulate herself and call herself lucky."

A while back a riot excited Peter and his mother, excited them and frightened them. The spectacle of the police being fought, of white-owned property being assaulted, stirred the boy a great deal: "I figured the whole world might get changed around. I figured people would treat us better from now on. Only I don't think they will." As for his mother, she was less hopeful, but even more apocalyptic: "I told Peter we were going to pay for this good. I told him they wouldn't let us get away with it, not later on." And in the midst of the trouble she was frightened as she had never before been: "I saw them running around on the streets, the men and women, and they were talking about burning things down, and how there'd be nothing left when they got through. I sat there with my children and I thought we might die the way things are going, die right here. I didn't know what to do: if I should leave, in case they burn down the building, or if I should stay, so that the police don't arrest us, or we get mixed up with the crowd of people. I've never seen so many people, going in so many different directions. They were running and shouting and they didn't know what to do. They were so excited. My neighbor, she said they'd burn us all up, and then the white man would have himself one less of a headache. The colored man is a worse enemy to himself than the white. I mean, it's hard to know which is the worst."

I find it as hard as she does to sort things out. When I think of her and the mothers like her I have worked with for years, when I think of Peter and his friends, I find myself caught between the contradictory observations I have made. Peter already seems a grim and unhappy child. He trusts no one white, not his white teacher, not the white policeman he sees, not the white welfare worker, not the white storekeeper, and not, I might add, me. There we are, the five of us from the 180,000,000 Americans who surround him and of course 20,000,000 others. Yet, Peter doesn't really trust his friends and neighbors, either. At nine he has learned to be careful, wary, guarded, doubtful, and calculating. His teacher may not know it, but Peter is a good sociologist, and a good political scientist, a good student of urban affairs. With devastating accuracy he can reveal how much of the "score" he knows; yes, and how fearful and sad and angry he is: "This here city isn't for us. It's for the people downtown. We're here because, like my mother said, we had to come. If they could lock us up or sweep us away, they would. That's why I figure the only way you can stay ahead is get some kind of deal for yourself. If I had a choice I'd live someplace else, but I don't know where. It would be a place where they treated you right, and they didn't think you were some nuisance. But the only thing you can do is be careful of yourself; if not, you'll get killed somehow, like it happened to my father."

His father died prematurely, and most probably, unnecessarily. Among the poor of our cities the grim medical statistics we all know about become terrible daily experiences. Among the black and white families I work with—in nearby but separate slums—disease and the pain that goes with it are taken for granted. When my children complain of an earache or demonstrate a skin rash I rush them to the doctor. When I have a headache, I take an aspirin; and if the headache is persistent, I can always get a medical check-up. Not so with Peter's mother and Peter; they have learned to live with sores and infections and poorly mended fractures and bad teeth and eyes that need but don't have the help of glasses. Yes, they can go to a city hospital and get free care; but again and again they don't. They come to the city without any previous experience as patients. They have never had the money to purchase a doctor's time. They have never had free medical care available. (I am speaking now of Appalachian whites as well as southern blacks.) It may comfort me to know that every American city provides some free medical services for its "indigent," but Peter's mother and thousands like her have quite a different view of things: "I said to you the other time, I've tried there. It's like at City Hall, you wait and wait, and they pushes you and shove you and call your name, only to tell you to wait some more, and if you tell them you can't stay there all day, they'll say 'lady, go home, then.' You get sick just trying to get there. You have to give your children over to people or take them all with you; and the carfare is expensive. Why if we had a doctor around here, I could almost pay him with the carfare it takes to get there and back for all of us. And you know, they keep on having you come back and back, and they don't know what each other says. Each time they starts from scratch."

. . .

I am a physician, and over the past ten years I have been asking myself how people like Peter and his mother survive in mind and body and spirit. And I have wanted to know what a twentieth-century American city "means" to them or "does" to them. People cannot be handed questionnaires and asked to answer such questions. They cannot be "interviewed" a few times and told to come across with a statement, a reply. But inside Peter and his brother and his sisters and his mother, and inside a number of Appalachian mothers and fathers and children I know, are feelings and thoughts and ideas—which, in my experience, come out casually or suddenly, by accident almost. After a year or two of talking, after experiences such as I have briefly described in a city hall, in a children's hospital, a lifetime of pent-up tensions and observation comes to blunt expression: "Down in Alabama we had to be careful about ourselves with the white man, but we had plenty of things we could do by ourselves. There was our side of town, and you could walk and run all over, and we had a garden you know. Up here they have you in a cage. There's no place to go, and all I do is stay in the building all day long and the night, too. I don't use my legs no more, hardly at all. I never see those trees, and my oldest girl, she misses planting time. It was bad down there. We had to leave. But it's no good here, too, I'll tell you. Once I woke up and I thought all the buildings on the block were falling down on me. And I was trying to climb out, but I couldn't. And then the next thing I knew, we were all back South, and I was standing near some sunflowers—you know, the tall ones that can shade you if you sit down.

"No, I don't dream much. I fall into a heavy sleep as soon as I touch the bed. The next thing I know I'm stirring myself to start in all over in the morning. It used to be the sun would wake me up, but now it's up in my head, I guess. I know I've got to get the house going and off to school."

Her wistful, conscientious, law-abiding, devoutly Christian spirit hasn't completely escaped the notice of Peter, for all his hard-headed, cynical protestations: "If I had a chance, I'd like to get enough money to bring us all back to Alabama for a visit. Then I could prove it that it may be good down there, a little bit, even if it's no good, either. Like she says, we had to get out of there or we'd be dead by now. I hear say we all may get killed soon, it's so bad here; but I think we did right to get up here, and if we make them listen to us, the white man, maybe he will."

To which Peter's mother adds: "We've carried a lot of trouble in us, from way back in the beginning. I have these pains, and so does everyone around here. But you can't just die until you're ready to. And I do believe something is happening. I do believe I see that."

To which Peter adds: "Maybe it won't be that we'll win, but if we get killed, everyone will hear about it. Like the minister said, before we used to die real quiet, and no one stopped to pay notice."

Two years before Peter spoke those words he drew a picture for me, one of many he has done. When he was younger, and when I didn't know him so well as I think I do now, it was easier for us to have something tangible to do and then talk about. I used to visit the alley with him, as I still do, and one day I asked him to draw the alley. That was a good idea, he thought. (Not all of my suggestions were, however.) He started in, then stopped, and finally worked rather longer and harder than usual at the job. I busied myself with my own sketches, which from the start he insisted I do. Suddenly from across the table I heard him say he was through. Ordinarily he would slowly turn the drawing around for me to see; and I would get up and walk over to his side of the table, to see even better. But he didn't move his paper, and I didn't move myself. I saw what he had drawn, and he saw me looking. I was surprised and a bit stunned and more than a bit upset, and surely he saw my face and heard my utter silence. Often I would break the awkward moments when neither of us seemed to have anything to say, but this time it was his turn to do so: "You know what it is?" He knew that I liked us to talk about our work. I said no, I didn't—though in fact the vivid power of his black crayon had come right across to me. "It's that hole we dug in the alley. I made it bigger here. If you fall into it, you can't get out. You die."

He had drawn circles within circles, all of them black, and then a center, also black. He had imposed an X on the center. Nearby, strewn across the circles, were fragments of the human body—two faces, an arm, five legs. And after I had taken the scene in, I could only think to myself that I had been shown "like it is in the alley"— by an intelligent boy who knew what he saw around him, could give it expression, and, I am convinced, would respond to a different city, a city that is alive and breathing, one that is not for many of its citizens a virtual morgue.

11 Fifth Avenue, Uptown*

James Baldwin

THERE IS A HOUSING project standing now where the house in which we grew up once stood, and one of those stunted city trees is snarling where our doorway used to be. This is on the rehabilitated side of the avenue. The other side of the avenue —for progress takes time—has not been rehabilitated yet and it looks exactly as it looked in the days when we sat with our noses pressed against the windowpane, longing to be allowed to go "across the street." The grocery store which gave us credit is still there, and there can be no doubt that it is still giving credit. The people in the project certainly need it—far more, indeed, than they ever needed the project. The last time I passed by, the Jewish proprietor was still standing among his shelves, looking sadder and heavier but scarcely any older. Further down the block stands the shoe-repair store in which our shoes were repaired until reparation became impossible and in which, then, we bought all our "new" ones. The Negro proprietor is still in the window, head down, working at the leather.

* From James Baldwin, "Fifth Avenue, Uptown," *Esquire*, 59 (July, 1960), 72–73, 76. Reprinted by permission of Robert Lantz–Candida Donadio Literary Agency, Inc. Copyright © 1960 by James Baldwin.

These two, I imagine, could tell a long tale if they would (perhaps they would be glad to if they could), having watched so many, for so long, struggling in the fishhooks, the barbed wire, of this avenue.

The avenue is elsewhere the renowned and elegant Fifth. The area I am describing, which, in today's gang parlance, would be called "the turf," is bounded by Lenox Avenue on the west, the Harlem River on the east, 135th Street on the north, and 130th Street on the south. We never lived beyond these boundaries; this is where we grew up. Walking along 145th Street—for example—familiar as it is, and similar, does not have the same impact because I do not know any of the people on the block. But when I turn east on 131st Street and Lenox Avenue, there is first a soda-pop joint, then a shoeshine "parlor," then a grocery store, then a dry cleaners', then the houses. All along the street there are people who watched me grow up, people who grew up with me, people I watched grow up along with my brothers and sisters; and, sometimes in my arms, sometimes underfoot, sometimes at my shoulder—or on it—their children, a riot, a forest of children, who include my nieces and nephews.

When we reach the end of this long block, we find ourselves on wide, filthy, hostile Fifth Avenue, facing that project which hangs over the avenue like a monument to the folly, and the cowardice, of good intentions. All along the block, for anyone who knows it, are immense human gaps, like craters. These gaps are not created merely by those who have moved away, inevitably into some other ghetto; or by those who have risen, almost always into a greater capacity for self-loathing and self-delusion; or yet by those who, by whatever means—War II, the Korean War, a policeman's gun or billy, a gang war, a brawl, madness, an overdose of heroin, or, simply, unnatural exhaustion—are dead. I am talking about those who are left, and I am talking principally about the young. What are they doing? Well, some, a minority, are fanatical churchgoers, members of the more extreme of the Holy Roller sects. Many, many more are "moslems," by affiliation or sympathy, that is to say that they are united by nothing more—and nothing less—than a hatred of the white world and all its works. They are present, for example, at every Buy Black street-corner meeting—meetings in which the speaker urges his hearers to cease trading with white men and establish a separate economy. Neither the speaker nor his hearers can possibly do this, of course, since Negroes do not own General Motors or RCA or the A&P, nor, indeed, do they own more than a wholly insufficient fraction of anything else in Harlem (those who *do* own anything are more interested in their profits than in their fellows). But these meetings nevertheless keep alive in the participators a certain pride of bitterness without which, however futile this bitterness may be, they could scarcely remain alive at all. Many have given up. They stay home and watch the TV screen, living on the earnings of their parents, cousins, brothers, or uncles, and only leave the house to go to the movies or to the nearest bar. "How're you making it?" one may ask, running into them along the block, or in the bar. "Oh, I'm TV-ing it"; with the saddest, sweetest, most shamefaced of smiles, and from a great distance. This distance one is compelled to respect; anyone who has traveled so far will not easily be dragged again into the world. There are further retreats, of course, than the TV screen or the bar. There are those who are simply sitting on their stoops, "stoned," animated for a moment only, and hideously, by the approach of someone who may lend them the money for a "fix." Or by the approach of someone from whom they can purchase it, one of the shrewd ones, on the way to prison or just coming out.

And the others, who have avoided all of these deaths, get up in the morning and go downtown to meet "the man." They work in the white man's world all day and come home in the evening to this fetid block. They struggle to instill in their children some private sense of honor or dignity which will help the child to survive. This means, of course, that they must struggle, stolidly, incessantly, to keep this sense alive in themselves, in spite of the insults, the indifference, and the cruelty they are certain to encounter in their working day. They patiently browbeat the landlord into fixing the heat, the plaster, the plumbing; this demands prodigious patience; nor is patience usually enough. In trying to make their hovels habitable, they are perpetually throwing good money after bad. Such frustration, so long endured, is driving many strong, admirable men and women whose only crime is color to the very gates of paranoia.

One remembers them from another time—playing handball in the playground, going to church, wondering if they were going to be promoted at school. One remembers them going off to war—gladly, to escape this block. One remembers their return. Perhaps one remembers their wedding day. And one sees where the girl is now—vainly looking for salvation from some other embittered, trussed, and struggling boy—and sees the all-but-abandoned children in the streets.

Now I am perfectly aware that there are other slums in which white men are fighting for their lives, and mainly losing. I know that blood is also flowing through those streets and that the human damage there is incalculable. People are continually pointing out to me the wretchedness of white people in order to console me for the wretchedness of blacks. But an itemized account of the American failure does not console me and it should not console anyone else. That hundreds of thousands of white people are living, in effect, no better than the "niggers" is not a fact to be regarded with complacency. The social and moral bankruptcy suggested by this fact is of the bitterest, most terrifying kind.

The people, however, who believe that this democratic anguish has some consoling value are always pointing out that So-and-So, white, and So-and-So, black, rose from the slums into the big time. The existence—the public existence—of, say, Frank Sinatra and Sammy Davis, Jr. proves to them that America is still the land of opportunity and that inequalities vanish before the determined will. It proves nothing of the sort. The determined will is rare—at the moment, in this country, it is unspeakably rare—and the inequalities suffered by the many are in no way justified by the rise of a few. A few have always risen—in every country, every era, and in the teeth of regimes which can by no stretch of the imagination be thought of as free. Not all of these people, it is worth remembering, left the world better than they found it. The determined will is rare, but it is not invariably benevolent. Furthermore, the American equation of success with the big time reveals an awful disrespect for human life and human achievement. This equation has placed our cities among the most dangerous in the world and has placed our youth among the most empty and most bewildered. The situation of our youth is not mysterious. Children have never been very good at listening to their elders, but they have never failed to imitate them. They must, they have no other models. That is exactly what our children are doing. They are imitating our immorality, our disrespect for the pain of others.

All other slum dwellers, when the bank account permits it, can move out of the slum and vanish altogether from the eye of persecution. No Negro in this country has ever made that much money and it will be a long time before any Negro does. The Negroes in Harlem, who have no money, spend what they have on such gimcracks as they are sold. These include "wider" TV screens, more "faithful" hi-fi sets, more "powerful" cars, all of which, of course, are obsolete long before they are paid for. Anyone who has ever struggled with poverty knows how extremely expensive it is to be poor; and if one is a member of a captive population, economically speaking, one's feet have simply been placed on the treadmill forever. One is victimized, economically, in a thousand ways—rent, for example, or car insurance. Go shopping one day in Harlem—for anything—and compare Harlem prices and quality with those downtown.

The people who have managed to get off this block have only got as far as a more respectable ghetto. This respectable ghetto does not even have the advantages of the disreputable one, friends, neighbors, a familiar church, and friendly tradesmen; and it is not, moreover, in the nature of any ghetto to remain respectable long. Every Sunday, people who have left the block take the lonely ride back, dragging their increasingly discontented children with them. They spend the day talking, not always with words, about the trouble they've seen and the trouble—one must watch their eyes as they watch their children—they are only too likely to see. For children do not like ghettos. It takes them nearly no time to discover exactly why they are there.

The projects in Harlem are hated. They are hated almost as much as policemen, and this is saying a great deal. And they are hated for the same reason: both reveal, unbearably, the real attitude of the white world, no matter how many liberal speeches are made, no matter how many lofty editorials are written, no matter how many civil-rights commissions are set up.

The projects are hideous, of course, there being a law, apparently respected throughout the world, that popular housing shall be as cheerless as a prison. They are lumped all over Harlem, colorless, bleak, high, and revolting. The wide windows look out on Harlem's invincible and indescribable squalor: the Park Avenue railroad tracks, around which, about forty years ago, the present dark community began; the unrehabilitated houses, bowed down, it would seem, under the great weight of frustration and bitterness they contain; the dark, the ominous schoolhouses from which the child may emerge maimed, blinded, hooked, or enraged for life; and the churches, churches, block upon block of churches, niched in the walls like cannon in the walls of a fortress. Even if the administration of the projects were not so insanely humiliating (for example: one must report raises in salary to the management, which will then eat up the profit by raising one's rent; the management has the right to know who is staying in your apartment; the management can ask you to leave, at their discretion), the projects would still be hated because they are an insult to the meanest intelligence.

Harlem got its first private project, Riverton—which is now, naturally, a slum—about twelve years ago because at that time

Negroes were not allowed to live in Stuyvesant Town. Harlem watched Riverton go up, therefore, in the most violent bitterness of spirit, and hated it long before the builders arrived. They began hating it at about the time people began moving out of their condemned houses to make room for this additional proof of how thoroughly the white world despised them. And they had scarcely moved in, naturally, before they began smashing windows, defacing walls, urinating in the elevators, and fornicating in the playgrounds. Liberals, both white and black, were appalled at the spectacle. I was appalled by the liberal innocence—or cynicism, which comes out in practice as much the same thing. Other people were delighted to be able to point to proof positive that nothing could be done to better the lot of the colored people. They were, and are, right in one respect: that nothing can be done as long as they are treated like colored people. The people in Harlem know they are living there because white people do not think they are good enough to live anywhere else. No amount of "improvement" can sweeten this fact. Whatever money is now being earmarked to improve this, or any other ghetto, might as well be burnt. A ghetto can be improved in one way only: out of existence.

Similarly, the only way to police a ghetto is to be oppressive. None of Commissioner Kennedy's policemen, even with the best will in the world, have any way of understanding the lives led by the people they swagger about in two's and three's controlling. Their very presence is an insult, and it would be, even if they spent their entire day feeding gumdrops to children. They represent the force of the white world, and that world's real intentions are, simply, for that world's criminal profit and ease, to keep the black man corraled up here, in his place. The badge, the gun in the holster, and the swinging club make vivid what will happen should his rebellion become overt. Rare, indeed, is the Harlem citizen, from the most circumspect church member to the most shiftless adolescent, who does not have a long tale to tell of police incompetence, injustice, or brutality. I myself have witnessed and endured it more than once. The businessmen and racketeers also have a story. And so do the prostitutes. (And this is not, perhaps, the place to discuss Harlem's very complex attitude towards black policemen, nor the reasons, according to Harlem, that they are nearly all downtown.)

It is hard, on the other hand, to blame the policeman, blank, good-natured, thoughtless, and insuperably innocent, for being such a perfect representative of the people he serves. He, too, believes in good intentions and is astounded and offended when they are not taken for the deed. He has never, himself, done anything for which to be hated—which of us has?—and yet he is facing, daily and nightly, people who would gladly see him dead, and he knows it. There is no way for him not to know it: there are few things under heaven more unnerving than the silent, accumulating contempt and hatred of a people. He moves through Harlem, therefore, like an occupying soldier in a bitterly hostile country; which is precisely what, and where, he is, and is the reason he walks in two's and three's. And he is not the only one who knows why he is always in company: the people who are watching him know why, too. Any street meeting, sacred or secular, which he and his colleagues uneasily cover has as its explicit or implicit burden the cruelty and injustice of the white domination. And these days, of course, in terms increasingly vivid and jubilant, it speaks of the end of that domination. The white policeman, standing on a Harlem street corner, finds himself at the very center of the revolution now occurring in the world. He is not prepared for it—naturally, nobody is—and, what is possibly much more to the point, he is exposed, as few white people are, to the anguish of the black people around him. Even if he is gifted with the merest mustard grain of imagination, something must seep in. He cannot avoid observing that some of the children, in spite of their color, remind him of children he has known and loved, perhaps even of his own children. He knows that he certainly does not want *his* children living this way. He can retreat from his uneasiness in only one direction: into a callousness which very shortly becomes second nature. He becomes more callous, the population becomes more hostile, the situation grows more tense, and the police force is increased. One day, to everyone's astonishment, someone drops a match in the powder keg and everything blows up. Before the dust has settled or the blood congealed, editorials, speeches, and civil-rights commissions are loud in the land, demanding to know what happened. What happened is that Negroes want to be treated like men.

Negroes want to be treated like men: a perfectly straightforward statement, containing only seven words. People who have mastered Kant, Hegel, Shakespeare, Marx, Freud, and the Bible find this statement utterly impenetrable. The idea seems to threaten profound, barely conscious assumptions. A kind of panic paralyzes their features, as though they found themselves trapped on the edge of a steep place. I once tried to describe to a very-well-known American intellectual the conditions among Negroes in the South. My recital disturbed him and made him indignant; and he asked me in perfect innocence, "Why don't all the Negroes in the South move North?"

I tried to explain what *has* happened, unfailingly, whenever a significant body of Negroes move North. They do not escape jim-crow: they merely encounter another, not-less-deadly variety. They do not move to Chicago, they move to the South Side; they do not move to New York, they move to Harlem. The pressure within the ghetto causes the ghetto walls to expand, and this expansion is always violent. White people hold the line as long as they can, and in as many ways as they can, from verbal intimidation to physical violence. But inevitably the border which has divided the ghetto from the rest of the world falls into the hands of the ghetto. The white people fall back bitterly before the black horde; the landlords make a tidy profit by raising the rent, chopping up the rooms, and all but dispensing with the upkeep; and what has once been a neighborhood turns into a "turf." This is precisely what happened when the Puerto Ricans arrived in their thousands—and the bitterness thus caused is, as I write, being fought out all up and down those streets.

Northerners indulge in an extremely dangerous luxury. They seem to feel that because they fought on the right side during the Civil War, and won, that they have earned the right merely to deplore what is going on in the South, without taking any responsibility for it; and that they can ignore what is happening in Northern cities because what is happening in Little Rock or Birmingham is worse. Well, in the first place, it is not possible for anyone who has not endured both to know which is "worse." I know Negroes who prefer the South and white Southerners, because "At least there, you haven't got to play any guessing games!" The guessing games referred to have driven more than one Negro into the narcotics ward, the madhouse, or the river. I know another Negro, a man very dear to me, who says, with conviction and with truth, "The spirit of the South is the spirit of America." He was born in the North and did his military training in the South. He did not, as far as I can gather, find the South "worse"; he found it, if anything, all too familiar. In the second place, though, even if Birmingham *is* worse, no doubt Johannesburg, South Africa, beats it by several miles, and Buchenwald was one of the worst things that ever happened in the entire history of the world. The world has never lacked for horrifying examples; but I do not believe that these examples are meant to be used as justification for our own crimes. This perpetual justification empties the heart of all human feeling. The emptier our hearts become, the greater will be our crimes. Thirdly, the South is not merely an embarrassingly backward region, but a part of this country, and what happens there concerns every one of us.

As far as the color problem is concerned, there is but one great difference between the Southern white and the Northerner: the Southerner remembers, historically, and in his own psyche, a kind of Eden in which he loved black people and they loved him. Historically, the flaming sword laid across this Eden is the Civil War. Personally, it is the Southerner's sexual coming of age, when, without any warning, unbreakable taboos are set up between himself and his past. Everything, thereafter, is permitted him except the love he remembers and has never ceased to need. The resulting, indescribable torment affects every Southern mind and is the basis of the Southern hysteria.

None of this is true for the Northerner. Negroes represent nothing to him personally, except, perhaps, the dangers of carnality. He never sees Negroes. Southerners see them all the time. Northerners never think about them whereas Southerners are never really thinking of anything else. Negroes are, therefore, ignored in the North and are under surveillance in the South, and suffer hideously in both places. Neither the Southerner nor the Northerner is able to look on the Negro simply as a man. It seems to be indispensable to the national self-esteem that the Negro be considered either as a kind of ward (in which case we are told how many Negroes, comparatively, bought Cadillacs last year and how few, comparatively, were lynched), or as a victim (in which case we are promised that he will never vote in our assemblies or go to school with our kids). They are two sides of the same coin and the South will not change—*cannot* change—until the North changes. The country will not change until it re-examines itself and discovers what it really means by freedom. In the meantime, generations keep being born, bitterness is increased by incompetence, pride, and folly, and the world shrinks around us.

It is a terrible, an inexorable, law that one cannot deny the humanity of another without diminishing one's own: in the face of one's victim, one sees oneself. Walk through the streets of Harlem and see what we, this nation, have become.

Section Three

The Ghetto As a Target of Reform

The enduring ghetto has soiled the ideals of America as an open, just, egalitarian society, to the chagrin of many urban reformers. Prodded by guilt, moral scruples, and outrage, and struck by the human waste entombed within ghetto walls, men and women of good faith have periodically expressed deep interest in ameliorating the plight of ghetto residents. Reformers have ranged from paternalistic upper-class patricians to concerned, dedicated professionals to ghetto residents themselves. Their goals have been even more varied, including moral regeneration of the resident, rehabilitation of the physical environment, destruction of the ghetto, and a combination of all three. The continued existence of the ghetto in all its virulent forms suggests the ultimate failure of the good-intentioned reformers.

In fact, the immediate needs of ghetto residents—jobs, loans, ticket fixes, food and drink, coal, money and midwife at birth, flowers and burial money at death—have often been serviced only by political machines that have a vested interest in perpetuating the ghetto. Nevertheless, reformers have publicized problems, sought solutions, and relayed warnings to the larger society. Recently, some soured liberals, discouraged by the shortcomings of the past and confused by the rhetoric of ghetto militants about local control, have despaired of assuming any further active role in ghetto reform. Black sociologist Kenneth Clark, criticizing this type of separatism as self-defeating to all groups in society, has called instead for a massive mobilization of public concern to break the shackles of the ghetto. In *Dark Ghetto* (p. 240) he wrote:

> White and Negro must fight together for the rights of human beings to make mistakes and to aspire to human goals. Negroes will not break out of the barriers of the ghetto unless whites transcend the barriers of their own minds, for the ghetto is to the Negro a reflection of the ghetto in which the white lives imprisoned.

The selections in this section illuminate the various approaches to ghetto reform and the changing attitudes of ghetto reformers during the nineteenth and twentieth centuries. Urban historian Raymond A. Mohl's essay on preindustrial reform efforts describes how poor people were categorized, analyzed, scrutinized, and made to conform with the mores of the dominant Anglo-Saxon society in order to qualify for relief. The austere, moralistic methods of early nineteenth-century philanthropists had their roots in pre-American British practices, and they lingered into the twentieth century. Commissioner of Labor Carroll D. Wright's "Housing of the Working People," written in 1895, represents a milestone in ghetto reform efforts. This *Special Report* utilized scientific methods of gathering empirical data on such matters as building plans and European innovations. Tainted at times by a moralistic and paternalistic tone, its recommendations—rehabilitation of buildings, formation of citizen groups to prod bureaucracies, and legislation with stronger enforcement provisions—were nevertheless wide-ranging and surprisingly sophisticated. James B. Lane's essay on Jacob A. Riis and *How the Other Half Lives* connects ghetto reform to the Progressive movement. Humanitarian reformers of Riis's era were a link between nineteenth- and twentieth-century liberalism—both of which included a faith in progress and reason. Riis and other Progressives called on liberal-minded citizens to hold in abeyance their fear of the state and use the government to reform the urban environment. Michael Young, a British ghetto reformer, has analyzed the findings of the United States Riot Commission Report of 1968. Young criticizes the Commission for underestimating the problems of governmental solutions and failing to take account of the creativity of ghetto residents in understanding what is best for themselves.

For further reading on related subjects see Robert H. Bremner, *From the Depths: The Discovery of Poverty in the United States* (1956); George Rosen, *A History of Public Health* (1958); Clifford W. Patton, *The Battle for Municipal Reform, 1875–1900* (1940); Nathan I. Huggins, *Protestants Against Poverty: Boston's Charities, 1870–1900* (1971); Roy Lubove, *The Progressives and the Slums: Tenement House Reform in New York City, 1890–1917* (1962); Lincoln Steffens, *The Shame of the Cities* (1904); Bruce M. Stave, *The New Deal and the Last Hurrah: Pittsburgh Machine Politics* (1970); Paul Jacobs, *Prelude to Riot: A View of Urban America from the Bottom* (1966); Lawrence M. Friedman, *Government and Slum Housing: A Century of Frustration* (1968); Guichard Parris and Lester Brooks, *Blacks in the City: A History of the National Urban League* (1971).

12 Social Welfare and Social Control in Nineteenth-Century America: The Preindustrial City*

Raymond A. Mohl

FEW DOMESTIC PROBLEMS plague contemporary American society as deeply as poverty, dependency, and social welfare. The "welfare mess" is a troublesome and persistent ingredient of the larger urban dilemma, but it is one most Americans have become pervasively aware of only in the last decade. Unfortunately, greater awareness has not led to greater understanding. Frances Fox Piven and Richard A. Cloward have recently written an important and insightful book which goes far to bridge that gap between awareness and understanding. Entitled *Regulating the Poor: The Functions of Public Welfare*, the Piven-Cloward book maintains, among other things, that relief systems have historically served two main functions: first, to maintain social and civil order, and second, to enforce work.[1] Denying that government welfare policies have become progressively more liberal and humane, the authors contend that relief has simply been an effective way of manipulating the poor, keeping them orderly, and forcing them into low-income,

---

* The author read a version of this article at the 1972 meeting of the Organization of American Historians. Copyright © 1973 by Raymond A. Mohl.

menial work. Piven and Cloward marshaled most of their historical evidence, however, from seventeenth- and eighteenth-century England and from the New Deal period in the United States; they ignored an enormous amount of relevant and applicable material from early American history, especially in the nineteenth century. By way of testing their hypothesis, I would like to suggest here, in an exploratory way, that the merchant elite and middle-class moral reformers of the early nineteenth-century preindustrial city utilized both public relief and private humanitarianism as a means of maintaining social order and enforcing the work ethic at a time when these pillars of a stable society seemed to be crumbling.

Between the American Revolution and the industrial takeoff of the mid-nineteenth century, American cities underwent a profound and, to contemporaries, disturbing transformation. A variety of social and economic changes combined to destroy the essentially stable and deferential society of the Colonial period. To be sure, most of the large Colonial towns experienced economic depressions, poverty, disease, overcrowding, crime, violence, and social conflict. Yet few of these problems threatened for long to upset the elite-dominated, community-centered nature of pre-Revolutionary urbanism. Colonial institutions tempered conflict and maintained more than a semblance of order and stability. But in the early decades of the nineteenth century, old and established institutions of family and faction, church and government, social class and community became ineffective and broke down under new urban conditions. With the decline in deference, social relationships became uncertain and old norms eroded. Small, usually orderly, and relatively well-regulated in Colonial years, the seaport cities became large, unstable, and socially fragmented.

Extremely rapid population growth speeded these changes in preindustrial American cities. A small city of little more than 30,000 in 1790, New York grew by more than 80 percent during the following decade. Baltimore almost doubled its population in the same ten-year period. Between 1790 and 1830 New York had an overall population growth rate of 549 percent. Over the same four decades Baltimore, Boston, and Philadelphia expanded at rates of 497 percent, 367 percent, and 266 percent, respectively. As economic historian George Rogers Taylor has suggested, these growth rates exceeded the total rate of population expansion, the growth rate of the same cities in the forty years after 1860, and the contemporary growth rate of large British cities. The growth rates of the port cities remained high between 1830 and 1860 as well.[2]

Rapid population increase contributed to the emergence of a disorderly society. While new transportation technology permitted upper- and middle-class movement to suburbs, even during these early years, the cities themselves became increasingly congested. Several wards of New York City, for example, had average densities above 170 persons per acre by 1840. Most big cities experienced housing shortages. By the 1830s European immigrants and native rural migrants crowded into boarding houses, cellars, attics, newly converted tenements, and makeshift quarters along waterfronts and on the outskirts of business districts. These new residential patterns destroyed the homogeneity of earlier years and altered everyday relationships among city dwellers. Heavy population concentrations fostered impersonality and stimulated social tensions. Population growth also forced physical expansion of urban centers—a haphazard process in the early nineteenth century. The gridiron pattern typically applied in Philadelphia and New York seemed efficient and businesslike, but the jumble of land uses and the absence of space for parks, squares, and neighborhood gathering places had a socially disintegrating effect.[3]

Increasingly heavy immigration during the period contributed not only to urban population growth, but to social fragmentation as well. Only a small stream in the 1790s, and interrupted several times in later years by war and depression, the immigrant influx hit flood tide after the 1820s. While almost 93,000 immigrants arrived in New York during the 1820s, more than 400,000 came during the 1830s. New York City annually received between one-half and two-thirds of all newcomers, although not all remained in the metropolis. By 1850 the foreign born made up almost half of New York's total population. By the same year Irish immigrants alone composed more than 25 percent of Boston's population. The newcomers—mostly Irish and German workers and laborers and their families—added ethnic and religious diversity, challenged earlier majorities of English, Protestant stock, and altered the social complexion of city life in the United States. Nativists argued, moreover, that because the primarily Catholic foreigners constituted "the materials for mobs and rebellions," they threatened social stability and cohesiveness. The Irish especially became the butt of nativist hostilities. Poverty-stricken, for the most part without marketable skills, seemingly averse to work, and morally offensive to old stock Americans, they crowded growing slums in seaport cities and contributed to urban disorder.[4]

Increasing class distinctions also fostered disorder. To be sure, upward economic mobility was always possible, but some historians have suggested than even eighteenth-century society was becoming more stratified and unequal. James Henretta, for instance, has shown that the class of propertyless laborers in Colonial Boston grew twice as rapidly as the city's total population. Others have demonstrated increasing disparities in wealth and property distribution as the nineteenth century advanced, especially in urban commercial and business centers. Despite the rhetoric of egalitarianism in the "age of common man," the fact is that a kind of permanent proletariat was emerging in early nineteenth-century cities—composed largely of day laborers and unskilled, propertyless workers, immigrants, and blacks. Combined with the decline of deference, the reality of a larger, often discontented, lower class eroded the fixity of the old order and the values and norms which had sustained it.[5]

Moreover, the disorder attendant on a large lower class was multiplied by geographic mobility and population turnover. According to early nineteenth-century observers, the lower stratum of society in New York City was characterized by a "floating" population of transients and migrants. One writer described the poor as "constantly on the wing." Many were immigrants passing in or out of the city; others were native Americans who drifted temporarily to the city from neighboring countryside, or who sought new opportunities in the west after exhausting possibilities in the city. The same pattern prevailed in other cities as well. Peter R. Knights, author of *The Plain People of Boston, 1830–1860,* found population turnover in Boston to be about 30 percent per year in the 1830s and 1840s and 40 percent per year in the 1850s. Even within the urban community the poor moved constantly from place to place. On three different days in January 1810, for example, the superintendent of New York's poorhouse listed one Ann Haviland, a widow on outdoor, or home, relief at three different addresses. And non–New Yorkers were always amazed at the spectacle of disorder presented every May 1, the city's traditional moving day, when, because of the uniform expiration of leases, rich and poor alike filled the streets moving furniture and belongings to new residences. Mobility undermined community as effectively as class distinction.[6]

Simultaneous economic changes had a similar impact. In pre-Revolutionary times work patterns reinforced the cohesive community. Men worked in small shops with a few other apprentices and journeymen, along with the shop owner—a master craftsman. Such work patterns transferred skills and, as Sam Warner has suggested for Colonial Philadelphia, the incentive for shop ownership to the rising generation of craftsmen. The Colonial city worker identified with his community and with the master craftsman—an employer who only temporarily stood above the worker in economic and social status. By the 1820s, however, cities like New York, Philadelphia, and Boston poised at the threshold of the industrial era. As the cities became important processing and manufacturing centers, the factory increasingly replaced the small shop, and machines, the skilled craftsman. Immigrants and farm girls took up places in the new factories, further altering work patterns. At the same time industrial beginnings produced new forms of economic complexity and interdependence. Workers, in turn, became increasingly subject to the business fluctuations, depressions, and unemployment which characterized the economic transformation of the period. Moreover, changes in the social organization of work brought specialization of tasks, lessened the importance of skill, and destroyed security, independence, and incentive for workers. The decline of handicraft industry, in other words, undermined the urban worker's identification with community. These changes had a very real impact on worker behavior, as evidenced by the emergence of a strong, but short-lived, trade union movement complete with picketing, strikes, and labor violence in the 1820s and 1830s. The development of factory-type work . . . also had an impact on urban business leadership . . . as . . . the old merchant elites suffered a relative decline in power, position, and social status.

Other developments also reflected the growing ferment and disorder of the preindustrial American city. Municipal governments failed to cope with a multiplicity of urban problems; city services lagged far behind residential need. The essentially negative municipal controls and restrictive regulatory policies of the Colonial era no longer sufficed in the larger, more diverse city of the early nineteenth century. Inadequate facilities for sewage and garbage disposal made cities like New York, as diarist George Templeton Strong wrote in the late 1830s, "one huge pigsty." Indeed, in the absence of real public responsibility, roving pigs rivaled city scavengers in efficiency —a sure indication, one British traveler suggested, of "something wrong" with municipal administration. Poor water supply and distorted medical conceptions rendered public health measures useless; epidemics of yellow fever and cholera periodically ravaged the cities. Despite constant complaints from citizens about crime and violence, no city had a professional police force before 1840. Volunteer fire companies concentrated more on fighting one another than the frequent blazes which could destroy whole sections of a city at a time. The city required positive government to counter disorder, but mayors and councilmen failed to provide it. As the sense of community broke down, so also did municipal government.[7]

Social and economic change, then, undermined the orderly, well-regulated society of the Colonial town. Institutions which had fostered community, tempered conflict, kept order, and maintained social control in the small city became ineffective in the distended, disorderly seaport cities of the early nineteenth century. As a Philadelphia group noted in 1827, the ties which connected society had become "relaxed." The new conditions of an expansive but unsettled urban society imposed qualitative changes on the lives of city dwellers. Established middle-class norms and values held little meaning for the European and native newcomers who crowded the cellars and tenements of the growing cities. The struggle for adjustment and survival absorbed most of their energies. Technology and immigration threatened the position of workers. Heterogeneity, diversity, and division marked emerging residential patterns.[8]

By the 1820s, according to a Boston civic leader, social and economic changes had destroyed the "compact, united, and friendly community" of earlier years. Some observers thought they detected a widening gap between rich and poor—a disturbing sign of disunity and declining identification with community. For the rich, they said, the self-interested and all-consuming concern for private wealth had corrupting influences. Yet, the poor, somehow lacking this same acquisitive drive, remained equally corrupt. The role of the family seemed diminished; educators and preachers complained about the lessened influence of parents over children. Alarmed middle-class moralists noted rising rates of urban crime, violence, delinquency, and immorality. Nativists worried intensely about "internal subversion" purportedly plotted by Catholics, Freemasons, and abolitionists. Heightened ethnic, religious, class, and racial tensions resulted in a wave of urban riots and violence, clearly reflecting social unrest and fragmentation. The mob threatened the fragile foundations of American liberty. For a society which prized uniformity, stability, and order, which saw conformity as synonymous with cohesiveness and community, these social changes were especially disturbing. For those who defined the public good in terms of self-interest, disorder meant bad business and violence posed a very immediate personal danger. For those who identified with a virtuous and communal past, the signs of social anarchy seemed very real.[9]

For the merchant elite and for most native, middle-class Americans, urban pauperism and dependency typified all that was wrong with society in the early nineteenth century. Like the contemporary British political economists from whom they borrowed intellectually, nineteenth-century Americans accepted the idea of permanent economic inequality among men, but postulated an essential distinction between poverty and pauperism. Poverty seemed natural and ineradicable, the normal condition of the laboring classes. Few expected unskilled workingmen and immigrants to live much above a subsistence level. Furthermore, the self-reliant, laboring poor outwardly conformed to the Protestant work ethic and presented little threat to established order.

Pauperism, however, meant dependency, a clearly unacceptable condition. It contradicted the basic assumptions and requirements of a stable society. Pauperism undermined virtue and order. It violated the work ethic; it represented a constant economic drain on productive members of society. It denied the optimistic and often-repeated assertions of American progress. Paupers were idle, ignorant, immoral, impious, and vicious, civic and urban spokesman said. They begged, stole, disturbed the peace, drank to excess, and, in the parlance of the times committed "shameful enormities." They sought charity but avoided work. They refused to conform. Because a good portion of them were the same foreigners blamed for other disturbing changes, they were labeled un-American too. Pauperism, in short, seemed a destructive evil which threatened social values and norms and thus became intolerable.[10]

As the well-regulated society began to break down after 1800, as growing cities became crowded with penniless, often unemployed immigrants, pauperism became increasingly observable, a daily evident symbol of social disorder. In cities like New York as many as one-fifth of the population went on relief during periods of severe economic crisis, such as that which prevailed in the half decade after the War of 1812.[11] The magnitude of the problem seemed ominous to middle-class businessmen, newspaper editors, and city officials; the visibility of the poor seemed threatening. For the nineteenth-century establishment, for those, that is, who sought restoration of old norms and familiar patterns, for those who sought an orderly society, an assault against pauperism and associated "vices" became a primary objective.

Almost uniformly, middle-class urbanites traced dependency to the poor themselves. They found causes of pauperism in voluntary idleness, drunkenness, impiety, extravagence, immorality, and the ease with which public and private charity could be obtained. Few failed to associate pauperism with the "vicious and immoral habits" observable in city slums. Character deficiency seemed the cause of economic insufficiency. Humanitarian leaders and city officials from Boston to Baltimore postulated these views with regularity. Despite the obvious relationship between lengthened welfare rolls and depressed economic conditions, by the 1820s pauperism came to be treated as a moral problem whose solution was central to the reestablishment of social order.

Given their concern about social disintegration and their assumptions about the causes of pauperism, the reformers had few alternatives. The conviction that the poor brought poverty upon themselves implied that work and moral improvement, rather than charity and relief, would cure dependency. Indeed, the certainty of relief in time of need, some reformers argued, tended to destroy character and self-reliance, but the fear of suffering was "a wholesome moral discipline" which forced the poor to work and save. Stemming from individual moral defects, pauperism could be ended only by compelling the poor to work and by character-building moral reforms.[12]

Social welfare developments in the early nineteenth-century city reflected these attitudes and social perceptions. Troubled by mounting evidence of entrenched pauperism in urban centers, state and municipal officials took actions tempering the humanitarianism which primarily underlay poor relief in Colonial years. The hardened moralism of the period demanded welfare cutbacks, limiting aid only to the "worthy" poor—presumably a relatively small group of people who became dependent through no fault of their own. To ensure that public aid was the last resort of the poor, life on relief had to be made less appealing—"less eligible," in the terminology of the time—than the worst kind of independent existence. Convinced that numerous "undeserving" applicants lived comfortably on welfare, public officials sought to purge the rolls as much as possible, forcing those remaining into a degrading institutionalized existence. Welfare "reform" in the 1820s in New York State, for example, although abolishing archaic settlement clauses, cut outdoor relief and required poorhouses in every county. A simultaneous investigation of Massachusetts' poor laws, conducted by Boston Mayor Josiah Quincy, similarly condemned outdoor relief and recommended poorhouses "having the character of workhouses, or houses of industry" as an economically and morally superior relief technique. An 1827 inquiry in Philadelphia concluded that outdoor relief destroyed ambition, fostering idleness and dependency. The tradition of local responsibility for the needy continued, but by the 1820s city governments hoped to deter relief seekers and save money by providing only for those willing to submit to the regimen and discipline of the poorhouse.[13]

During these years city officials turned the relief system into a work-enforcing device. In a competitive, wage-oriented economy work became a prime requisite for the maintenance of public order. Legislation in most states permitted local officials to impose a work requirement for relief. Every urban almshouse became a workhouse; forced labor became routine. Before 1800 in New York City, for example, poorhouse rules demanded that inmates work; the purpose was "to inure them to labour." In the 1820s the Baltimore poorhouse instituted a system of charges for maintenance and credits for work; under this system, which was also adopted in Philadelphia, paupers were not dismissed from the institution until they had worked off the costs charged against them. The work test applied indiscriminately to all paupers—children, aged, blind, and disabled as well as able-bodied. When Boston's city government established a "house of industry" in the 1820s, a local organization enthusiastically supported the idea: "It is believed," the organization stated, "there are but few of our poor who, notwithstanding the imbecility induced by previous habits, cannot do something, and very many of them a great deal towards their own support." In 1830 the New York City common council not only tried to maximize pauper labor by turning "to some advantage the labour of the more feeble," but argued as well that work positively improved health and character. In 1834 the Philadelphia Guardians of the Poor refused to replace the almshouse "treadmill" with a steam engine, preferring human power because of the "constant employment" it necessitated. In every city plagued by pauperism in the first half of the nineteenth century, outdoor relief was limited or terminated and work became the indispensable condition for institutional aid.[14]

The work test, moreover, seemed to have other positive advantages. Municipal leaders clearly saw it as a deterrent to relief, one which would encourage relief applicants to seek, as city fathers in New York said in 1821, "a course of voluntary industry of their own choice to a systematic Service under the Overseers in the Poorhouse." The very mention of the workhouse, a Boston philanthropic group contended, "impressed with a salutary terror the minds of several, who might justly be considered candidates for admission to it." As Robert M. Hartley of the New York Association for Improving the Condition of the Poor put it, almshouse employment had to be made "more irksome" than independent labor. Thus relief costs would go down, while the "idle and vicious poor" would be forced into jobs in order to survive.[15]

Similarly, many private charitable groups encouraged and enforced work among the poor. Many acted upon arguments popularized by such men as the Reverend Ezra Stiles Ely, New York's poorhouse preacher. Although man was naturally idle, he said, societal pressures, primarily the refusal of charity, could force the idler into industriousness. "If man will not work, when able," Ely concluded, "he should not eat." Work, in other words, could end pauperism and dependency. Thus groups like New York's Society for the Promotion of Industry, the Boston Employment Society, and the Philadelphia Society for the Employment and Instruction of the Poor sought to channel dependents into jobs, but menial jobs at wages well below the ordinary. Such work, the Philadelphia society contended, fostered individual self-respect, which alone made "the gatherer of offal the superior of the pauper."[16]

For much the same purposes, several cities spawned societies for the encouragement of faithful domestic servants, urging household and kitchen help to submissive, industrious, and orderly habits. Work-enforcing attitudes influenced the treatment of children of the poor as well, who were considered juvenile delinquents if they were "idle." The juvenile reformatories built in major eastern cities in the years after 1825, therefore, considered instilling work habits as central to the reformation process, and these institutions became, in the words of one report, places of "never ceasing occupation." In the New York City House of Refuge, presumably delinquent children spent two hours per day in school, the rest at work. Essentially, the work was preparation for future menial jobs—girls did washing, ironing, cooking, baking, and plaiting of glass; boys worked as shoemakers, tailors, and construction laborers. These numerous philanthropic organizations, and others like them, promoted an early form of "work fare." Conformity to the work ethic would wean the poor from former bad habits, build character and self-reliance, and help stabilize the deteriorating social order.[17]

For the noninstitutionalized poor, urban philanthropists created a multitude of voluntary associations supplementing institutional "work fare" and designed to promote moral reform. By the 1820s urban humanitarians had abandoned older benevolent precepts—that charity was a religious obligation and a human duty. Accepting lower-class vices as the causes of pauperism, they again and again asserted the need for encouraging opposing virtues. While some reformers urged paupers to work, others sought to purge the poor of their sins and vices, bring moral uplift to the slums, and end poverty with virtue and religion. The assumptions of such a program to regulate lower-class behavior stimulated, even demanded, a far-reaching humanitarian activism—an activism institutionalized in a fantastic array of benevolent societies for every imaginable humanitarian purpose. Concerned about social order and drawing upon new social perceptions about the causes of pauperism, these groups consciously combined charity with moral and religious exhortation. Convinced that relief undermined character and multiplied the poor, many abandoned charity altogether for moral and religious reform. They used benevolence for what they considered important social purposes —to restore urban order and ensure security for established society. Evangelical preacher Lyman Beecher saw in these voluntary societies "a sort of disciplined moral militia" which would "uphold peace and good order in society" and "save the nation from civil war and commotion." They became, as one historian has suggested, "special kinds of defense organizations." In the early nineteenth century the network of benevolent associations replaced the less formal, but now ineffective, institutions and controls of Colonial years.[18]

The new philanthropic associations became primary instruments for the achievement of civil and social order. Fairly typical of urban benevolence in the early nineteenth century, the Boston Society for the Moral and Religious Instruction of the Poor (later the Boston City Missionary Society) began in 1816 with the conviction that moral reforms would end the temporal problems of the city's poor while improving their chances in eternity. Headed by prominent merchants, professionals, and clergymen of Boston, the society embarked upon a wide-ranging reform program. Since, as the society argued, "nine tenths of the pauperism in our country is occasioned by vice," true benevolence demanded moral and religious instruction rather than charity and relief for the poor. Thus the organization sponsored Sunday schools, distributed Bibles and religious tracts, hired missionaries to visit and exhort the urban poor, established a chapel and "temperance" boarding houses for seamen, and promoted antiliquor and antiprostitution campaigns. Reflecting the protective functions of philanthropy, the society envisioned positive returns from such programs: elimination of "numberless outrages" in the city, the "protection and security of property," and reduction of "the greater part of the public expenses for the support of the poor."[19]

Similar objectives prevailed among numerous special-purpose welfare and reform organizations. Education for the poor, for instance, was thought of primarily as a means of creating a moral, docile, hardworking, and law-abiding lower class. The New York African Free School typically aimed to make blacks "safe and useful members of society" and "quiet and orderly citizens." The New York Free School Society attempted to disseminate "fixed habits of industry, decency, and order." The Boston Children's Friend Society promoted moralistic schooling among the poor to "give stability to our valued institutions." The Boston Farm School urged education for potential delinquents from the slums as a means of "increasing the security of life and property."[20]

Likewise, it was argued that Sunday schools, which proliferated rapidly in every city after 1816, promoted "habits of order, submission, [and] industry," checked "destructive habits," increased "the public safety," and made the poor contented with their "station" in life. "Are you friends to *social order*?" asked a writer in a religious periodical, *The Evangelical Guardian*, in 1818. Then "engage in Sunday schools that you may be instrumental in teaching the rising generation how to preserve that order." As the Boston Sunday School Union noted in 1836, the poor were taught "self-control, and subjection, and the lesson of subordination."[21] As disseminators of societal traditions and values, schools in the preindustrial city provided formal indoctrination in middle-class morality. By demanding ethical conformity, by providing models of decency and decorum, by imposing values upon the lower classes from above, they also become protectors of social order. As one public school society argued, the moral training of the poor became "an act of self-preservation."[22]

A widespread campaign to evangelize city slums revealed similar purposes. Formed in 1816, the American Bible Society and a myriad of local auxiliaries optimistically attacked pauperism and urban disorder with scripture. When the New York Bible Society in 1820 asked why the city's courts overflowed with vicious criminals and its streets with beggars and paupers, the answer seemed logical and self-evident—"it is because," the society said, "Bibles are not sufficiently distributed among them." Active in the growing southern manufacturing city of Richmond, the Bible Society of Virginia urged biblical learning as the best method of restraining "bad passions" and producing "reverence of the laws." Bible reading made men virtuous and useful, sober and industrious; it stimulated "steady habits and correct moral deportment"; it served "the purposes of virtue and social order" and strengthened "the fabric of civil society."[23]

Bible Society views were reinforced by a simultaneous proliferation of religious tract societies. Short pamphlets of four to twelve pages, tracts contained pointed moral messages and were widely disseminated in the larger cities. The New York Religious Tract Society alone distributed more than 2 million such pamphlets between 1812 and 1825. Their social purposes were obvious. A religious tract in every home, contended an evangelical advocate, was the surest guardian against "vice, anarchy, and violence," the best safeguard against revolution.[24] In addition, city mission organizations built free churches in the slums, sponsored Sunday schools and Bible lectures, held prayer meetings for seamen, and sent visitors to exhort and pray with the poor in their homes. One of the primary functions of such missions was to "save the bulwarks of freedom . . . from threatened overthrow." Few disagreed with Philadelphia Presbyterian preacher William Engles, who noted in 1833 that these urban missionaries helped "secure the national stability."[25] At the same time some city governments paid the salaries of poorhouse preachers. The New York City Common Council supported such a practice because, the council said, religion was "highly beneficial not only to the morals, but to the industry of the Lower Classes." Sabbatarians offered their program as "one of the most efficient expedients for the prevention of pauperism."[26] Similarly, temperance advocates argued that lower-class drinking habits destroyed incentive to work, undermined morality, and thus severed a main prop of the social order.[27] The removal by evangelical means of such vices as alcoholism, idleness, crime, and Sabbath-breaking would bring salvation to the poor, eliminate pauperism, and improve civil order and social stability.

It occurred to some city leaders that work and moral reform might fail to convert urban paupers into upright, hardworking citizens. Covering this eventuality, an alternative argument justifying charity and relief emerged by the 1820s. Some contended that the almshouse and private charitable institutions served as a kind of safety valve, that the availability of relief acted as an effectual check against crime, violence, and disorder. The Boston Society for the Religious and Moral Instruction of the Poor, for instance, justified public institutions in 1824 with such an argument: "Doubtless it were better for the community to sustain some loss in the expenses of establishments that insure public safety," the society suggested, "than live in continual dread of violence, or exposed to depredation."[28] Although inconsistent with the idea of limiting charity and relief to the helpless poor and forcing the able-bodied to work, this alternative attitude suggests the extent of middle-class fear of urban disorder and instability.

Thus social welfare, in its various manifestations, became a technique for regulating the poor and keeping them orderly. Almshouses became workhouses. The voluntary philanthropic and religious associations became instruments in the more general attack on pauperism and dependency, protective devices against urban disorder. "Benevolent" citizens as well as city functionaries viewed the poor with a new set of assumptions in the early nineteenth century, assumptions which dictated urban antipoverty programs centering on forced labor and moral reform. Threatened by the symptoms of social and economic change, and concerned about the breakdown of urban order, they built a network of new institutions to restore the familiar, stable, well-regulated society they had known in the past. In attacking pauperism, they struck out at what seemed the most disturbing element in the changing city. Their perceptions of their society and their assumptions about pauperism narrowly limited their choice of solutions. But by moralizing about the poor, they conveniently overlooked the social and economic inequities of the urbanizing, industrializing, capitalistic environment. They gave high priority to social order, but generally neglected fulfillment of human needs.

These problems seem just as real in mid-twentieth century. Nurtured by the idea of the United States as the land of opportunity, Americans continue to moralize about the poor and ignore more fundamental causes of dependency. Indeed, the demand to get the lazy bums off welfare rivals in intensity the calls to lower taxes and support your local police. The bulk of modern welfare programs have been stretched upon a framework fashioned by nineteenth-century moralism. Welfare "reform" has become synonymous with "work fare." And it may be, as Piven and Cloward have suggested, that the welfare system continues to function as a means of social control, with relief rolls expanding during and after periods of large-scale disorder and violence, but contracting and forcing former recipients into menial jobs as social turbulence subsides. Today's "welfare mess" has very obvious antecedents in the preindustrial city of the early nineteenth century.

Notes

1. Frances Fox Piven and Richard A. Cloward, *Regulating the Poor: The Functions of Public Welfare* (New York, 1971). See also their article, "The Relief of Welfare," *Trans-Action*, 8 (May, 1971), 31–39, 52–53.

2. David T. Gilchrist, ed., *The Growth of the Seaport Cities, 1790–1825* (Charlottesville, Va., 1967), 38–46; George Rogers Taylor, "American Urban Growth Preceding the Railway Age," *Journal of Economic History*, 27 (September, 1967), 309–39.

3. Robert Ernst, *Immigrant Life in New York City, 1825–1863* (New York, 1949), 48–60; Gilbert Osofsky, "The Enduring Ghetto," *Journal of American History*, 55 (September, 1968), 243–255; James Ford et al., *Slums and Housing: With Special Reference to New York City* (2 vols., Cambridge, Mass., 1936), 1: 72–121; Sam Bass Warner, Jr., *The Private City: Philadelphia in Three Periods of Its Growth* (Philadelphia, 1968), 50–56.

4. Kate H. Claghorn, "The Foreign Immigrant in New York City," *United States Industrial Commission Reports* (Washington, D. C., 1901), 15: 464; Gilchrist, ed., *Growth of the Seaport Cities*, 32–33; Oscar Handlin, *Boston's Immigrants: A Study in Acculturation* (rev. ed., New York, 1968), 243; *The [Eighth] Annual Report of the Boston City Missionary Society* (Boston, 1849), 12.

5. James Henretta, "Economic Development and Social Structure in Colonial Boston," *William and Mary Quarterly*, 22 (January, 1965), 75–92; Jackson Turner Main, "Trends in Wealth Concentration Before 1860," *Journal of Economic History*, 31 (June, 1971), 445–447; Douglas T. Miller, *Jacksonian Aristocracy: Class and Democracy in New York, 1830–1860* (New York, 1967).

6. *Christian Herald and Seaman's Magazine* (New York), 8 (June 16, 1821), 71; 9 (February 1, 1823), 553; Peter R. Knights, *The Plain People of Boston, 1830–1860: A Study in City Growth* (New York, 1971), 58; Account Book of Cash Distribution to the Poor, 1809–1816, entries for January 11, 20, 30, 1810, vol. 0383, Alms House Records, New York City Municipal Archives and Records Center; Bayrd Still, *Mirror for Gotham* (New York, 1956), 114–115; Kenneth and Anna M. Roberts, trans. and eds., *Moreau de St. Mery's American Journey, 1793–1798* (Garden City, N.Y., 1947), 165.

7. Allan Nevins and Milton Halsey Thomas, eds., *The Diary of George Templeton Strong* (4 vols., New York, 1952), 1: 110; William Dalton, *Travels in the United States and Part of Upper Canada* (Appleby, England, 1821), 5.

8. *Report of the Committee Appointed by the Board of Guardians of the Poor of the City and Districts of Philadelphia, to Visit the Cities of Baltimore, New York, Providence, Boston, and Salem* (Philadelphia, 1827), 24.

9. George Ticknor, "Memoir of the Buckminsters," *Christian Examiner*, 47 (1849), 173, quoted in Stanley K. Schultz, "Breaking the Chains of Poverty: Public Education in Boston, 1800–1860," in Kenneth T. Jackson and Stanley K. Schultz, eds., *Cities in American History* (New York, 1972), 307.

10. See Joseph Tuckerman, *Eleventh Semiannual Report, as a Minister at Large in Boston* (Boston, 1833); William Douglas, *Annual Report of the Providence Female Domestic Missionary Society* (Providence, 1843).

11. See, for example, *Minutes of the Common Council of the City of New York, 1784–1831* (21 vols., New York, 1917–1930), 8: 204; Thomas Eddy to De Witt Clinton, February 15, 1817, De Witt Clinton Papers, Columbia University Library; *New-York Evening Post,* March 12, 1817.

12. William O. Bourne, *History of the Public School Society of the City of New York* (New York, 1870), 90. See also New York Society for the Prevention of Pauperism, *Documents Relative to Savings Banks, Intemperance, and Lotteries* (New York, 1819), 21.

13. *Journal of the Assembly of the State of New-York,* 47th session (1824), 1: 386–398; *Laws of the State of New York,* 47th session, November 27, 1824; Josiah Quincy, *Report on the Pauper Laws of Massachusetts* (n.p., 1821), 9; *Report of Philadelphia Guardians of the Poor,* 23–25.

14. *Ordinances, Rules and Bye-Laws, for the Government of the Alms-House, and House of Employment, of the City of New-York,* June 16, 1784, broadside, in New-York Historical Society; *Report of a Committee Appointed by the Guardians for the Relief and Employment of the Poor of Philadelphia, &c, to Visit the Almshouses of Baltimore, New York, Boston and Salem, November, 1833* (Philadelphia, 1834), 9, 13; *The Laws Relating to the Relief and Employment of the Poor, in the City of Philadelphia, and the District of Southwark, and the Townships of the Northern Liberties and Penn* (Philadelphia, 1835), 22–23; *Seventh Annual Report of the Directors of the Boston Society for the Religious and Moral Instruction of the Poor* (Boston, 1824), 5; New York City Common Council, *Report of Special Committee on Pauperism, May 31, 1830* (n.p., n.d.), 9–10; Benjamin J. Kelbaner, "Employment of Paupers at Philadelphia's Almshouse Before 1861," *Pennsylvania History,* 24 (April, 1957), 138.

15. *Minutes of the Common Council of New York,* 12: 158; *Seventh Report of Boston Society for Religious and Moral Instruction of Poor,* 5; Robert M. Hartley, "Removal of Alms House from Bellevue," New York *Journal of Commerce,* August 30, 1845.

16. Ezra Stiles Ely, *Visits of Mercy* (2 vols., Philadelphia, 1829), 1: 86–87; *Report of the Managers of the Philadelphia Society for the Employment and Instruction of the Poor, Presented at the Annual Meeting of the Society—1851* (Philadelphia, 1851), 13.

17. On domestic servants see *First Annual Report of the Society for the Encouragement of Faithful Domestic Servants in New-York* (New York, 1826); *First Report of the Board of Managers of the [Philadelphia] Society for the Encouragement of Faithful Domestics* (Philadelphia, 1830). On juvenile delinquents and work see Joseph M. Hawes, *Children in Urban Society: Juvenile Delinquency in Nineteenth-Century America* (New York, 1971), 259; *An Address from the Managers of the House of Refuge to Their Fellow Citizens* (Philadelphia, 1826), 9; *First Annual Report of the Managers of the Society for the Reformation of Juvenile Delinquents, in the City of New-York* (New York, 1825), 12–13.

18. Lyman Beecher, *A Reformation of Morals Practicable and Indispensable. A Sermon Delivered at New-Haven on the Evening of October 27, 1812* (Andover, 1814), 18; Lyman Beecher, "Prosperity and Importance of Efforts to Evangelize the Nation," *The National Preacher* (New York), 3 (March, 1829), 154; Fred Somkin, *Unquiet Eagle: Memory and Desire in the Idea of American Freedom, 1815–1860* (Ithaca, N.Y., 1967), 34.

19. *Third Annual Report of the Boston Society for the Moral and Religious Instruction of the Poor* (Boston, 1819), 22.

20. New York *Daily Advertiser,* October 27, 1789; Charles C. Andrews, *The History of the New-York African Free Schools* (New York, 1830), 47; Bourne, *Public School Society,* 7; *Eleventh Annual Report of the Boston Children's Friend Society* (Boston, 1844), 7; *Report on a Farm School* (n.p., n.d.), 8.

21. *American Sunday School Teachers' Magazine* (New York), 1 (January, 1824), 60; *Third Report of Boston Society for Moral and Religious Instruction of Poor,* 11; Thomas Raffles, *The Sunday School Teacher's Monitor, together with Hints for Self-Examination, Addressed to Persons of Various Classes, in Connection with Sunday Schools* (New York, 1817), 2; New York *Commercial Advertiser,* May 8, 1816; *The Evangelical Guardian* (New York), 1 (February, 1818), 458; *Seventh Annual Report of the Board of Managers of the Boston Sabbath School Union* (Boston, 1836), 5.

22. Bourne, *Public School Society,* xx.

23. *The First Report of the New-York Bible Society* (New York, 1820), 16; *The Second and Third Annual Reports of the Managers of the Bible Society of Virginia* (Richmond, 1816), 14; *The Third Annual Report of the Managers of the Marine Bible Society of New-York* (New York, 1819), 8; *The Eighth Report of the Bible Society of Philadelphia* (Philadelphia, 1816), 16; New York *Christian Herald,* April 5, 1823, 9: 690.

24. *The Fifth Annual Report of the New-York Religious Tract Society* (New York, 1817), 45, 47; *The Thirteenth Annual Report of the New-York Religious Tract Society* (New York, 1825), 5. See also *Fifth Annual Report of the Executive Committee of the New England Tract Society, May 26, 1819* (Boston, 1819), 8.

25. Richard S. Storrs, *Man's Duty, in Relation to the Lord's Work. A Semi-Centennial Discourse, Delivered before the Massachusetts Home Missionary Society, in Boston, May 29, 1849* (Boston, 1849), 24; William M. Engles, *The Patriot's Plea for Domestic Missions* (Philadelphia, 1833), 4. For typical city missionary activities see *Proceedings of the First Anniversary of the New-York Evangelical Missionary Society of Young Men* (New York, 1817); *[First] Report of the Boston Society for the Moral and Religious Instruction of the Poor* (Boston, 1817); *First Annual Report of the Board of Directors of the Boston Seaman's Friend Society* (Boston, 1829); *The [First] Annual Report of the Boston City Missionary Society, for the Year 1841* (Boston, 1842).

26. Report of Committee of Charity on Petition of the Trustees of the African Church, December 8, 1817, box 3175, City Clerk Documents, New York City Municipal Archives and Records Center; Gardiner Spring, *An Appeal to the Citizens of New-York, in Behalf of the Christian Sabbath* (New York, 1823), 16.

27. See, for example, Alexander Gunn, *A Sermon, on the Prevailing Vice of Intemperate Drinking* (New York, 1813); *Journal of the Assembly of the State of New York,* 47th session (1824), Part II, Appendix B, 44; *First Annual Report of the New York City Temperance Society* (New York, 1830); L. M. Sargent, *An Address Delivered Before the Seaman's Bethel Temperance Society* (Boston, 1833).

28. *Seventh Report of Boston Society for Religious and Moral Instruction of Poor,* 8.

13 Housing of the Working People*

Carroll D. Wright

Sanitary Laws

Wisely conceived and well-enforced sanitary laws are a supreme necessity of modern civilization. The let-alone policy, if admitted, would mean that urban populations would periodically suffer from fearful epidemics, and that a vast number would fall into pauperism and moral degradation under the irresistible impulsion of unhealthy environments. Legislatures have thus seen the necessity of endowing metropolitan centers with large powers for their self-protection. In New York these powers are especially drastic. Recently a better code has been established in London, but most of the continental countries have not yet fully risen to the occasion. A difficulty in many cities both here and abroad is that sufficient power of initiative has not been given to the sanitary authorities. Bothersome enabling acts must frequently be secured before urgent work can be done. Gen-

* From Carroll D. Wright, "Housing of the Working People," *8th Special Report of the Commissioner of Labor* (Washington, 1895), 23, 55, 88–89, 419, 421–22, 434, 436, 441–43.

erally speaking, urban sanitary law in the United States and Great Britain is fairly complete, but almost universal complaint is heard that it is not fully enforced. Many of the most competent witnesses before the English royal commission, in 1885, stated that further regulations were of minor importance as compared with the necessity of enforcing those already in existence. Added vigilance and increased inspection were enjoined by the commissioners in their report as a means of improving the house accommodations of working people.

In one notable way sanitary law may further good housing. As stringency increases and owners are compelled to keep their property in good repair they are obliged to exercise greater care in selection of tenants. The undesirable classes are thus likely ultimately to find themselves corralled in specific neighborhoods. They can then be the more easily looked after.

. . .

When houses or neighborhoods become irremediably bad, the only logical thing to do is to wipe them out of existence. It is true this form of procedure is costly, but late awakenings are always expensive. The supreme necessity of safeguarding public health is a sufficient motive for action, but the welfare of individual dwellers is also happily subserved. The right of expropriation is a weapon of last resort, and perhaps alone can efficiently check the unscrupulous rapacity which allows property to degenerate into an incurably unhealthy state.

. . .

In New York there are probably thirty associations engaged in ascertaining infractions of the laws, and otherwise aiding the sanitary authorities. The president of the board of health has sometimes found some of these organizations a little querulous and troublesome, but in general he believes them to be of very considerable utility. The Sanitary Aid Society has been one of the most important of this class of volunteer bodies. It was founded about nine years ago, and has at various times instituted a house-to-house visitation, gathered statistics of the most flagrant violations of sanitary laws, especially in that most overcrowded part of the city, the Tenth ward, and with this material has urged the health board to extra activity and reenforced it in its pleas for a larger sanitary inspection corps. In a measure, the society has assisted in cleansing and remodeling many of the most dangerous of the overcrowded tenements, and in abating nuisances which were a constant menace to the city. Among its other activities it has opened a model lodging house, thus attacking the problem of overcrowding from both sides.

The Sanitary Protective League, the Ladies' Health Protective Association, a most aggressive and successful organization of women who extend their activities much beyond the sanitation of houses, and the society in which Dr. Leo is the moving spirit, and which concerns itself particularly with the care of newly arrived immigrants and other victims of the sweatshop, are conspicuous examples of sanitary aid societies in the American metropolis.

The New York Association for Improving the Condition of the Poor has now completed its fifty-first year of existence. Among the objects of the society are enumerated—"improving the sanitary condition of the dwellings of the poor and the elevation of their home life, their health, and their habits." Taking the report of 1891 for example, it is found that 506 complaints were received of the insanitary condition of tenement houses, streets, and alleys. Four hundred and fourteen appeared to be good causes and were reported to the board of health, 4 to the department of public buildings, 7 to owners directly, and the remainder were not reported. The board of health found that in 293 cases there was good cause for complaint. In 89 instances nuisances were abated; in 25 cases the complaints were considered ill-founded, and 7 cases were still under inspection. Leaking roofs, defective water-closets, premises generally filthy, and wet cellars were the chief causes cited.

Vigilance is necessary to maintain a proper hygienic standard in the housing of the poor. From the very magnitude of their work the regular sanitary administrations find themselves crippled from lack of resources and of inspectors sufficient to fully accomplish the work. The organization and maintenance of such societies is a necessity in order to secure the wise enforcement of health laws and the advance of sanitary education in any city. The prime conditions of success are hearty cooperation with regularly constituted authority, and an intimate knowledge of the conditions and needs of the homes of the poor.

. . .

Economic and Ethical Aspects

Will improved housing pay? This is a question of cardinal importance, and only in case an affirmative response is forthcoming can we augur a successful issue to the housing problem. If the solution of the problem is to depend upon philanthropy alone it is safe to say that very small progress can be made. If city dwellers are to be better housed better housing must pay.

There can be no question as to the remunerative character of housing operations conducted in the interests of the artisan and other well-paid laborers. Money invested for this purpose brings a sure, safe, and stable return. There is, therefore, absolutely no reason why every workingman in receipt of a fair wage should not be able to command a favorable living environment. It is a well-known fact that rents paid for inferior houses are often quite as high, and in some cases higher, than those paid for a good class of dwellings. . . .

. . .

There is no doubt at all that working people of all classes, except the very lowest and most degraded (and these can not be called working people, for they work only as a last necessity), appreciate good accommodation and are willing to pay for it. . . . Over crowding and living in filthy surroundings are sometimes represented to be matters of habit or preference with certain nationalities. The almost universal testimony of all who have seriously tried to improve the environments of city dwellers goes far toward proving the reverse to be true.

. . .

Undoubtedly, even the lowest class should be stimulated by offering them the best accommodation that can be remuneratively afforded. Strong willed, intelligent people create or modify environment, while the weaker and unthinking become largely subject to it. This is the correct way of expressing the relation of individuals to environment. The importance of healthy living surroundings can find no stronger principle of sanction than that offered by this great law of human progress.

. . .

Bad housing is a terribly expensive thing to any community. Moreover, it explains much that is mysterious in relation to drunkenness, poverty, crime, and all forms of social decline.

Conclusions

. . .

The duty of every community to provide itself with an efficient sanitary code and to see that the same is enforced is apparent enough; neither is there any excuse for failing to make stringent building regulations so that the future may be guaranteed. . . . It has been suggested that property holders should be called upon to produce upon demand a sanitary certificate. Houses being, in one sense, commodities, this method of treatment would simply put the owners of bad property in the same light before the law as the venders of decayed fruits or vegetables.

It is scarcely an excuse to say that a tenant is willing to take risks. He may be ignorant, or he may be apathetic and careless about hygienic surroundings for himself and family. The community has a right to protect itself so that such people may not become public charges through sickness. But it is not the landlord alone after whom it is necessary to look. Tenants should be coerced into keeping themselves and their surroundings reasonably clean, as is done in Berlin, where, after warning, unusually slovenly families are turned out of their dwellings and subjected during a certain period to the special surveillance of the police. In this way the upgrowth of slums is prevented. Tenants generally feel that when they pay their rent their dwellings belong to them, and that if they wish to sublet any part thereof that is their affair. This custom ought to be regulated and the practice of overcrowding repressed with a strong hand. The slum must go. Not only is it a menace to public health, but it is a moral fester wherein character is being continually debauched and the evils which afflict civilization recruited. . . .

There is another feature of this problem which stands clearly outlined. Investigation shows indubitably that the percentage of earnings of heads of tenant families which is absorbed in payment of rent in all large cities is far too high. It is no wonder that overcrowding within the dwelling as well as overcrowding on space becomes an almost universal practice. The price of land cannot be artificially lowered nor can wages be advanced by public decree. For governing bodies to assume the task of housing so large a quota of the population as would be represented, without any commerical return, might operate indirectly to enhance wages, but, like other artificial stimuli, would very soon lose its good effects.

Scanty wages are a powerful element in human misery. Weak characters are apt to become despondent and allow themselves to drift with the tide, and end too often in a state of chronic wretchedness. Those whose earnings are not only scanty but fitful have a supreme necessity to live near the localities where labor may be obtained. This means that they must be housed where land is valuable, and for that reason where it is hard to build new houses and make them pay. Here is, indeed, the crux of the problem. Does the present inquiry furnish any suggestion for its solution? A hint has already been offered from the commercially successful experience of agencies in Edinburgh and Glasgow, cities certainly where the average earnings of unskilled labor are much lower than they are in any American center of like population. Old property was bought which either had been closed as unfit for human habitation and its value thus artificially depressed, or which was in a dilapidated condition and yielded insignificant returns. Such properties were remodeled, filled with the class of laborers referred to, and placed under the administration of lady rent collectors. Efforts of this kind, however, are limited by the public spirit, philanthropic sentiment, and courage existing in a given community. Probably not a tithe of the necessary effort can be organized.

A way, however, seems to be opening up wherein the elements just mentioned do not largely enter. For the workingman's purposes space is measured by time not by distance. Underground and overhead electric transportation means the lessening of distances, and brings a large range of territory within living areas which hitherto has been outside possible consideration. The effect of rapid transit ought normally to be that artisans, or the higher earning portion of working people, will more and more house themselves in the suburbs of cities, where they may purchase homes upon reasonable conditions. Widening habitable areas to workingmen in cities would not only relieve congestion of population, but it must in time reduce the demand for houses in those spots where massing most frequently occurs, consequently reducing rents so that those with lower earnings might then find fair accommodation at reasonable rates. The cheapening of property in these neighborhoods would enlarge the action of that form of philanthropy which organizes itself into agencies for purchasing and reconstructing old tenements, putting ladies in charge, and contenting itself with a normal commercial return. The artificial enhancement of rents, due most largely to these necessities of the poorer laborers, is already operating to relieve congestion in certain parts of New York City. Clothing manufacturers and others conducting house industries are sending their goods to the country districts to have them made. The workmen are going with the goods.

Increasing sanitary stringency, encouragement afforded by savings banks, life insurance, and other institutions in lending money at low rates, the spread of knowledge and awakening of public interest . . . , and the support of model effort are indications pregnant with hope and possibility.

The problem of the housing of working people includes sanitary, economic, and ethical issues of the highest importance, but a final solution can only be wrought out along economic lines. The general teaching of the present inquiry, as regards model housing enterprises, affords in most respects a certainty, and in others more than a reasonable probability, that this can be done in the future, as . . . it has been done in the past.

14 Unmasking the Ghetto: Jacob A. Riis and How the Other Half Lives*

James B. Lane

IN 1890 JACOB A. RIIS's exposé of New York City's tenement-house slums, *How the Other Half Lives,* dramatically awakened interest in urban reform. In fact, Riis's most impressive accomplishment as a crusader for social justice during the late-nineteenth century was his ability to subject affluent Americans vicariously to the reality of poverty. For example, the genteel and urbane poet James Russell Lowell, after perusing *How the Other Half Lives,* wrote its author that he "had but a vague idea of these horrors before you brought them home to me." By bringing ghetto districts to life, Riis made the city more comprehensible to his readers, and therefore not quite so fearful. His popular book, appearing at the dawn of the Progressive movement, ushered in a generation of examination and reform, and personal involvement with the problems of the urban poor.[1]

Riis's background had equipped him well for the task of bridg-

* Reprinted with permission from James B. Lane, "Unmasking Poverty: Jacob A. Riis and *How the Other Half Lives,*" *Maryland Historian* (Spring, 1971), 27–39.

ing the chasm of communication between the rich and the poor. Reared in the small preindustrial town of Ribe, Denmark, he learned to revere the traditional institutions of family, church, community and nation. From his romantic, sentimental mother and cultured, ascetic father—a schoolmaster who enjoyed the status but not the wealth of Ribe's upper-class society—Riis developed an idealistic, adventurous, optimistic personality.[2] His values fit well with the dual pillars of the nineteenth-century American ethos, the faith in progress and the belief in the moral responsibility of the individual. In 1870, at the age of twenty-one, Riis emigrated to New York and for the next seven years drifted in semi-poverty from job to job, searching for a creative outlet for his formidable energies. During this time he practiced carpentry, mined for iron, picked vegetables, sold flat irons, hawked copies of Charles Dickens's *Hard Times*, trapped muskrats, edited a small newspaper and showed advertisements with a stereopticon display. He endured these frustrations with his confidence intact, and the seven-year ordeal gave him an intimate insight into the problems that shackled immigrants.[3]

In 1877 Riis became a police reporter for the New York *Tribune*. His beat was in Manhattan's East Side slum district, Mulberry Bend, where 290,000 people were packed into one square mile of land, often twenty to a room in foul, unlit dwellings. For Riis journalism served two functions: to secure a comfortable place in American society, and for venting his outrage at the tragic scenes which he daily witnessed among the jerry-built rear tenements, the narrow back alleys, the rat-infested schools, the leperous lodging houses and the stale-beer dives. The squalor and human misery unnerved the reporter and, in his words, "gripped my heart until I felt that I must tell of them, or burst, or turn anarchist, or something."[4]

During his years as a police reporter Riis learned to incorporate the mood and essence of the slum into the rigid requirements of his news stories. He learned that the way to sidestep newspaper censors was to clothe reformist rhetoric in patriotic and respectable terms. Thus his indictments of public apathy in the face of grievous ills would appear to be neither polemic nor radical tract. He learned to make articles sensational enough to whet the popular appetite without overstepping the proprieties of genteel taste in a way that might be repulsive or disgusting to the upper and middle classes.

By subtle phrase or archtypical anecdote Riis invoked a didactic moral from a factual story.[5] In an article about mothers who abandoned their ill-nourished children to the foundling asylum he wrote: "The rich have other ways of covering up their sins than by scattering the evidence about the streets."[6] In another story he recounted how a handicapped workman died needlessly in a railway accident and how the company did not even inform the man's family of the disaster. Riis concluded the article with the dead man's family's reaction when the reporter told them the sad news. He wrote that "their grief would have wrung tears from a stone. Life had seemed bright to the little family since he got work again. Now darkness had settled on it forever. But the company's shares were all right."[7]

One of the first persons to photograph the interior of tenements, in 1888 Riis put together a stereopticon slide display that gained the attention of Dr. A. F. Schauffler, the director of the City Mission Society. Endorsing Riis's narrated program as indisputable evidence of intolerable urban squalor, Schauffler added in a letter of recommendation to church and civic leaders that none of the material would "shock the taste of any in the audience."[8] During an ensuing series of lectures Riis found that the candid, pathetic revelations of misery fascinated his listeners. Sensing in this response the possibilities of marketing his material in book form, he secured a copyright to the title, "The Other Half, How it lives and dies in New York, with one hundred Illustrations, Photographs from real life, of the haunts of poverty and vice in a great city."[9]

In 1889 Riis wrote several articles on the theme of the "Two Americas." Crystallizing the insights gained as a newspaperman, he personalized his experiences into impressionistic vignettes. To buttress his anecdotes he drew upon statistics from the Department of Health and from philanthropic organizations in which he was involved, such as the Charity Organization Society and the Children's Aid Society.[10] In vivid and passionate phrases he guided his readers through the tenements. "Do not stumble over the children pitching pennies in the hall," Riis wrote, "not that it would hurt them. Kicks and cuffs are their daily diet." He told of one small child whose job it was to transport beer from a saloon to workers in a nearby factory. One day the lad drank too much beer himself, fell asleep in a cellar, where rats gnawed him to death. Warning the public about the slum-bred evils, he referred to the million New Yorkers who lived in overcrowded tenements as "that other half, uneasy, suffering, threatening anarchy and revolt, the despair of our statesmen and the joyful opportunity of the [machine] politician." Their habitat was a social cancer born of public neglect and nurtured by private greed that touched "the family life with deadly moral contagion."[11]

Although he was an idealist and moralist himself, Riis nevertheless refrained from pinning hopes for improvement on humanitarian appeals alone. Just as compelling, he argued, were motives of public health, public safety, economic self-interest and good government. Everyone had a stake in combatting the slums, he stated in *How the Other Half Lives,* because they caused epidemics, paupers, corruption and moral decay. The tenements "hold within their clutch the wealth and business of New York, hold them at their mercy in the day of mob-rule and wrath," he warned. To remove this blight would require a multi-pronged assault combining charity work, individual regeneration, governmental action and shrewd business enterprise. The existing Sub-Treasuries with their bullet-proof shutters, Gatling guns and hand-grenades were scant insurance against a bitter harvest.[12]

Prior to 1890 most social critics had contrasted the pastoral ideal with the depravity of the city. Riis, on the other hand, focused on the concept of two Americas, not rural and urban but rich and poor.[13] "The half that was on top cared little for the struggles, and less for the fate of those who were underneath," he wrote, "so long as it was able to hold them there and keep its own seat." Riis had many of the anti-urban biases that were so common at the time; but he counseled his readers to accept, not abandon, the city and "make the best of a bad bargain." He found that metropolitan centers tended to be impersonal and fraught with temptations for the weak, but concluded that they were not incompatible with the traditional ties of family, church and community.[14]

In subtitling his book *Studies Among the Tenements of New York,* Riis meant to focus on the effect that bad housing had on immigrant families, especially the so-called children of the tenements.[15] "All life eventually accommodates itself to its environment, and human life is no exception," he claimed. Without sufficient space to move, fresh air to breathe, or aesthetic pleasures to enjoy, he warned, people would lose their capacity for any "gentle thought and aspiration above the mere wants of the body. . . ." By the standards of the slum a respectable neighborhood was one that had a trace of greenery and no more than four saloons to each block. Yet in the midst of these degrading circumstances Riis marveled at the countless personal struggles of heroism "against fearful odds" to overcome the oppressive milieu.[16]

Riis traced the genesis of the tenement to the spacious homes of New York's former Knickerbocker aristocracy, who sold out to real-estate dealers early in the nineteenth century. Reacting to the new conditions of industrialization and immigration, the owners sub-

divided the floors, partitioned the rooms and constructed rear tenements "in the old garden where the stolid Dutch burgher grew his
tulips or early cabbages. . . ."[17] Five families moved in where one had
lived, and then still more came.[18]

Using his favorite device of acting as a tour-guide, Riis re-
created Mulberry Bend, which lurked in the shadows of his newspaper office and was to the Danish reporter the apotheosis of evil and
neglect. During the 1860's governmental officials had declared that
almost all of the Bend's 609 tenements were a menace to public
health. But in 1889 they still stood. Riis wrote that "the whole district
is a maze of narrow, often unsuspected passageways—necessarily, for
there is scarce a lot that has not two, three, or four tenements upon
it, swarming with unwholesome crowds." Sections of the Bend had
appropriate sobriquets such as Bottle Alley and Bandit's Roost.
Gangsters and prostitutes were common in this locale, but the most
heinous criminals, in Riis's opinion, were the absentee landlords who
perpetuated the conditions.[19]

In graphic detail Riis took his readers into a back alley which
was "just about one step wide, with a five-story house on one side
that gets its light and air—God help us for pitiful mockery!—from this
slit between brick walls." One wall had no windows; a fire escape
straddled the two sides, touching each. The sun, he said, "never
shone into the alley from the day the devil planned and man built it."
Inside a typical dwelling was a darkened hallway and the odors of
poisoned sewage and an adjacent saloon. "Here is a door. Listen!
That short hacking cough, that tiny, helpless wail—what do they
mean?" Riis asked rhetorically. Another child dying. "With half a
chance it might have lived; but it had none. That dark bedroom
killed it," he concluded.[20]

Summer in the tenements was the worst time of the year. The
heat made indoor life almost insufferable, and the crowded quarters
invited epidemics. Riis told of a woman who attempted to kill her
own child after she failed to obtain food with which to nourish the
infant. On another occasion Riis and a doctor visited a three-room
flat that housed six adults and five children who slept on straw-filled
boxes. Near the stove a baby lay dying from malnutrition and a lack
of fresh air. The physician's thermometer revealed that the temperature of the room was 115 degrees. Such pains of life and the shortage
of good water drove people to the plentiful taverns, often the only
cheerful and "humanly decent" place on the block. Yet Riis believed
that the saloons undermined decency by breaking up families, corrupting youngsters and further pauperizing the downtrodden. The

tavern, Riis moralized, "saps the very vitals of society, undermines its strongest defences, and delivers them over to the enemy."[21]

In the Fourth Ward, in an area which residents named Blind Man's Alley, there lived a colony of blind beggars. Daniel Murphy, their landlord, made a half-million-dollar profit from his occupants, and then in his old age he lost his sight also. When the Board of Health forced him to repair his property, Murphy protested that his tenants were "not fit to live in a nice house." Once every June the city distributed twenty thousand dollars to the blind. On that evening the sightless beggars sang and drank and played their fiddles in celebration. Riis recounted on one such occasion that "even the blind landlord rejoices, for much of the money goes into his coffers."[22]

Riis's description of living conditions undoubtedly startled most of his readers but commanded their attention, and his personal sketches of slum residents gained their affection. In bold strokes he described the multitude of cultures and personalities among New York's polyglot population, which he called "this queer conglomerate mass." Concerning the mixed crowd of Italians, Irish, Germans, Eastern Europeans, Poles, Chinese, Bohemians and other national groups, Riis declared with considerable exaggeration that "the one thing you shall vainly ask for in the chief city of America is a distinctively American community. There is none; certainly not among the tenements."[23]

Measuring immigrant societies against his own cultural traditions, which had more in common with the upper class than the "Other Half," Riis's yardstick of approval corresponded in part to how well an ethnic group adopted American habits and values. Although he showed much compassion for the plight of immigrants, he was somewhat cavalier in describing their manner of living and used simplistic clichés in caricaturing groups. To Riis the Italians seemed clannish, the Bohemians easygoing, and the Jews grasping. He had the least sympathy for the Chinese, perhaps because he saw little hope of assimilating them into American life. "Between the tabernacles of Jewry and the shrines of the Bend," he wrote, "Joss has cheekily planted his pagan worship of idols, chief among which are the celestial worshipper's own gain and lusts." He desired the Americanization of the immigrant, and so he was insensitive at times to habits that were barriers to this goal.[24] Yet he did not so much denigrate ethnic customs as social patterns that were exaggerated or even created by conditions in the American ghetto. The dislocations of the slum caused many foreign-born residents to cling tenaciously to old-world customs. Often their offspring mocked them and abandoned respect for all primary-group ties. Both of these extremes Riis thought to be dangerous.[25]

Riis's commentary on New York's black residents mixed compassion with condescension. This dichotomy sprang from his partial acceptance of erroneous racist stereotypes and concurrently his deeper commitment to the premise that environment was the controlling factor in personality development.[26] Riis presented a stereotyped image of the black man cheerfully working at menial jobs for which "his past traditions and natural love of ease" perhaps fit him best. He wrote, however, that "his ludicrous incongruities, his sensuality and his lack of moral accountability, his superstition and other faults . . . are the effect of temperament and of centuries of slavery. . . ." What happened, Riis concluded, was that the Negroes emulated the worst characteristics of their former masters, as evidenced by their love of expensive luxuries. He looked with horror on the mixing of black men and white women at the lewd dance halls that were "the worst of the desperately bad." The mingling of "the utterly depraved of both sexes, white and black, on such ground, there can be no greater abomination," Riis chided.[27]

Despite misgivings which Riis harbored as a result of his inaccurate and simplistic assessment of black culture, in *How the Other Half Lives* he came out squarely against the closed system of housing which Negroes faced when they emigrated to New York. Landlords, in their lust for profits, deliberately and brutally drew color lines and heightened racial tensions, Riis wrote, in order to make "the prejudice in which he traffics pay him well." He rejected the myth that Negroes were inherently dirty, pointing out that black tenements on 99th Street were cleaner than the Italian ghettos. If vile surroundings debased men, Riis believed, then good housing could uplift them.[28]

How the Other Half Lives also contained descriptions of tenement sweatshops. Riis demonstrated how unscrupulous entrepreneurs in the clothing industry took advantage of the plentiful labor supply and the financial distress and isolation of their Eastern European employees to circumvent factory and child-labor laws. With "merciless severity" the sweater smothered "every symptom of awakening intelligence in his slaves." During a visit to a two-room apartment the author came upon a family of five who worked from daybreak until nine at night, sewing, finishing, and ironing trousers. They sold them to a manufacturer at a profit of five cents a dozen. Supplementing this income by taking in boarders, the family earned twenty-five dollars a week and paid twenty dollars a month rent for the two rooms. Riis concluded: "At the least calculation, probably, this sweater's family hoards up thirty dollars a month, and in a few years will own a tenement somewhere and profit by the example set by their landlord in rent-collecting."[29]

Rivaling the clothing sweatshops in human misery were the tenement cigar factories. Legions of workers, primarily Bohemians, made cigars by stripping tobacco leaves, breaking bits into filler, and then wrapping it up into a finished product. Landlords often held this class of tenants "in virtual serfdom" by binding their rent to the terms of their employment. The exploitation of the Bohemians, according to Riis, constituted "a slavery as real as any that ever disgraced the South." Entire families labored from seventy-five to one hundred hours a week each. A typical household received only eleven dollars for the three thousand cigars they made each week, and then they had to pay $12.25 a month rent to the manufacturer. Such outrageous and barbarian treatment, Riis predicted, might cause the Bohemians, a gregarious and passionate people, to rebel against the system which perpetuated such injustices upon them.[30]

All the immigrant groups in the tenements shared common problems, and the weak perished. Riis cogently told of the toll in wasted lives. In 1889 one hundred forty thousand people were jammed into the city's jails, workhouses, almshouses, foundling homes, insane asylums or charity hospitals. In addition fourteen thousand men each night slept in unsanitary lodging houses. One of ten New Yorkers ended up in Potter's Field, the burial ground of paupers. Riis wrote: "The Potter's Field stands ever for utter, hopeless surrender. The last the poor will let go, however miserable their lot in life, is the hope of a decent burial."[31]

Children were the most helpless against the slum. Life denied most of them the joys of childhood or the benefits of formal education. Many worked almost from infancy to help their family keep from starving. Young girls often labored eighty hours a week to earn a paltry two dollars and had to pay fines for tardiness and other mistakes. Orphans who escaped the foundling asylum often became "Street Arabs" or runaway vagabonds, who lived or died in the streets according to their cunning. Gangs of young toughs were common on every corner. They offered the sons of immigrants a source of identity, companionship and pride; but Riis lamented that their objectives were usually crime and bravado.[32]

With the intolerable conditions of the slum and the widening gap between rich and poor, Riis held up the spectre of revolution if reform was not forthcoming. "The sea of a mighty population, held in galling fetters, heaves uneasily in the tenements," he warned. The time for counseling patience or preaching a hollow Christianity had passed. Churches had to cease being slum landlords and accessories to an inadequate system. They needed to take up the social gospel in order to keep the faith and save themselves. The only possible paths were justice or violence.[33] Riis warned the wealthy of the consequences of inactivity in an oft-quoted parable:

A man stood at the corner of Fifth Avenue and Fourteenth Street the other day, looking gloomily at the carriages that rolled by, carrying the wealth and fashion of the avenue to and from the big stores downtown. He was poor, and hungry, and ragged. This thought was in his mind: "They behind their well-fed teams have no thought for the morrow; they know hunger only by name, and ride down to spend in an hour's shopping what would keep me and my little ones from want a whole year." There rose up before him the picture of those little ones crying for bread around the cold and cheerless hearth—then he sprang into the throng and slashed around him with a knife, blindly seeking to kill, to revenge.[34]

How the Other Half Lives called for an end to the economic policy of laissez-faire which Riis branded as a smoke screen for selfishness. "It is easy enough to convince a man that he ought not to harbor the thief who steals people's property," he asserted, "but to make him see that he has no right to slowly kill his neighbors, or his tenants, by making a death-trap of his house, seems to be the hardest of all tasks." He concluded that the health and security of all Americans depended on decent housing, since slum conditions constituted a clear danger to social and political institutions. Nearly all of his specific reform proposals were unoriginal, but his compelling diagnosis of the problems was a take-off point for examinations into solutions.[35]

Riis defined the slums as the symbol and gauge of society. Their inhabitants were neither immoral dolts who deserved their fate nor happy and noble people. Rather they were what environment made them, potentially dangerous but capable of becoming good citizens. Riis wanted to wipe out poverty before the culture of the slum affected younger generations and hardened into permanent patterns for individuals, families, communities and ultimately, the nation. Riis called on Americans not to construct a new system but to modernize their methods and realize the goals of the past. He concluded his book with this warning: "—Think ye that building shall endure/which shelters the noble and crushes the poor?"[36]

How the Other Half Lives received favorable critical acclaim and quickly gained great popularity, thereby establishing Riis as an expert on urban life.[37] Reviewers compared it to two similar contemporary books about the poor, John Peter Altgeld's *Live Questions* and William Booth's *In Darkest England.*[38] And they contrasted it to Ward McAllister's *Society As I Have Found It,* which described the manners of New York's upper class. McAllister's portrayal of opulence and ostentatious display reenforced Riis's central theme of poverty in the midst of plenty.[39] One dissenting critic, however, pointed out Riis's "lack of broad and penetrative vision, a singularly warped sense of justice at times, and a roughness amounting almost to brutality."[40] This criticism, especially if directed at the author's treatment of Chinese and black New Yorkers, was warranted. And while not unsympathetic toward European immigrants, *How the Other Half Lives* contained racial slurs that others could use to support nativistic shibboleths and restrictionist legislation.[41] Ironically, the racial stereotypes, which detracted from the book's validity, probably widened the book's appeal with upper-class readers.

Within Riis's mind warred two contradictory impulses regarding ghetto residents, one benign and the other backward-looking. On the one hand, he was an environmentalist and rejected explanations of poverty based upon inherent biological differences among races. Since all people were basically alike in potential, Riis argued, tenement-house ghettos were unnatural aberrations. On the other hand, the Danish-American reformer believed in the cultural superiority of Anglo-American institutions and in a genteel code of conduct. Describing habits of ghetto residents which he found loathsome, such as sloth, vice, clannishness, intemperance and superstition, he explained that they were vestiges of Old World ways or spurious by-products of the ghetto. But at times his indictments of ethnic customs revealed a class and race snobbery. This trace of condescension toward "this queer conglomerate mass" became much less pronounced later in life, but Riis never totally suppressed it.

In any case the publication of *How the Other Half Lives* helped strike the spark which ignited a progressive spirit in many Americans. Many more people knew the human side of the slum, rather than viewing the poor as a vast, faceless mass. Riis evoked the compassionate lump in the throat, the tear of sorrow or perhaps guilt, in the place of vague uneasiness. He stirred the conscience of a generation of young activists, many of whom worked to blot out the ills which Riis described. Such men as Louis H. Pink, a settlement worker and housing expert, John Jay Chapman, an innovator in neighborhood

development, and Ernest Poole, an author, social worker and socialist reformer, and many more attested to the effect of *How the
Other Half Lives* in jolting them out of their complacency.[42] Ener-
getic, moralistic, sentimental, chauvinistic, and above all optimistic,
in spirit Riis represented the mood of the Progressive movement, a
movement which his proselytizing did much to create and sustain.

Notes

1. James Russell Lowell to Jacob A. Riis, November 21, 1890, Jacob
A. Riis mss, Library of Congress. Curiously historians have recognized the
importance of *How the Other Half Lives,* while treating Riis as being *sui
generis,* or as a nineteenth-century man, as if the Progressive movement
itself were not the ultimate expression of the nineteenth-century faith in
reason, morality, progress and culture. See Robert H. Bremmer, *From the
Depths: The Discovery of Poverty in the United States* (New York, 1967);
Roy Lubove, *The Progressives and the Slums: Tenement House Reform
in New York City, 1890–1917* (Pittsburgh, 1962).

2. Jacob A. Riis, *The Making of an American* (New York, 1901), 5–
35; Lubove, *Progressives and the Slums,* 55–56.

3. Riis, *Making of an American,* 35–191; Jacob A. Riis, "Diary,"
Jacob A. Riis mss, New York Public Library.

4. New York *Mercury,* November 1, 1885; Jacob A. Riis, *How the
Other Half Lives* (New York, Hill and Wang ed., 1957), 6–8; Riis, *Making of an American,* 192–99, 267.

5. Roger S. Tracey, untitled manuscript, Riis mss, Library of Congress (L.C.); Louise Ware, *Jacob Riis: Police Reporter, Reformer, Useful
Citizen* (New York, 1939), 82.

6. New York *Sun,* May 16, 1885.

7. New York *Mercury,* June 14, 1885.

8. New York *Sun,* February 12, 1888; A. F. Schauffler to Jacob A.
Riis, Feb. 29, 1888, Riis mss, L.C.

9. George N. Thomssen to Jacob A. Riis, April 27, 1888, Riis mss,
L.C.; Library of Congress, "Document," Riis mss, L.C.

10. Jacob A. Riis, "Homeless Waifs of the City," *Harper's Young
People,* January 22, 1889, Riis mss, L.C.; Jacob Riis to Mary Riis, January
11, 1914, Riis mss, L.C.

11. Jacob A. Riis, "The Tenement-House Problem," Parts I and II,
Christian Union, 1889. Both are in Riis mss, L.C.

12. Riis, *How the Other Half Lives,* 2–4, 14–15.

13. Examples of books of the first type are Charles Loring Brace,
*The Dangerous Classes of New York and Twenty Years' Work Among
Them* (New York, 1880); Josiah Strong, *Our Country: Its Possible Future*

and *Its Present Crisis* (New York, 1885); Samuel L. Loomis, *Modern Cities and Their Religious Problems* (New York, 1887).

14. Lubove, *Progressives and the Slums*, 45–46, 55–56; Riis, *How the Other Half Lives*, 1–2.

15. The tenement-house problem was not restricted to New York City, as Riis well knew. Arthur Mann, describing a section of Boston during the 1880s, wrote that "the very wretchedness of the area attracted gamblers, pimps, prostitutes, sailors out on a spree, and human wrecks of one kind or another." Mann, *Yankee Reformers in the Urban Age* (Cambridge, Mass., 1954), 4.

16. Riis, *How the Other Half Lives*, 120–22.

17. Ibid., 6–7.

18. Ibid., 8.

19. Ibid., 43.

20. Ibid., 31–34.

21. Ibid., 48–49, 124–29, 159–63.

22. Ibid., 24–26.

23. Ibid., 15–16.

24. Ibid., 41, 67–76.

25. Ibid., 39–41, 91; see also Oscar Handlin, *The Uprooted* (Boston, 1951), 170–71.

26. Riis sometimes portrayed black men as strong but dim-witted. In 1885, writing of a man who got up unhurt after he fell headfirst from a third-story window, Riis stated, "No one but a Negro could possibly have performed that feat." New York *Mail and Express*, September 19, 1885.

27. Riis, *How the Other Half Lives*, 111–17.

28. Ibid., 110, 112, 118. Unable to imagine the assimilation of Negroes into American society, Riis later endorsed the gradualist philosophy of Booker T. Washington as holding out the best hope for the advancement of the black race. Jacob Riis, *Theodore Roosevelt, The Citizen* (Washington, 1904), 369; Jacob Riis to Elisabeth Riis, February 20, 1905, Riis mss, L.C.

29. Riis, *How the Other Half Lives*, 89–94.

30. Ibid., 108–09.

31. Ibid., 65, 184–85, 193–99.

32. Ibid., 148–55, 164–70, 177–78.

33. Ibid., 200, 203, 226.

34. Ibid., 199–200; see also Robert H. Wiebe, *The Search for Order: 1877–1920* (New York, 1967), 89.

35. Riis, *How the Other Half Lives*, 205, 207–22.

36. The final quotation is from a poem by James Russell Lowell. Ibid., 226. See also Lubove, *Progressives and the Slums*, 55, 65; Oscar Lewis, *La Vida* (New York, 1965), xliii–xliv.

37. Charles N. Glaab and A. Theodore Brown concluded in 1967: "It was, so to speak, a book whose time had come in 1890." Glaab and Brown, *A History of Urban America* (New York, 1967), 241.

38. Altgeld's *Live Questions* was a reprint of the Illinois Governor's speeches and articles. *In Darkest England* was ghost-written by William T. Stead for the Salvation Army leader Booth. See Harry Barnard, *Eagle Forgotten: The Life of John Peter Altgeld* (New York, 1938), 132, 144; Robert H. Bremner, *From the Depths: The Discovery of Poverty in the United States* (New York, 1967), 29.

39. Brooklyn *Times,* December 15, 1890; *True Nationalist,* November 29, 1890, Riis mss, L.C.

40. "How the Other Half Lives," *The Critic,* 17 (December 27, 1890), 332.

41. John Higham, *Strangers in the Land: Patterns of American Nativism,* 1860–1925 (New York, Atheneum ed., 1968), 40. See, for example, Henry Cabot Lodge, "The Restriction of Immigration," *North American Review,* 152 (1891), 34.

42. Louis H. Pink, "Reminiscences," Columbia Oral History Project, New York; Van Wyck Brooks, *The Confident Years: 1885–1915* (London, 1953), 73–74; Truman F. Keefer, *Ernest Poole* (New York, 1966), 11, 25; Louise C. Wade, *Graham Taylor: Pioneer for Social Justice* (Chicago, 1964), 96.

15 The Liberal Approach: Its Weaknesses and Its Strengths; A Comment on the U.S. Riot Commission Report*

Michael Young

THE EVENTS IN modern Memphis and Atlanta, followed by their chorus of funeral fires, have been almost as tragic for distant spectators as they have been for the actors. They have further sharpened the absorption of the world in the affairs of an America whose title to world leadership is that it is even more obviously "humanity in miniature" than when Myrdal used the phrase in 1942. Not only does it contain a myriad peoples representative of different countries and of different colours, but these peoples are between them facing in the concentrated form that underlies all drama the world's most fundamental moral issue: Will the Christian doctrine that we are all God's children triumph again in race relations as it has done against always tenacious resistance in so many other spheres? The doctrine has not just survived the decline of the church and the weakening of faith in the existence of God; this bit of Christianity has taken on a new strength in a post-Christian era. The chil-

* Reprinted from Michael Young, "The Liberal Approach: Its Weaknesses and Its Strengths; A Comment on the U.S. Riot Commission Report," by permission of *Daedalus*, Journal of the American Academy of Arts and Sciences, Boston, Mass., vol. 97, Fall 1968, *The Conscience of the City*, pp. 1379–89.

dren (at least if they are of the same colour) espouse their brotherhood more devoutly after the death of their father. When secularised
by the long line of liberals who followed John Stuart Mill, this mighty
doctrine destroyed the British Empire. The oppressors communicated
the idea to the oppressed, and the oppressed communicated it back
to the oppressors. Could the idea be mightier still and bring together
in a brotherhood a variety of men without "distinction as to complexion"? We know it has failed to do so in Southern Africa. Will it
succeed in America, now the chief guardian of the old doctrine in
the new form it has taken in the American Creed? The stakes for all
of us are gigantic. The chances of moderating colour conflict in the
world and, in the long run, of avoiding the deadliest kind of war,
depend upon the ability of Europe to live in brotherhood with Africa
in America. The chances for humanity in general depend upon humanity in miniature.

This is perhaps as obvious (or more so) writing from today's
England as it is from elsewhere. Ten years ago it might have been
different; anti-Americanism was so rife and coloured people in the
country so few that if the riots had happened then there might have
been some perfidious crowing. But now we are a miniature of the
miniature. Coloured immigration, the legacy of Empire, has un-
covered as much prejudice among limey whiteys as among yankee.
The prejudice has helped to create ghettos in Brixton and North
Kensington, Sparkbrook and Southall. A Labour Government, defer-
ring to the racism of its own supporters (many of whom are also
supporters of Enoch Powell), has done nothing major to prevent
these districts from becoming future Notting Hills except to restrict
further immigration and this in disregard of promises made to the
Kenyan Indians. When we watch the news from American cities on
television, we know that we may be seeing our own future. We know,
too, that if America can provide a model of reconciliation, it will be
one on which we can build.

The report of the Kerner Commission is, therefore, almost a domestic document, even if it has not been produced by Her Majesty's
Stationery Office, and I am going to comment on it as freely as if it
were. It is immensely welcome. Joe McCarthy is still a haunting presence in Britain, as well as in America, and after the summer of 1967
the fear was that extremism would breed extremism, that the Goneril
of a Stokely Carmichael would be matched by the Regan of a Reagan,
or worse. The report might have edged that way, as some thought
it would when the Commission's membership was first announced;
if it had, the dreaded polarisation of black and white would have

been pushed a good deal further. The Right would have had an official stance. We can, therefore, take great comfort from what the report is *not* and rejoice that instead of a manifesto for the Right the Commission has issued a mammoth manifesto of liberalism. It is a reaffirmation of the American Creed at a period in the world's history when it could not have been more timely, one that is, if anything, even more so after Memphis. This is such virtue that the report, despite its repetitiveness and other more serious weaknesses, ranks as a great and moving document. This is especially true of Part I, "What Happened?" The whole report sustains faith in America.

But even so one cannot help wishing that it had been someing more. The report has avoided the extremism of white and black marvelously well, and yet (as in such critical times it must be difficult to avoid doing) has gone in for a sort of extremism all the same, the extremism of the middle. A certain kind of primitive liberalism is there almost to the last "t." Having decided to attribute the blame to white society, as was surely right and courageous, the Commission has made everything else it says consistent—in fact far too consistent to be convincing. White society created the ghetto: "White institutions created it, white institutions maintain it, and white society condones it." Yes, but white society is not consistent. It also does not condone the ghetto. The report notes that "Burn, baby, burn" was originated by a disc jockey. It does not recognise, or at any rate does not say, that white society and, above all, the ethos of equality I mentioned a moment ago created more than the Kerner Commission. It has sustained Negro protest. It has sustained a civil rights movement that has, after all, enjoyed more success in the last ten years than in the previous hundred. Where else did the ethos come from?—certainly not from Africa. It may seem that again and again nothing fails like success, that expectations are always outpacing achievement, but this should not detract from the achievement, which is primary. If the blame is white society's, so is the credit. If the riots partly stemmed from the Vietnam War (because the war detracted from the legitimation of white society), it is still immensely creditable to have produced a report like this while the war continues.

It is the same with one of the basic diagnoses of the report: That there is a kind of iron law at work that, unless the whole liberal bill is acted upon, will produce a steady worsening of the situation. There is, for instance, "accelerating segregation of low-income, disadvantaged Negroes within the ghettos of the largest American cities," and within them an increase of crime, drug addiction, family instability, and illegitimacy. Schools and housing deteriorate. Needs increase, but the income to meet them goes down as the tax base is eroded by the exodus of white people and industry to the suburbs, and so on.

True enough; but the other side of the picture—the striking economic progress there has been—is not so prominently displayed. For many years now, calves have been calving double in America. Negroes have gained along with whites. The Commission recognises this when it says that "most whites and many Negroes outside the ghetto have prospered to a degree unparalleled in the history of civilization." (Should it not be *most* Negroes though?) But in the next sentence triumph suddenly becomes disaster: "Through television—the universal appliance in the ghetto—and the other media of mass communications, this affluence has been endlessly flaunted before the eyes of the Negro poor and the jobless ghetto youth." The Commission has so fully, and in a way admirably, identified itself with the ghetto people that the members seem to feel their same despair. Neither can gain on the swings *or* on the roundabouts. If America does not get richer, there will not be enough money to spare for the ghetto; if America does get richer, the ghetto people will by contrast feel poorer than ever. Relatively speaking, the poor blacks will whatever happens be as poor as ever.

Yes, yes, one keeps wanting to say, *but* why won't they go on to draw the proper conclusion? Of course poverty can never be abolished. Unless Pareto's Law can be deprived of effect, incomes will continue to conform to a normal distribution, and the people in the bottom tail of that distribution will be in poverty, the same in a hundred years as now. The proper conclusion in this context is surely that a major goal is to bring about the same distribution of incomes among the blacks as among the whites. As far as the poor are concerned, this means that the representation of Negroes in, say, the bottom 20 per cent of income distribution should be reduced to the proportion that they form of the general population; if Negroes are 11 per cent of the total population, there should not be more than 11 per cent of them in poverty. If this be one of the major goals, then a vital social indicator would show how far it is approaching or receding from year to year. Since it does not state the goal, the report naturally does not give any prominence to the indicator. It says that "the proportion of Negroes employed in high-skill, high-status, and well-paying jobs rose faster than comparable proportions among whites from 1960 to 1966." It then relegates to a footnote the statement that "the proportion of non-white families living in poverty dropped from 39 per cent to 35 per cent from 1964 to 1966." There is clearly a long way to go, but at least the movement is in the right direction.

The progress, such as it is, means that there has been some improvement in the Negro standard of life relative not just to their standards in the past, but also to the present standards of whites. The self-blame that liberals are liable to is so evident in the report that this progress is not at any point featured. The missing man, as Nathan Glazer has pointed out, is the Negro who is not in ghetto poverty at all. "Thus, between 2.0 and 2.5 million poor Negroes are living in disadvantaged neighborhoods of central cities in the United States. These persons comprise only slightly more than 1 per cent of the nation's total population, but they make up about 16 to 20 per cent of the total Negro population of all central cities, and a much higher proportion in certain cities." But what of the other 80 per cent? The Commission's focus on the ghetto poor and their belief that things are getting worse there have prevented them from asking this question. It is a crucial one. The Commission seems to recognise this in passing, when it says of the better-off Negro, without giving any weight to it, that "relative affluence seems at least to inhibit him from attacking the existing social order and may motivate him to take considerable risks to protect it," or when it speaks more particularly of the beneficial influence of Negro policemen and counter-rioters, like Hesham Jaaber in Elizabeth, New Jersey, the Positive Neighborhood Action Committee in Detroit, and effective individuals like the twenty-four-year-old E. G. in Detroit, or the two young Plainfield Negroes described as D. H., the newspaper reporter, and L. C., the chemical worker. The outcome of present discontents depends upon the extent to which the 80 per cent become involved in political and other action to relieve the plight of themselves and their fellow Negroes in and out of the ghetto. Without allotting them a central role, there can be no grand strategy for changing the conditions that gave rise to the riots of 1967 and 1968.

These are my first and minor criticisms, and they relate to the general analysis of the place of the Negro in American society. My second set is about the recommendations. They, too, seem to me to embody a primitive kind of liberalism. The members of the Commission are all distinguished men of affairs, with intimate experience of politics and administration. Yet they write as if they were outside instead of inside the establishment; it is not only state and city police who are operating on different wave lengths. Why this should be so I cannot from this distance fathom, unless it be that at the moment there is, apart from this brand of liberalism, no other well-accepted body of thought on race relations for such a body to reflect. It may seem especially strange to me because I am used to reports of Royal Commissions, which lean too far the other way; their members sometimes appear to be so sensitive to the problems of government that they might be its mouthpiece.

The chief marks of the informed outsider's view on almost anything important are these: that a very great deal is attacked as wrong, and very drastic and speedy action is said to be needed to avert disaster. The mark of the insider's view is his awareness of the harsh necessity of choice. No government can ever do a lot quickly. Since resources are always limited, and their possible uses unlimited, policy-makers and administrators have constantly to choose or, in other words, to decide which alternatives have priority. This is obvious stuff of course, and it is only mentioned because the Kerner Report, to take it at its face value, has overlooked the obvious. It has failed to cost its massive list of recommendations either in terms of money or of manpower of different levels of skill, and it has failed to say what priority should attach to each in the use of resources or in the order in time in which they should be acted upon. Its value to governments—federal, state, or local—is therefore bound to be less than it could have been. They all want to know how to make a dollar go furthest; how, that is, to achieve the most for the least. But perhaps it is not too late. Could some of the members of the Commission be recalled—joined this time by some social scientists, with priority for an economist proficient in the cost-benefit analysis for which America is rightly so famous, and for a sociologist well-versed in the debate about social indicators—and asked to say how and why they would spend sums of various orders from the amount at present spent on the Vietnam War downwards? This kind of work is going on in many places, but the results could be usefully pulled together in a second volume of the report. And could the new national commission be matched by a series of local commissions that would have exactly the same task for their cities? It might be objected that this would be to arrogate the functions of government at the national or local level. The objection is not convincing. How much money there will be and how it is spent will be decided in good part by political pressures. But there is still need not just for political pressure on behalf of this or that sectional interest, but for a great deal more thought about the cost-effectiveness of the different steps that might be taken to improve the lot of the Negro American. Continued study is, as the Commission said, essential.

Since I have attacked the Commission on a major point, I feel bound, even as an outsider myself and very much of a one at that, to say something about how I would respond to the same challenge. What would my priorities be? I am going to mention a short list under two main headings: the police and the system of local administration.

The Police

Much of what the Commission says about the police is admirable. The report fully recognises the importance of the part the police play in and out of the ghetto, in times of civil peace as much as in times of civil disorder. Professor Reiss' judgment is endorsed. "The slum police precinct is like the slum school. It gets, with few exceptions, the worst in the system." The worst is too often also the most racist. It is therefore not surprising that the first grievances of the Negro communities in the cities surveyed were police practices. Anyone who reads the horrifying accounts of the behavior of police (whether or not they had Confederate pennants on their cars) in Bridgeton, New Jersey, or in the 10th Precinct Station in Detroit will sympathise. Improvement of police standards would probably do more than any other single change to take heat out of the situation and restore a little of the respect for authority that is evidently so lacking and so needed. More adequate police protection would also encourage the 80 per cent to side more openly with the forces of law and order.

The report thus makes a whole slate of recommendations: for assignment to the ghettos of "officers with superior ability, sensitivity and the common sense necessary for enlightened law enforcement"; for giving them special incentives, getting patrolmen out of the car and into the neighborhood; and for moderating aggressive "stop-and-frisk" practices. It puts forward an excellent proposal for recruiting as "community service officers" many more young Negroes between seventeen and twenty-one without the ordinary standard police qualifications and then giving them the opportunity to "graduate" into full police officers; and a hundred other proposals besides. The Commission even wants the police to take on more willingly a host of non-police services, including the settlement of marital disputes.

This is all very sensible. Such a new model policeman would certainly make a striking difference to the urban scene. He (or she?) would be the visible representative of authority capable of giving aid and service as well as enforcing the law. But if he is to take on so much more on behalf of society, what more is society going to give him in return? Apparently nothing. The tone of comment on the police is almost uniformly unsympathetic. The Commission has identified with the ghetto Negro, but perhaps just because it has succeeded in that, it has failed to identify also with the police. To appreciate their difficulties as they see them, one has to read between instead of on the lines. No surveys are reported on police attitudes.

The new model police are needed right enough. But where are they to come from in sufficient quantity and, above all, quality? The Commission does not say. It notes, but without any emphasis, that "Blue Flu" raged among the police in Detroit before the riots and that the poor pay of the police is one reason why "better qualified Negroes are often more attracted by other, better paying positions." But why not again draw the obvious conclusion? My first priority would be an improvement in the pay and conditions of the police force at all levels. It would no doubt involve federal subvention. But my guess is that a dollar spent on that would do more than a dollar spent on anything else to reduce the threat of further riots and, more positively, to improve race relations. The relative pay of the police can no longer be considered an index of civil order.

There is an important related matter on which there is no comment at all. Seen from England, the most extraordinary omission in the whole report is the failure to say anything about the need for civil disarmament, and this even though it was written before Memphis. There are unprecedented riots; police and National Guardsmen, with guns everywhere, are terrified of "snipers"; suburban housewives and others start arming themselves; rumours of armed bands marching into or out of the city terrify everyone; and yet even such a report as this does not mention arms control once.

It does say that "a climate that tends towards approval and encouragement of violence as a form of protest has been created by white terrorism directed against non-violent protest." But has not violence also been encouraged by the approval given to its instrument?

To institute arms control would, therefore, be my second priority. I know this is an easy thing to suggest from this disarmed island. The police here can be without guns partly because there are so few guns among the populace, and there are so few of them among the populace partly because hunting was traditionally a prerogative of the aristocracy and landed gentry. The American's right to carry arms is indeed partly a reaction against the aristocratic tradition in England in the eighteenth century. Anyway, you have a National Rifle Association, and we do not. But after the riots and the assassinations (of which we have surely not seen the last) is it not time to take issue with pressure group and tradition? Quite apart from prohibiting Sears Roebuck and the like from selling guns, could not all arms, under pain of penalty, be lodged in police-controlled stores from which they could only be withdrawn "on parole" for specified periods for use on hunting trips or other legitimate purposes? Once the citizenry were disarmed, the police whom they protect could be also. I think that whether and how the police are armed is a better index of the state of civil order than their pay. General Throckmorton ordered the weapons of all military personnel unloaded in Detroit. It would indeed be a day for America and the world if the police could be ordered not just to unload, but to disarm.

Local Administration

"Program" is an American word for which I can find no translation in our brand of English. "Programme" is certainly quite different and "scheme" somewhat so. I am glad there is none. The report is packed with programs for this and that, and full, too, of complaints about the confusions which they engender. The Commissioners are outspoken about the fault.

> The spectacle of Detroit and New Haven engulfed in civil turmoil despite a multitude of federally aided programs raised basic questions as to whether the existing "delivery system" is adequate to the bold new purposes of national policy. . . . There are now over 400 grant programs operated by a broad range of federal agencies and channeled through a much larger array of semi-autonomous state and local government entities. Reflective of this complex scheme, federal programs often seem self-defeating and contradictory: field officials unable to make decisions on their own programs and unaware of related efforts; agencies unable or unwilling to work together; programs conceived and administered to achieve different and sometimes conflicting purposes. . . . The existing welfare programs are a labyrinth of federal, state and local legislation.

To find a way through the labyrinth there has been the usual device of the labyrinthine. "Some two dozen inter-agency committees have been established to coordinate two or more federal aid programs."

But surely what is needed is not 400 new inter-agency programs for coordinating existing programs, not more coordination but more actual unification of administration. To hope for this at the federal or even at the state level is perhaps to hope for too much. Could there not, however, be unification at the local level? The Commission does recognise the need for this at the most local level of all. The Neighborhood Action Task Force it proposes wherever there are many "low-income minority citizens" would be a sort of neighbourhood council. But its proposed functions are vague; it is not even recommended that each Task Force set young Negroes to work during the summer building their own swimming pools and other amenities. Its relationship to the city government is also vague. How could such a "community cabinet," as it is called, focus all those programs if immediately above the neighbourhood the agencies responsible for them remain scattered through a dozen pages of the telephone directory? Should one not aspire to one or at any rate a few for the whole of local bureaucracy? This would imply that most federal aid would be channeled through the city administration and that federal agencies at the local level would be defederalised and made part of the municipality. Such issues are not mentioned by the Commission. Being men of experience in politics, they presumably know what devils they would be letting loose if such issues had been mentioned, and they also realise that any reform of local bureaucracy which was more than tinkering would take so long to accomplish in the face of entrenched opposition that the summer of 1980 could have come and gone before there was very much to show for the expenditure of a great deal of energy. Presumably, therefore, one has to rule out unification of local planning and administration with single local governments covering the areas of whole conurbations, suburbs and all. What I would naturally propose for this tidy England is presumably sheerly impracticable for America. Yet if that is so at least there is a great advantage that can be secured from the plurality of government that exists. It seems to me that the Commission, in preferring the Integration Choice to the Enrichment Choice (as it was surely right to do for the long run), has played down the value that could be derived in the meantime from the deployment of Black Power and its use for constructive work in the neighbourhoods and cities where Negroes are in sufficient density to grasp it. Successful new model governments led by Negroes would be symbols for racial pride to concentrate on, commanding general respect from whites as well as blacks.

My last priority would therefore be for the exercise of the utmost positive discrimination in favour of Negro political leadership, embracing the 80 per cent as well as the 20 per cent in Cleveland or

Gary or anywhere else where there is a chance of creating the kind of political machine the Negroes have so far lacked. It could be aided, too, if private corporations (particularly if the Vietnam War can be ended) were drawn in and given responsibility for organising the employment of Negroes for rebuilding in the ghettos. One of many other priority steps that would help would be the abolition of the lunatic and unjust "Man-in-the-House" rule for the payment of welfare benefits. Many of the ills from which the ghetto suffers derive from fatherless families, and yet here is government actually sowing the dragon's teeth. This same issue was one of the most bitter political issues in Britain in the 1930's. Nothing but good has come from the subsequent abolition of the "Means Test" which used to embody that same residue from the Elizabethan Poor Law. I am sure that a similar reform in America would produce the same benefits for family life.

I said earlier that I was not going to spare criticism, and I have not. But despite that, I want to end by reiterating that this is a great document, even a noble one. It speaks with the voice of an enlightenment that could keep social chaos at bay, for America and for the world.

Section Four

The Creative Ghetto

The ghetto inhabitants' creative responses to their environment have been the most effective weapons in ghetto reform. To cope with ghetto life, residents have banded together in organizations and emphasized community pride and group solidarity. When the primary group institutions of family and church and school have been threatened in the stark ghetto setting, residents have taken steps to revitalize them or replace them with more appropriate institutions. Among the many manifestations of the creative ghetto are political organizations, schools, film and writers' workshops, drug and medical clinics, storefront community centers, tenant unions, and underground newspapers. The history of the creative ghetto emphasizes that the culture of the ghetto is more subtle and rich than merely being a maelstrom that entraps and dehumanizes its victims. As Kenneth Clark declared in *Dark Ghetto* (pp. 11–12),

> The ghetto is ferment, paradox, conflict, and dilemma. Yet within its pervasive pathology exists a surprising human resilience. The ghetto is hope, it is despair, it is churches and bars. It is aspiration for change, and it is apathy. It is vibrancy, it is stagnation. It is courage, and it is defeatism. It is cooperation and concern, and it is suspicion, competitiveness, and rejection. It is the surge toward assimilation, and it is alienation and withdrawal within the protective walls of the ghetto.

The first selection, by historian Timothy L. Smith, analyzes the creation of educational institutions in immigrant ghettos. The community-sponsored educational opportunities at once preserved the cultural identity of ghetto residents and allowed them to compete more successfully in the new American environment. Robert Rockaway's selection on Jewish welfare and cultural activities in Detroit portrays a common feature of ghetto life—conflict among residents from different towns or countries, despite bonds of race, religion, or ethnic culture. The split between the established German Jewish community and the newly arrived Russian Jews was an important accompaniment to self-help welfare activities in Detroit's Jewish ghetto. Novelist José Yglesias' article on the Young Lords describes the work of a revolutionary street organization in turning the destructive forces of the ghetto to constructive purposes. In battling apathy, hostility, ridicule, and an inert New York bureaucracy, the Young Lords used tactics ranging from blustering publicity gimmicks and rhetorical education campaigns to practical lobbying techniques and breakfast programs for the young. Piri Thomas' article is a review of *From the Ashes: Voices of Watts,* an anthology of poetry, short stories, essays and television scripts emanating from the Watts writers' workshop, which Budd Schulberg established after the 1965 Los Angeles riot. Thomas, a multi-talented author, poet, playwright, and painter, declares that ghetto dwellers of all races share common problems and goals in their quest for dignity and justice. Both he and the contributors to *From the Ashes: Voices of Watts* provide tangible evidence of the reservoir of talent and creativity simmering in the ghetto.

For further reading see Carl Wittke, *We Who Built America* (1939); Moses Rischin, *The Promised City: New York's Jews, 1870–1914* (1962); Arthur Goren, *New York Jews and the Quest for Community: The Kehillah Experiment, 1908–1922* (1970); Eliot Lord,

John J. D. Trenor, and Samuel Barrows, *The Italian in America* (1905); Humbert S. Nelli, *Italians in Chicago, 1880–1930: A Study in Ethnic Mobility* (1970); Elena Padilla, *Up from Puerto Rico* (1958); John H. Bracey, Jr., August Meier, and Elliot Rudwick, eds., *Black Nationalism in America* (1970); Lee Rainwater, ed., *Soul* (1970). Among the important literary works that elucidate the creative ghetto are Alfred Kazin, *Walker in the City* (1951); Bernard Malamud, *The Assistant* (1957); John Fante, *Dago Red* (1940); Langston Hughes, *Big Sea* (1940); Malcolm X and Alex Haley, *The Autobiography of Malcolm X* (1965); Piri Thomas, *Down These Mean Streets* (1967) and *Savior, Savior, Hold My Hand* (1972).

16 Immigrant Social Aspirations and American Education, 1880–1930*

Timothy L. Smith

STATISTICS FOR LITERACY and school attendance in the federal census of 1910 suggest that immigrant families showed as much or more zeal for education as those in which the parents were native Americans. Not just in the South, where the school system was weak and the former slave population large, but in every section of the country, the percentage of children of foreign or mixed parentage aged six to fourteen who were enrolled in school closely approximated that for children of native Americans. And the literacy of the immigrants' offspring was uniformly higher, even in the populous Middle Atlantic and North Central states, where newcomers from central and southern Europe were many, and traditions of education among the Yankee population strong.[1] The relative preponderance of first- and second-generation immigrants in public school teaching underlines the point. In 1908, in Duluth, Minnesota, 10 per cent of 460 teachers in the kindergarten and elementary grades

* Reprinted with permission from Timothy L. Smith, "Immigrant Social Aspirations and American Education, 1880–1930," *American Quarterly,* 21 (Fall, 1969), 523–27, 531–39, 541–43. Copyright, 1969, Trustees of the University of Pennsylvania.

were themselves immigrants, and the fathers of another 42 per cent were foreign-born.[2] Such figures help explain why those who campaigned to restrict immigration on the argument that newcomers were illiterate cited statistics only for the foreign-born themselves, ignoring the achievements of their children.[3] Woodbridge M. Ferris, Governor of Michigan during the copper strike of 1913–14, appealed soon after for a great expansion of night school programs for immigrants from central and southern Europe on the grounds that their desire for education far outran the provisions the community was making for them. During the year-long strike, he noted, the children enrolled in the public schools of the polyglot Marquette peninsula recorded an average attendance of 97 per cent, a result which an army of truant officers could not have achieved if the parents had lacked enthusiasm.[4]

Apparently, not only parents but also the single men who joined them in forming after 1890 the new Italian, Greek, Slavic, Finnish, Hungarian and Jewish ethnic associations displayed a remarkable commitment to education. When, for example, in 1889, Protestant women in Rochester, New York, opened an Italian mission, ninety men enrolled at once in the English class which met three nights a week. The attendance by the year's end averaged seventy, though the total Italian population of the city that year was barely five hundred.[5] Peter Roberts noted in 1904 that ambitious young Slavs in the anthracite mining towns of eastern Pennsylvania crowded out the night schools which private agencies conducted there, after they learned that the public ones could enroll only persons under twenty-one years of age.[6] By 1910 a former Polish peasant, who had begun life in America as a Michigan farmhand thirty years before, was operating a printing firm in Toledo, Ohio, which issued every year more books than any publishing house in Poland.[7] John Jurin, a coppersmith's apprentice from Croatian Slavonia, was unable to read or write his own language when he came to Chicago on the eve of World War I. Members of a Croatian dramatic club helped him first to become literate in his native tongue, and then taught him English. He wound up editor of the newspaper which the club published during the 1930s, earning his living all the while at his trade.[8] Stoyan Christowe, a Bulgarian who came from a Greek village to St. Louis at about the same time, soon fled the inferno of jack-hammers and hot rivets which he encountered on his first job, but he did not forget the advice of an older immigrant that he study English. "I applied myself to it with the diligence of a scientist," he wrote later. He pored over the dictionary and the grammar, and read newspapers and magazines continually. "I never threw away a package, a can or a box without reading whatever labels were pasted upon them," Christowe said. "The words that were unfamiliar to me I wrote on small square pieces of paper in red or green pencil. These I tacked to the walls of the bunk until every available inch of space was covered. In whatever direction I looked I saw words."[9]

Intensified concern for schooling seems to have been an integral part of the social experience of migration from central and south-eastern Europe at three important junctures: on the eve of departure from the homeland villages, when some chose to go and some to stay; in the first years after resettlement in America, when the lessons to be learned were many and the rewards were large for those who learned them quickly and well; and, thereafter, among the residents of the former Old World villages, where letters from those who stayed overseas as well as the example of others who returned helped the peasant class to understand the role of education in personal, communal and national advancement. The records also indicate that the laymen and clergymen who established programs of parochial education in Roman Catholic, Greek Catholic, Eastern Orthodox and Protestant immigrant congregations linked their efforts closely to the social aspirations which had drawn the newcomers from the villages far away.

Behind the concern for learning lay three interlocking motives. The one most explicit in their literature and also most deeply rooted in Old World experience was simply the desire to earn a better living and, if possible, to gain both riches and fame. The second, and the one which seems to have been most prominent in religious congregations in America, was the need to shape a structure of family and communal life which would fit the requirements of mobile and urban existence. The third was specifically ethnic: the quest of a definition of national identity which would fulfill the sense of duty to their homeland or to their people that memory inspired and still not contradict their new allegiance to America.

The most obvious factor in the educational awakening on both sides of the Atlantic was the migrating peasant's desire to make money, and so to get ahead. Italian or Slavic workers who came intending to stay in America, and who brought over their wives or sweethearts as soon as they had gotten a foothold, were keenly aware of hardship. They often protested their exploitation by native Americans or by fellow-countrymen who had arrived earlier.[10] Nevertheless, they knew their condition was vastly improved over the poverty they had experienced in Calabria, Dalmatia, Carniola or the Carpathian mountains. As for the "birds of passage," Romanian old-timers who came from Bukovina or the Banat intending only temporary employment here recall that each man's slogan on departure was "a thousand dollars and my ticket home."[11]

Both the permanent and the temporary migrants realized that to learn to speak and read English was to make their investment of time, expense and emotion gilt-edged. The earliest volumes of virtually every Slavic newspaper that religious or secular organizations published in America carried lessons in English, announced the publication of simple dictionaries or grammars, and exhorted readers to learn the new tongue as a means of getting and holding a better job. The night-school movement, for which public officials and industrial executives generally took credit, began in many cities under the auspices of immigrant associations themselves.[12] Polish farmers who took over poorer farmsteads in the Connecticut Valley around Hadley, Massachusetts, after 1900 acknowledged that monetary values prompted them to flock to evening classes, and to require faithful attendance by their younger children in the public schools.[13] Even in the anthracite country, where the availability of employment for twelve-year-olds caused a sharp drop-off of attendance above the primary grades, Peter Roberts' tabulation showed that 55 per cent of all the children enrolled in the two public elementary schools in Mahanoy City were of Slavic parentage. Proportionate enrollment was similar in five nearby mining towns, despite the fact that several thousand Slovak and Polish children in the region attended parochial day-schools.[14]

The early parochial schools, moreover, stressed the learning of English quite as much as the preservation of Old World culture. The seventy thousand pupils attending Polish Roman Catholic schools in Chicago in 1901 studied religion and Polish language and history in their parents' native tongue, but the language of instruction in geography, American history, bookkeeping and algebra was English. The first Hungarian and Slovak Roman Catholic congregations in Cleveland employed English-speaking Benedictine nuns as teachers; the priest or some interested layman came in periodically to instruct the youngsters in Magyar or Slovak.[15] Roberts noted that Slavic Roman Catholic priests in the anthracite country often limited parochial education to the first three or four grades because they were unable to secure instructors of their faith and nationality who could teach the children in English.[16] Laymen insisted on an adequate program of secular instruction. A Milwaukee Polish editor declared around 1907 that many of his readers had begun to discover that their parish schools were doing a poor job, and were demanding improvements. "With the exception of those where the priest himself" was "a sincere educator," he charged, children were getting superficial instruction in reading, writing, arithmetic, geography and history. Moreover, the memorization of the catechism and of dogmatic formulas was, he said, "far from being really religion." The editor advised the public school authorities that if they would add Polish language to their curriculum in Slavic neighborhoods, many parents would send their children to public school.[17]

The fact that the so-called "new immigrants" arrived in largest numbers from central and southeastern Europe during the same decades when the progressive movement in American education was placing much heavier emphasis upon vocational training helped to confirm their utilitarian attitude toward schooling.[18]

. . .

. . . the experience of migration required priests and laymen, parents and children to adjust to urban and industrial conditions. For those who undertook the venture, money, education and respectability formed a trinity of controlling aspirations which we have too long associated with the term "the Protestant ethic." The successful immigrant's value system seems on closer inspection to have been simply a new combination of preferences which shrewd peasants had shared for generations, and which Orthodox, Catholic and Jewish no less than Protestant faith managed to sanctify.[19]

A second major social aspiration which helps to explain the extensive educational interests of immigrants from central and eastern Europe was their desire to establish and preserve a new order of family and communal life. The small-family unit in America at first stood free of the kin-group system which prevailed in Old World villages, but it did not stand alone. The immigrant family simply drew sustenance from an improvised rather than an inherited community—usually a religious congregation, though sometimes an anti-clerical ethnic association replaced the old village as the web of communal life. The new bonds were psychic, rather than geographic, and their organizational forms were in every case voluntary, oriented to the future and, therefore, generally receptive to social change. The leading laymen in a congregation were usually heads of families, not bachelors. The officers were often the first successful businessmen —tavern keepers, coal-dealers, travel agents and the like—in whose households emotional security and a hopeful outlook prevailed.[20]

Priests who were directly responsible for parochial education in these communities were not all mere guardians of tradition. Father

Paul Tymkevich, pastor of a Ruthenian Greek Catholic congregation in Yonkers, New York, formed around 1900 a cooperative association which erected a model tenement house for 39 families, complete with a tavern on the ground floor. Then he instituted in his own home a boarding school for older boys from the anthracite country. He sent them to the Yonkers public high school for their general education and after hours gave them instruction in the faith, language and traditions of their fathers. Tymkevich told Miss Balch that although his people had gained economically by coming to America, their customs did not fit them for life in the city. "The first step in civilization is to acquire habits," he said, "and where can they acquire them? On the streets? In the saloon?" What they needed most, he believed, was educated leaders from among their own ranks, "to form themselves upon, to give them a standard of ambition." At about the same time Ivan Ardan, another Greek Catholic Ruthenian pastor, encouraged the establishment of self-improvement clubs in the larger towns of the anthracite country. One of them maintained by 1904 a library of three hundred volumes. Generally under the supervision of the priests, these clubs aimed to "qualify Slav immigrants for the duties of citizenship."[21]

In the study of immigrant acculturation, the attention which scholars have paid to Jewish examples has raised the proper question but produced a distorted answer. The question is, how did positive faith in education as a means of personal gain become dominant in young families, where the crucial shaping of childhood attitudes had to take place? The answer has been that Jews who came to North America enjoyed a special combination of favorable circumstances. Sex ratios among adults were more balanced, leaving fewer unattached males in each community; whole families tended to migrate together; a proportionately much higher number intended on their first arrival to settle permanently here; Jewish group life was by tradition essentially ethnic, rather than nationalistic, reflecting more a religious and cultural than a political ideology; and, finally, their religious tradition was even in the anthropological sense a literary one, for in the lowliest Galician *shtetl* the man of prestige was the one who knew The Book.[22]

But a like devotion to family life, often in a religious setting which idealized literary culture, prevailed among immigrants of other central European backgrounds as well. Certainly the group life of those of Orthodox and Greek Catholic faith, whether they were Romanians, Ruthenians, Greeks, Serbians or Slovaks, was anchored in a distinctively literary religion. The Bible held an important place, but even more important were the words and the music of the Divine Liturgy, which laymen memorized in all the various forms it assumed for the successive seasons of the Christian year.[23] Moreover, significant numbers of husbands and wives of all nationalities migrated together in the early years, declaring by that fact their intention to settle permanently here. The marriage records of the congregations they established indicate that a continuous stream of girls began arriving soon after from homeland villages to become wives of the bachelor lads who were numerically preponderant in the pioneer group. These first families of Hunkytown and Dagoville became within each nationality the "American" models for those of their countrymen who came over later.

Protestant and Roman Catholic congregations also nurtured the growing commitment to education. Associations of Slovak, Lithuanian and Polish laymen often organized schools to teach both English and their native language and culture long before priests arrived from the Old World. A primary objective of the earliest Hungarian Reformed congregations, established in Pittsburgh and Cleveland with the help of American Presbyterian and Reformed home mission funds, was to educate their children in the religious and national traditions of their homeland and in American ways as well.[24]

Immigrants of Greek Catholic faith, whether they called themselves Rusins, Ruthenians, Ukrainians, Carpatho-Russians, Slovaks or Hungarians, almost invariably sent their children to public schools, as did the Eastern Orthodox Serbs, Romanians and Russians, and the Lutheran Finns. All these, however, insisted upon frequent and sometimes daily attendance at the church for catechetical instruction, precisely as Orthodox Jewish parents sent their youngsters from public schools to the synagogue in the late afternoon or on Sunday.[25]

An optimistic outlook characterized family life in all these religiously oriented ethnic communities. As among the Jews of Galicia, Slovakia or sub-Carpathian Ruthenia, so among Slavs, Magyars, Italians, Greeks and Finns, the decision to migrate had been a personal one. It brought men and women to America whose family traditions as well as individual dispositions inclined them to seize the main chance with faith and hope, at whatever sacrifice of the traditions they had known or the familiar associations they had enjoyed.[26] An immigrant priest in New York City told Emily Greene Balch that Slovak brides in small mining or factory settlements of the West often matched their husbands' income by keeping boarders. As their children reached school age, however, the parents usually gave up the extra income and moved to the city to assure their youngsters good schools and kindergartens.[27] As late as 1922, Jerome Davis found that although single men still comprised the majority in Russian and Carpatho-Russian neighborhoods in Jersey City, nearly all the women kept boarders or else did outside work in order to help with the expenses of their children's education. He visited a family living in a one-room tenement whose two older youngsters were making good grades in public school, although the parents were illiterate and "the cost of food and clothes for the children, who wanted to be dressed as well as the others, . . . made saving impossible."[28] Peter Roberts believed that the occasional outbursts of criminal behavior among the offspring of immigrants stemmed from the frustration of the "desire to excel," of the "intensive longing" for better things which fathers had passed on to their sons.[29]

The notion of persistent conflict over educational goals between immigrant parents and their children during the early years of the settlement of each group in America finds scant support in the several kinds of testimony I have been able to read. The contrary, rather, seems more typical. The highly unbalanced sex ratios which at first prevailed among these groups may have provided the stress necessary to break down the tradition of patriarchal domination and to secure rapid acceptance of the more democratic and child-centered family ideals which characterized urban America. The husband had typically emigrated first. He found a job, saved the money to pay back what he had borrowed for passage, then sent home a ticket for his wife or sweetheart, or for a girl picked out for him by someone in his old village. In the process, of course, he learned the ABC's of urban life. When, at last, he met his long-awaited companion at the railway station, he often took her directly to buy a complete outfit of American clothes. Then followed an evening at the tavern and a day at the church or synagogue, where she met his friends, most of whom were single. In the following weeks, he showed her how to operate a stove, to open windows and door-latches, and to regulate the gas lights of an urban tenement; and he taught her enough English to communicate with postmen, streetcar conductors and push-cart peddlers.[30] He was unquestionably the leader, then, as "American" husbands were, and so felt little pain at the surrender of the tradition of formal mastery. His wife, for her part, accepted willingly the burden of keeping boarders, sensing at once the vast improvement in her position as compared with that of her homeland cousins, who still must toil in the fields from dawn to dusk. For she was now the indispensable manager of a successful business venture and, the competition in a predominantly bachelor society being what it was, the object of her husband's romantic love. As time passed, such parents cultivated together dreams for their children's future, and along with their priests or other communal leaders took pride in seeing the youngsters acquire the traits necessary to success in the new land. The child-centered family thus became as characteristic among immigrants from central Europe, I think, as among Anglo-Saxon Protestants.

An essential psychological element in the success of many of the children was the fact that their real world, the one where they felt both the security and identity which flow from a structured system of values and relationships, was the private one of the family, the ethnic association and the religious congregation. Here a youngster knew he belonged. In the youth auxiliary of the *bratsva* or ethnic lodge, he found his true brothers. And surrounding him were men and women who noted with pride his every success. The society outside, by contrast, was an arena, not a community. A bright young man practiced in the arts of marginality could manipulate its elements impersonally, to his own advantage, without feeling any of the native-born Protestant's compulsion to impose upon it the structure of values which in his private world he found to be relevant and true.[31]

The adjustment to urban and secular society of the son of the villager who had been born in Lika-Krava, therefore, may have been easier than that of the son of one from Waterville, Vermont. Perhaps the recent popularity among intellectuals of white, Protestant and Anglo-Saxon backgrounds of the notion that alienation and conflict were the central aspects of immigrant history represents more a projection of their own experiences than the real situation among Italians, Greeks, Slavs and Jews. I believe that the error, if it is one, has persisted because historians of secular commitment but of Jewish ancestry—sons and grandsons of immigrants whose sense of alienation is a cultural heritage centuries old—have given it such frequent and thoughtful exposition.[32]

A third important factor which quickened the impulse to education among Americans from central Europe was their half-conscious groping toward a bipolar sense of national identity, one which embraced cultural pluralism in the New World while supporting movements for national independence at home.

The use of education to enhance group status in polyglot America was apparent from the outset. Organizations such as the National Slovak Society, the Slovenian Catholic Union, the Finnish temperance societies and the Polish National Alliance insisted at their founding that one of their principal aims was to prepare their members for American citizenship.[33] Father Joseph Buh, pioneer Slovene priest on the Minnesota Iron Ranges, in an editorial he wrote in 1895 with the title "Let Us Be Proud—About What?" declared that American Slovenes must develop scholars from among their own youth if they wished to enhance their nationality's status in the land they had adopted.[34] A year later the "Polish Educational Society" of Milwaukee called a mass meeting at Kosciusko Guard Hall to protest derogatory statements before the United States Congress, which was considering legislation to restrict the immigration of illiterate persons. "Polanders as a nation are great friends of education," their memorial declared. Their activities in America included "organizing educational societies, supporting numerous newspapers and magazines, attending lectures delivered in their own language, and building and providing for schools for their children."[35] In Rochester, New York, Louis J. Vannuccini, a future high school teacher, proposed in 1905 the organization of the "Italian Civic and Educational League," which united the lay societies of several parishes in furthering the general interests of the nationality and in promoting education.[36] Meanwhile, a "Lithuanian Education Society" flourished in Brockton, Massachusetts. The group erected a building dedicated exclusively to housing the classes in English and citizenship, the travelogues, and the discussions of job opportunities in various American industries which Yankee do-gooders had initiated among them some years earlier.[37]

Whether its purposes were primarily religious or political, each immigrant brotherhood eventually organized an auxiliary society for young people. The Slavs usually called theirs *sokols* [falcons], in imitation of European pan-Slav organizations of that name. The lay leaders of the First Greek Catholic Union, for example, a mutual benefit insurance society formed in 1892 among Ruthenians and Slovaks from the northeastern counties of Old Hungary, performed many of the functions of a Bishop, including educational ones. They assigned pastors to congregations, issued ABC books, readers and catechisms, and founded before World War I both a weekly newspaper and a monthly magazine for their flourishing *sokol*. Later they issued a substantial periodical for children as well.[38]

Group interaction, whether by imitation or competition, nourished such national pride, and so spurred on the growing educational concern. Finnish Lutherans wished their children to surpass the Swedes and Danes in public school, and they often did. German Catholics built their own secondary schools and supported Catholic colleges such as St. John's University, at Collegeville, Minnesota, in direct competition with the Irish. Poles and Czechs withdrew from German congregations and lodges so as to further the advancement of their own people, as well as to preserve their native languages and traditions. Slovenes and Slovaks strove thereafter to equal the cultural accomplishments of the Czechs, and Lithuanians, who at first had often worshiped with the Poles, drew apart for a competition in which both sides scored points through educational achievement.[39] When intensely anticlerical organizations adopted socialist platforms, as happened in the Slovene National Benefit Society, the Jewish workers circles and the Finnish workers clubs, they renounced parochial in favor of public schools, but promoted after-hours an ethnic as well as a class-conscious education for their members' children.[40]

Among the Italians, as with German and Polish Roman Catholics, national consciousness was often too strong to permit them to send their children to the "Irish" parish schools. Educational traditions were so weak among immigrants from southern Italy, however, and their numerous congregations were so small, that the development of their own parish institutions was retarded. The leading Italian editor in Chicago, Oscar Durante, complained in 1893 that other nationalities were "dishonoring" his countrymen for their failure to send their children to school and "make them good American citizens." Shortly thereafter, the Chicago Board of Education received from a Committee of the United Italian Societies of Chicago a request to remove Durante from his position as truant officer because he had not been able to prevent many parents from keeping their children out of school. In a bitter response, the editor said the committee had only contributed further to the low social esteem in which the American public held his countrymen.[41] Meanwhile, he and other leaders of north Italian extraction "promoted and seconded the movement in favor of the compulsory education law" in order to force the Calabrian and Sicilian *Contadini* to send to school the swarms of children whom they had previously "allowed to go wild on the public streets."[42] Alessandro Mastrovalero, editor of another Chicago newspaper, *La Tribuna,* and a former resident at Hull House, became the Italian truant officer in 1897. For a decade thereafter, both in that office and through the columns of his newspaper, Mastrovalero championed liberalism and nationalism in Italy, and promoted public education for Italians in the United States.[43] In response, Italian priests in Chicago and elsewhere intensified their efforts to promote parochial schools. They received steady encouragement from the Italian consulate, and much help from the Scala-

brini Society, an order of missionary priests with headquarters at
Florence. By 1906, one-fourth of the 330,000 Italian children who
were attending school in Chicago were in parish institutions.[44]

• • •

During World War I, as students of central European history
well know, the nurseries of nationalism which Slovaks, Ruthenians
and South Slavs maintained in Pittsburgh and Cleveland bore fruit
at last. T. G. Masaryk, architect of the modern state of Czechoslo-
vakia, visited the United States early in 1918 and worked out agree-
ments with Slovak leaders in the newly formed Czechoslovak National Council as well as with Ruthenians in the First Greek Catholic
Union. These called for political autonomy of the two peoples in
the new republic and the use of their own languages in the schools
and in public offices. A Pittsburgh attorney, Gregory T. Zlatkovic,
returned to his native Carpathian mountains, dreaming of leading a
political and cultural awakening among the Ruthenian villagers who
had so long suffered from the educational privation which Magyar
rule had imposed. Zlatkovic's political plans came to naught, but the
event helped stir the Carpatho-Russians, as by then they were often
called, to accept the help of the Czech civil servants who during the
next two decades sought to provide them with a respectable educational system.[45] A similar event occurred in Albania. During World
War I, Orthodox Bishop Fan S. Noli, a Harvard graduate who had
become the political and spiritual leader of the Boston Albanians,
returned to his homeland determined to bring about both an educational and agricultural reform. He served for a time as prime minister
of the country, importing schoolbooks and other educational materials printed on the presses of the Boston Albanian newspaper and
intended originally for use in American parishes.[46]

The cultivation of the sense of nationality through church and
fraternal educational programs in America thus fulfilled two diver-
gent purposes, though the immigrants themselves did not find them
contradictory. America was in their eyes above all a land of many
cultural traditions. Freedom, for men who had long struggled for it
in the Austro-Hungarian and Russian empires, meant not only opportunity for personal advancement but liberty to maintain the cultural
life of their ethnic group as well—in short, cultural pluralism. Nationalism, in the sense of a political commitment to establish an independent homeland for their people, was focused almost entirely on
the Old World. Native Americans and Jews who disclaimed Zionism
have rarely understood the capacity of religion to hold in balanced
tension these two diverging goals of immigrant ethnic groups. Pa-

rochial education, like most of the other cultural and social programs which the new citizens from central and southeastern Europe carried on, was from their point of view a nursery of two patriotisms, to both of which the immigrants were fondly attached. Woodrow Wilson was one of the few who perceived this fact. He and his political successors, Al Smith, Franklin Roosevelt and John Kennedy, were able to act upon that perception in many fields, and so to bring the vast majority of new immigrants into the mainstream of American politics.

These aspirations, then—the economic, the communal and the civic—propelled immigrants from central and southern Europe toward growing concern for education, both within their ethnic associations, and in the public and parochial schools. Quite as much as any coercion from compulsory education acts or any pressure from professional Americanizers, the immigrant's own hopes for his children account for the immense success of the public school system, particularly at the secondary level, in drawing the mass of working-class children into its embrace. By their presence, and by their commitment to these several ambitions, the first generation of immigrant children prompted educators, in administrative offices as well as classrooms, to a thousand pragmatic experiments geared to the interests and the needs of their students. Self-styled patriots and scholars devoted to the special value of the liberal arts later found the results displeasing, though for different reasons of course. But the event contributed heavily to the national consensus about progressive reform in both school and society which has dominated American social ideals throughout the 20th century.

Notes

1. United States, *Thirteenth Census* (1910), *Abstract . . . with Supplement for Minnesota* (Washington, D. C., 1913), 227–28, 245.

2. United States Immigration Commission, *Reports* . . . (41 vols., Washington, D. C., 1907–10), 31: 119–20.

3. An example is United States Industrial Commission, *Reports . . . on Immigration . . . and on Education* . . . (19 vols., Washington, D. C., 1901), 15: xxi, and in Pt. II, Ch. v, esp. pp. 280–83.

4. Minnesota Education Association, *Proceedings . . . 1915* (St. Paul, Minn., 1915), 34, 35.

5. Blake McKelvey, "The Italians of Rochester: An Historical Review," *Rochester History*, 22 (October, 1960), 5.

6. "The Slavs in Anthracite Communities," *Charities*, 13 (December 3, 1904), 222.

7. Peter Roberts, *The New Immigration. A Study of the Industrial and Social Life of Southeastern Europeans in America* (New York, 1912), 100–01.

8. Conversation of the author with Mr. and Mrs. John Jurin, Chicago, May 29, 1965. Mr. Jurin placed the files of the newspaper *Znanje,* 1935–38, and manuscript copies of many plays in the Immigrant Archives, the University of Minnesota.

9. Stoyan Christowe, *This Is My Country* (New York, 1938), 161–62.

10. For examples of the literature stressing hardship, see Mike Trudics (as told to Alexander Irvine), "Life Story of a Hungarian Peon," *Independent,* 63 (September 5, 1907), 557–64; and almost any issue of such socialist publications as *Glas Svobode,* a Chicago Slovene newspaper, 1902–8 (on microfilm at the Immigrant Archives, the University of Minnesota).

11. Notes on the author's interview with seven pioneer immigrants at the Romanian Orthodox *Vatra,* Grass Lake, Mich., May 30, 1965.

12. Cf. Raymond E. Cole, "The Immigrant in Detroit (Prepared for the Detroit Board of Commerce . . . Committee for Immigrants in America, May, 1915)," in Americanization Committee of Detroit, MS Archives (Michigan Historical Collections, the University of Michigan), folder for 1914–15.

13. Boston *Evening Transcript,* August 4, 1909, quoted in Emily Greene Balch, *Our Slavic Fellow Citizens* (New York, 1911), 474.

14. Peter Roberts, "The Slavs in Anthracite Communities," *Charities,* 13 (December 3, 1904), 221–22.

15. Balch, *Slavic Fellow Citizens,* 416.

16. Peter Roberts, *Anthracite Coal Communities; A Study of the Demography, the Social, Educational and Moral Life of the Anthracite Regions* (New York, 1904), 173–75.

17. Balch, *Slavic Fellow Citizens,* 477–78.

18. Lawrence Cremin, *The Transformation of the School: The Progressive Movement in American Education, 1876–1957* (New York, 1961), 23–50, and my article, "The Progressive Movement in American Education, 1880–1900," *Harvard Educational Review,* 31 (Spring, 1961), 170–78.

19. Ernest C. Pixotto, "Impressions of Dalmatia," *Scribner's Magazine,* 40 (July, 1906), 4–5, 16.

20. I have attempted a fuller explanation of the general role of the religious congregation among migrating peoples in one article on recent and one on Colonial times: "Religious Denominations As Ethnic Communities: A Regional Case Study," *Church History,* 35 (June, 1966), 207–26; "Congregation, State, and Denomination: The Forming of the American Religious Structure," *William and Mary Quarterly,* Third Series, 25 (April, 1968), 155–76.

21. The quotations are from Balch, *Slavic Fellow Citizens*, 419, 424 and Roberts, *Anthracite Coal Communities*, 46, 197–98. See also on Tymkevich, Emily Greene Balch, "A Shepherd of Immigrants," *Charities*, 13 (December 3, 1904), 193–94; Ivan Ardan, "The Ruthenians in America," *Charities*, 13 (December 3, 1904), 250–51.

22. Mark Zborowski and Elizabeth Herzog, *Life Is with People: The Jewish Littletown of Eastern Europe* (New York, 1955).

23. See, in general, Nicholas Zernov, *Eastern Christendom: A Study of the Origin and Development of the Eastern Orthodox Church* (London, 1961), 238–75, *passim*.

24. Louis A. Kalassay, "The Educational and Religious History of the Hungarian Reformed Church in the United States" (doctoral thesis, University of Pittsburgh, 1939), 82–83.

25. Roberts, *Anthracite Coal Communities*, 156–57.

26. Florence Woolston, "The Quest of Opportunity," *Technical World*, 16 (October, 1911), 135–44; Balch, *Slavic Fellow Citizens*, 107–8 (describing the interest of Slovak bankers in lending money to emigrants), 132–37; John I. Kolehmainen, "Finnish Overseas Emigration from Arctic Norway and Russia," *Agricultural History*, 30 (October, 1945), 224–32; Salom Rizk, *Syrian Yankee* (New York, 1943), 71–72. Cf. Oszkár Jászi, *The Dissolution of the Habsburg Empire* (Chicago, 1929), 231–33, on the bite of poverty in Hungary.

27. Balch, *Slavic Fellow Citizens*, 351–52.

28. Jerome Davis, *The Russian Immigrant* (New York, 1922), 81–82.

29. Roberts, *New Immigration*, 324–25.

30. Woolston, "The Quest of Opportunity," 135–44; Vera St. Ehrlich, *Family in Transition: A Study of Three Hundred Yugoslav Villages* (Princeton, N. J., 1966), 83, 91, 138, 285.

31. Milla Z. Logan, "On My Father's Mountain," *Common Ground*, 6 (Autumn, 1945), 67–73.

32. Sanford E. Marovitz, "The Lonely New Americans of Abraham Cahan," *American Quarterly*, 20 (Summer, 1968), 197.

33. See Peter Rovnianek, "Slovaks in America," *Charities*, 13 (December 3, 1904), 204; Balch, *Slavic Fellow Citizens*, 381; John I. Kolehmainen, "Finnish Temperance Societies in Minnesota," *Minnesota History*, 22 (December, 1941), 391–403.

34. *Amerikanski Slovenec*, September 27, 1895, 2.

35. United States, Fifty-Fourth Congress. First Session, Senate Doc. No. 307, "Memorial . . . by Citizens of Polish Nationality of Milwaukee . . . ," June 6, 1896.

36. McKelvey, "The Italians of Rochester," 8.

37. Roberts, *New Immigration*, 186.

38. First Greek Catholic Union, *Golden Jubilee Book* (Munhall, Pa., 1942), *passim*.

39. Šarká D. Hrbkova, "Bohemians in Nebraska," *Bohemian Review*, 1 (July, 1917), 10–14; Victor Greene, "The Attitude of Slavic Communities to the Unionization of the Anthracite Industry Before 1903" (doctoral thesis, University of Pennsylvania, 1963), Chs. 1, 2.

40. On Finnish socialists see *Sosialisti* (Duluth, Minn., newspaper organ of Finnish section of the International Workers of the World), December 11, 1914, 3; *Aakkosia Sosialistien Lapsille*, ed. A. B. Makela (Hancock, Mich., n.d.), 39–48.

41. *L'Italia*, September 16, 1893, trans. in Chicago Foreign Language Press Survey, microfilm edition (from whence subsequent citations from Italian-American newspapers are taken), reel 30.

42. *L'Italia*, July 21, 1894.

43. *L'Italia*, March 23, November 25, 1899, and May 24, 1902.

44. *L'Italia*, October 3, 1910; Icilio Felici, *Father to the Immigrants, The Servant of God: John Baptist Scalabrini, Bishop of Piacenza* (trans. G. B. Scalabrini, New York, 1955), 163–64.

45. Mark Stolarik, "The Role of American Slovaks in the Creation of Czecho-Slovakia, 1914–1918" (master's thesis, University of Ottawa, 1967), 57–81; on the Ruthenians see contemporary observations in "Carpathian Russians and the Czechoslovaks," *Bohemian Review*, 2 (November, 1918), 70–72; and a recent summary by Walter K. Hanak, "The Subcarpathian-Ruthenian Question: 1918–1945" (pamphlet, Munhall, Pa., 1962).

46. Antonio Mangano, *Charities and the Commons*, May 2, 1908, 176–77.

17 Ethnic Conflict and Self-Help in Detroit's Jewish Ghetto, 1881–1914*

Robert Rockaway

THE FIRST JEWISH VICTIMS of Russian oppression arrived in Detroit in 1881.[1] This was the vanguard of an influx of Eastern European Jews which continued unchecked until the outbreak of World War I, and which had an enormous impact on the city and its established Jewish community. Together with the Russians, numbers of Jews began emigrating from Rumania and Galicia because of the discrimination and economic hardship prevalent in those countries.

Most of the more than two million Jews who came to the United States between 1881 and 1914 disembarked at the American ports of New York, Boston, Philadelphia, and Baltimore. The vast majority of these Eastern Europeans were penniless when they arrived in America and were forced to establish residence at their port of entry.

There were a number of reasons Eastern Europeans came to

* Reprinted with permission from Robert Rockaway, "Ethnic Conflict in an Urban Environment: the German and Russian Jew in Detroit, 1881–1914," *American Jewish Historical Quarterly*, 40 (December, 1970), 133–147, 150.

Detroit during this period. After becoming economically secure, some of these newcomers ventured further west, and Detroit was sometimes their second stop.[2] Other immigrants, experiencing economic hardships at their first place of settlement, thought Detroit offered the widest economic opportunities and chances for success.[3] The growth of the auto industry increased opportunities for employment and soon Detroit was considered to be a mecca for those immigrants who wished to improve their condition.[4] The residence in Detroit of relatives, friends or *landsleit* (fellow countrymen) who could help them settle motivated many additional Jewish immigrants to come to the city.[5] Finally, some immigrants were sent to Detroit by Jewish relief agencies located in other American cities.[6] The Jewish population of the city increased from approximately 1,000 persons in 1880 to 10,300 in 1900, and between 34,000 and 35,000 by 1914.[7]

Throughout this period the attitudes of the German Jews of the city toward their brethren from Eastern Europe were ambivalent. The influx of these aliens reminded them that they were Jews too, and as Jews had obligations toward these "oriental" newcomers; but it also heightened the feelings of insecurity these more Americanized Jews felt regarding their position in the general community.

From the time the first Eastern European Jews came to Detroit, the German Jewish community felt obliged to assist them. ". . . the Jew is the keeper of his brother and is responsible for him," said Rabbi Leo Franklin of Temple Beth El in 1900;[8] and despite obvious differences between the Orthodox and Reform Jewish communities, the city's German Jews were kept cognizant of this tradition.

. . .

The German Jews of Detroit were also very sensitive about their image in the community. Their efforts to assist the Russian Jews were motivated to a degree by the anxiety that unless these immigrants were physically and spiritually aided their strange behavioral patterns would prove embarrassing and provide an excuse for anti-Semitism. "We belong to the minority, and the minority is always judged by its lowest representatives. Our great duty, therefore, is to raise our race . . ." ". . . the Jew, being a minority, must elevate his lowest type, if the higher classes are to attain their legitimate place in the popular estimation. . . . It has become a question of self-defense. . . . To the recipients of our help, but also to ourselves, we owe it, because we are a minor element in the community. . . . When there is no lowest type even minorities are safe." "The conditions among the newcomers breed discontent—which opens the way for outlawry and anarchism. These must be alleviated as quickly as possible lest the acts of these Jews bring discredit on *all* Jews."[9]

Most members of Detroit's Reform Jewish community had little understanding of the perspective and feelings of the Eastern European Jews. Seen as coming from a country and environment considered to be backward, unenlightened and "oriental" (non-western), these poverty-stricken refugees were viewed as being a completely different and inferior species of Jew who operated on a lower plane of morality than his more Americanized counterpart. Repulsed by what they considered to be crude and unpolished manners and behavior, some German Jews contemptuously referred to these newcomers as "kikes."[10] A much more pervasive attitude among Detroit's German Jewish community was one of paternalism. The immigrants were frequently viewed as wards or children who had to be guided, guarded, and protected. Naive and lacking sophistication, the aliens were considered a malleable quantity which could be regenerated and made "socially useful." Once this was achieved it was assumed that the newcomers would be far "better, wiser, and happier."[11]

The cultural gap between the two groups of Jews was especially manifest in the attitudes of the German Jews who administered the communal relief funds and those of the Eastern European recipients of the charity. It was natural that the Eastern European Jew should apply to the Jewish charitable agencies in America the standards that were applicable in his native milieu. The principle of investigation—quite superfluous in a primary group community—was alien to his philosophy and repugnant to his sensibilities. And the record and account keeping system of the American agencies impressed him as being a feelingless, thoroughly un-Jewish principle in action.

In order to be eligible for assistance, the recipient in Detroit first had to apply to the Jewish charity, at which time someone was appointed to investigate the case. If deemed worthy, the needed help was provided.[12] The German Jews who administered the Jewish charitable associations in Detroit frequently did not understand why the Eastern European Jews exhibited resentment and aversion toward these procedures. These practices were considered efficient, modern, practical, and "scientific" ways of dispensing relief and they viewed the charities established by the Eastern Europeans as being inefficient, poorly run, and unstable. As the numbers of impoverished immigrants who applied for relief continued to grow, an increasing burden was placed on the city's Jewish charities. This pressure together with a rising sense of aversion to the attitudes and behavior of the Eastern Europeans was bound to have some effect on the conduct of those persons who administered the relief funds. The spirit of kin-like obligation that may have motivated some of the earlier benevolence was replaced by mistrust and resentment. Some officials began to view their Eastern European pensioners as nothing more than "schnorrers" while others behaved in a callous manner and over-reacted to minor infractions of rules and regulations. There were instances where a failure to comply with directions or requests led to the severing of all forms of assistance. In one extreme case serious consideration was given to a proposal for sending a woman pensioner back to Russia because her "rooms [were] poorly kept," and her "children [were] not at school."[13]

The attitude of Detroit's Eastern European Jews toward their benefactors was a combination of gratitude and resentment. For many, the assistance they received meant the difference between want and security, but their gratefulness was frequently tinged with bitterness because of the manner with which the charity was dispensed. "After all, we were Jews, too."[14] Many immigrants felt that the officers of Detroit's Jewish charitable organizations were "a hard-hearted lot, without sympathy, and without the spirit of true charity in their hearts," who humiliated them and made them feel like beggars. "Yes! You are right. The charities was [sic] organized for the purpose of bettering the conditions of the poor workingmen. I am one of those workingmen but I do not like to beg."[15]

There were a number of understanding German Jews active in charitable work who recognized that the adjustment to American life would prove difficult for the newcomers. They realized that the needs of the Eastern Europeans were different than their own, and where possible they sought to accommodate them. The Orthodox Jews' demand for kosher food was respected, and their wish to work on Sunday rather than Saturday was strongly defended. Most important were the efforts made to protect the dignity of the impoverished immigrant. Procedures were inaugurated to avoid the assembly of persons on relief at the Jewish Institute "where one may learn of the disgrace of the other," and jobs were frequently created to prevent persons from needing any relief. All of these steps were undertaken to protect the sensibilities of the Russian Jew and guard against his feeling inferior and humiliated.[16] Despite these exertions, the undercurrent of resentment, on the part of Detroit's Russian Jews toward the German Jewish directors of the city's largest Jewish charity, grew so strong that by 1914 there was a "virtual boycott of the facilities" of the United Jewish Charities.[17]

The assistance given to the Eastern Europeans took two forms:

material aid, and "raising the moral tone" of the immigrants, as it was called. This latter form of help consisted of efforts to Americanize the newcomers as quickly as possible.

To achieve this goal, the German Jews of Detroit began teaching the new arrivals and their children the rudiments of citizenship and English. This meant arranging facilities, providing classes and teachers,[18] publicizing the availability of these facilities to the immigrants and stressing the necessity of their taking advantage of these opportunities, and finally, seeking the cooperation of the city's Orthodox congregations in fostering this program.[19] The success of these efforts was attested to by the *Detroit Free Press* which marveled at how quickly the city's Jewish immigrants attained a knowledge of American customs and the English language.[20]

Recognizing the need for a durable and systematic method of aiding the refugees, the Beth El Hebrew Relief Society of Temple Beth El established a permanent committee to help the Russian immigrants. This organization found housing and jobs, and gave funds and pensions to the destitute aliens throughout the 1880's.[21] The members of this Society felt, however, that they alone could not cope with all the problems and needs of the immigrants, and two new organizations comprised of members of Temple Beth El were established—a Ladies Auxiliary Society (later known as the Hebrew Ladies' Sewing Society) in 1882, and the Self-Help Circle in 1889.[22] The Ladies' Sewing Society, organized specifically for "visiting and succoring a number of the Russian Jewish masses here in exile, and who were near their accouchement and for whom it was necessary to provide both nourishment and clothing," also supplied money and clothing to needy refugees and occasionally assisted in resettling the new arrivals. The Self-Help Circle was founded to help the refugees learn domestic sciences so that they could provide for their own and their families' needs.[23]

By 1890 the inflow of Russian Jewish refugees to Detroit had become so great that a special Russian Refugee's Committee was organized by members of Temple Beth El. Among its affiliates were representatives of the B'nai B'rith, Kesher Shel Barzel, Free Sons of Israel, and Sons of Benjamin lodges. This consolidation was an attempt to coordinate all the diverse efforts to aid the refugees; and committees on relief, employment, education, finance, and auditing were formed. This Committee was especially instrumental in succoring the first Russian Jewish agricultural colony in Michigan at Bad Axe and provided much needed material and moral support through the first decade of its existence.[24]

The continuing migration of impoverished Eastern European Jews to Detroit created a chaotic situation for the various Jewish philanthropies. By 1898 there were at least ten separate Jewish charities in the city, some run by the German Jewish and others by the Russian Jewish community. Not only was there a great amount of duplication and working at cross-purposes, but there were simply not enough funds to provide for all the needs of the immigrants. Out of the movement to end this confusion was born the United Jewish Charities (UJC) of Detroit. . . .[25]

As was typical of "progressive" charitable thought during the late nineteenth and early twentieth centuries, the stated objects of the UJC were "to make men and women out of our dependent classes . . . to build character . . . to arouse a sense of manhood and womanhood among the poor."[26] Thus, a moral goal was interwoven with the desire to provide material assistance. Another aim of the founders was ". . . to help the poor to help themselves," and to help persons become as self-supporting as possible. The concept of "self-help" was an important motivation among Detroit's German Jewish philanthropists because they wanted to alter the stereotype of the ghetto dweller as an unskilled peddler or rag picker. To this end, they provided classes in manual training and encouraged the newly arrived immigrants to acquire skills in some sort of trade. Detroit's German Jews felt that a person was less likely to be unemployed if he had a craft or skill.[27]

In 1903, Seligmann Schloss donated $5,000 to the United Jewish Charities for the construction of a building which was to be the organization's permanent home. The cornerstone was laid on April 21, 1903, and the building formally dedicated on September 27, 1903. At the dedication of the building, to be known as the Hannah Schloss Memorial, Mr. Schloss announced his intention to pay for the entire cost of the construction, $12,700. This building contained classrooms, a day nursery, model kitchen, model dining room, and a library; and the UJC and constituent societies had headquarters there. A new wing, the money for which was contributed by Bernard Ginsburg, was dedicated in December 1908. The new wing and the Schloss Building were henceforth termed the Jewish Institute.[28]

The Jewish Institute was essentially a settlement house. The city's German Jews conceived of it as being a community center and charity headquarters whose function was to provide aid and services for those Jews who lived in the "ghetto" districts of Detroit. Within the Hannah Schloss building were classes in English, dancing, boy's drill, stenography, domestic science, and manual training. There were also boys' self-governing clubs, immigrant clubs, a library, a day nursery for working mothers, fresh air (camping) activities, and social and cultural programs for residents of the area. In addition, there were relief departments, hospital and clinical services, employment and legal aid departments, and a gymnasium. The building also had bathing facilities, the only such within miles, and four to six thousand baths a year were taken.[29]

• • •

Among those who followed closely the unfolding of the Jewish tragedy in Russia was the wealthy industrialist Baron Maurice de Hirsch. He created two institutions: the Baron de Hirsch Fund of New York and the Jewish Colonization Association (ICA) of Paris, in 1890 and 1891 respectively. These two agencies aimed at regulating mass emigration from Europe overseas, selecting the proper type of migrants, transporting them to their goals, and placing them in industry and handicrafts or settling them on farms. The Baron de Hirsch Fund was concerned with the transportation of immigrants from American ports to places where they might find work and make themselves self-supporting; vocational training of immigrants and the grant of tools to enable them to earn a living; instruction in English and the duties of American citizenship; and loans to immigrants from Russia and Rumania who were agriculturists and prepared to settle within the United States. The ICA was designed to promote and regulate Jewish migration from Europe and Asia, particularly from regions in which the Jews suffered political and economic disabilities; and it aimed at setting up Jewish colonies in North and South America.

Most of those Jews who came from Eastern Europe from 1900 to 1914 settled on the Atlantic seaboard, New York City alone absorbing some 70 per cent. The congestion in New York presented a very serious problem. The Baron de Hirsch Fund advocated dispersal in order to relieve the overcrowding in New York's East Side, but the net results it achieved were insignificant. Although thousands were transferred yearly, tens of thousands came to America and crowded into the large cities along the Atlantic coast. A decisive step to solve this problem was taken with the creation, in January, 1901, of the Industrial Removal Office [= IRO]. This organization operated in the following manner: 1) orders for employment were obtained by traveling agents, who established connections with local Jewish organizations, especially outside of the big cities along the Atlantic seaboard; 2) the B'nai B'rith lodges set up local committees charged with procuring orders for employment; 3) a New York bureau was set up to handle requests from the traveling agents and the local committees, and to select suitable individuals among the immigrants. The initial success of the IRO aroused lively interest, and many communities pledged their cooperation. In 1903, the work was put on a sound basis. Three organizations, the ICA of Paris, the Jewish Agricultural and Industrial Aid Society, and the Rumanian Relief Committee, undertook to secure the necessary finances. David Bressler became the general manager of the IRO. Despite its considerable efforts, the IRO was unable to shift large numbers of the Eastern European Jewish immigrants inland. From 1901 to 1912, 59,729 people were sent out of New York City. The number of cities and towns reached was 1,474, located in every state of the union. Among the major difficulties confronting the IRO was the fact that the Eastern Europeans refused to leave the Jewish environment found in the large metropolitan areas on the East Coast. They feared they would suffer spiritual isolation by moving to unknown cities away from centers of Jewish life.

The Detroit office of the IRO was established in 1902 under the auspices of the United Jewish Charities; and some of the officers of the UJC were active in its operation. Relations between the home office in New York and Detroit were cordial up to 1913, and the work of the Detroit agents was highly respected by the national officers. By 1914, however, friction resulted from the increasing reluctance of the Detroit office to accept larger numbers of unskilled laborers, and the growing feeling among UJC officers that Detroit was doing more than other cities in accommodating the immigrants.[30]

Approximately 4,000 individuals were sent to Detroit by the IRO from 1902 to 1914. Most of these were unmarried men, or men who had left their families in New York or in Europe. Since the majority of these men decided to remain in Detroit, where the married men were later joined by their families, it would not be unreasonable to estimate that the IRO was responsible for 10,000 to 12,000 Jewish immigrants coming to the city by 1914. The majority of these immigrants were from Russia, were young, ranging in age from twenty-one to forty, and were skilled at some trade.

The IRO operation in Detroit was well organized and efficient. Before the immigrant arrived, arrangements had usually been made for his lodging, care, and employment. Once in the city the migrant could expect additional assistance in the form of loans, housing, and legal and financial advice.[31] Even while assisting the newcomers the Detroit office was haunted by the fear that they would become public charges. The officers of the local IRO entertained misgivings about the character and capabilities of their Eastern European charges, and to diminish this danger, the removals had to meet certain criteria before they were accepted.

Only men who were in good health were to be sent. The Detroit office continually refused to accept responsibility for unhealthy immigrants and sent those who had ailments or diseases back to New York.[32] The agents also stipulated that all removals sent to Detroit be skilled in a trade.[33] If they felt that the labor market was tight or economic conditions appeared to be worsening, the Detroit agents advised New York not to send any immigrants at all.[34] The Detroit IRO was equally adamant about admitting removals who had no one in the city to receive them. Unless someone in Detroit was willing to accept responsibility for the immigrant once he arrived, the Detroit office refused to accept him.[35] In all these instances the predominant concern was that the immigrants not become a burden on the city's Jewish or public charities.[36]

Differences in religious outlook, nationality, class, and manners were factors in stimulating conflict between the German and Russian Jewish residents of Detroit. The initial reaction of the German Jews in Detroit was the same as that of their brethren in other parts of the United States—exclusion. The strong sense of peoplehood felt by the city's German Jews, however, forced them to justify their position. They frequently complained, not unjustly, that there was a dearth of funds available to care for the new refugees, and that sending them to Detroit would insure their becoming a burden of the Jewish community, or worse, public charges. Another reason given was that poor economic conditions in Detroit would prove disastrous for the successful establishment of new immigrants. "Brethren, no matter how bad conditions are in Russia, they are worse in Detroit."[37] Despite these exhortations, Eastern European Jews continued to come to Detroit. Once the immigrants were in the city, the German Jews sought to avoid close association with them and to delineate the differences between themselves and the newcomers, for the edification of the general public.

The religious position of the two groups precluded any meaningful dialogue or association in this sector of communal affairs. To many Orthodox Jews from Eastern Europe, religion was a way of life and pervaded many of their daily activities. Many Orthodox Jews shunned any contact with the Temple and considered Detroit's Reform Jewish community to be "socially degenerate." American social graces such as mixed dancing and card playing were viewed by Orthodox Eastern European Jews as a sure sign of moral decay. The participation in these activities by the Americanized German Jews of the city led one newcomer to call Detroit "the modern Sodom."[38]

In turn, the city's Reform Jews generally adhered to the position that religion had a place in life, but not life in religion. They separated the religious from the secular and felt themselves to be accepting an American definition of separation of church and state.[39] They therefore perceived Orthodox behavior as slavish and incompatible with American traditions. Orthodox Judaism was seen as being backward and filled with superstition, while its practitioners were characterized as being "ghetto people," hypocrites, and ignoramuses.[40]

> Our religion is distinctively American, totally differing from the boneless Orthodoxy of the old world, which cringes before kings and princes. Judaism may here blossom forth in all its strength and beauty.[41]

The Reform community suffered a special anguish when those religious customs which they considered to be especially incongruous in an American setting were broadcast by the daily press. At these times, Reform Jews were quick to remind the general public "that the ways of these people are not our ways, nor their thoughts our thoughts."[42] The religious animosities, occasionally flaring into bitterness and acrimony, divided the two communities and prevented any meaningful cooperation along religious lines.[43]

By the 1890's it was quite clear to Jew and non-Jew alike that factors of wealth and social standing also separated the German Jews from the Eastern European immigrants. Some members of the Reform Jewish community aggravated the situation by accenting the differences.

> Were it not for the poor Russian Jews who come here there would be hardly any need of Hebrew charitable organizations in this city. Of the pensioners supported by the Jewish charitable societies 98 per cent are Russians. It is very rare that a German Israelite seeks relief from anybody. . . .[44]

Conscious of the economic and social differences between themselves and their German Jewish brethren, most of Detroit's Eastern European community were reluctant to enter into social relations with the Reform Jews, and the German Jews did little to show that they desired such a relationship. In fact, they made it known that they were opposed to mixing socially with the newcomers from Eastern Europe. Hoping to breach the mounting social divisiveness, a few of the more farsighted Reform leaders founded the Fellowship Club, in 1903, with the aim of encouraging German and Russian Jew to mix on a social level. Despite this attempt, the social antipathies increased. This trend became so obvious that the Rabbi of Temple Beth El felt obligated to protest against the blatant social discrimination being practiced by members of his congregation. The *Jewish American* even had to caution the Reform Jewish community about the growth of "anti-Semitic feelings" among its members.[45]

· · ·

A . . . lasting form of cooperation occurred in projects which enhanced the image of the German Jews, aided in Americanizing the Russian Jews, or which tended to benefit the entire community. Thus, community-wide charitable efforts, a project to found and maintain a Young Men's Hebrew Association, and the desire to establish a Detroit *kehillah*, all attracted a measure of Reform and Orthodox cooperation. These endeavors also met with success because the leaders of the various Jewish factions were farsighted enough to realize that cooperation in communal efforts to aid the poor and underprivileged far outweighed individual differences.[46]

Despite these community-wide efforts, the social, economic, and religious differences which separated Jew from Jew in late nineteenth century Detroit continued to grow in the early twentieth century. The city's major Jewish charity remained under the control of a small clique of affluent German Jews who were generally out of sympathy with the Orthodox Jews' background, culture and ideals; and the latter reacted by virtually boycotting it. The few attempts at bridging the social barriers between German and Russian Jews failed to achieve the desired results, and the majority of the city's German Jews refused to associate with the immigrants. Thus, for all intents and purposes, the Jews of Detroit formed two separate communities at the outbreak of World War I.[47]

Notes

1. *Detroit Evening News,* December 29, 1881, 2; *American Israelite,* January 20, 1882, 238.

2. Robert A. Rockaway, "The Detroit Jewish Ghetto Before World War I," *Michigan History,* 52 (Spring, 1968), 28.

3. Industrial Removal Office, *Annual Report for the Year 1905* (New York, 1905), 6; David Bressler to Miriam H. Hart, May 4, 1911; Philip Seman to Miriam H. Hart, August 11, 1912; David Bressler to

Miriam H. Hart, May 29, 1913; "Detroit File," Industrial Removal Office Papers (IRO), American Jewish Historical Society.

4. David Bressler to Miriam H. Hart, November 13, 1911; Miriam H. Hart to Philip Seman, May 28, 1913; David Bressler to Miriam H. Hart, May 29, 1913; "Detroit File," IRO; Jewish Colonization Society, *Amerikanishe Shtedt* (in Yiddish) (Petrograd, 1911), 16–20.

5. Birdie Pick to David Bressler, March 30, 1908; April 2, 1903; April 15, 1908; Blanche J. Hart to David Bressler, October 29, 1908; David Bressler to Miriam H. Hart, May 4, 1911; Miriam H. Hart to David Bressler, May 3, 1911; May 5, 1911; Philip Seman to Miriam H. Hart, January 12, 1913; August 8, 1912; February 25, 1913, "Detroit File," IRO.

6. *American Israelite,* June 15, 1899, 2; Detroit *Jewish American,* October 25, 1901, 4; Blanche J. Hart to David Bressler, January 3, 1905; Miriam H. Hart to David Bressler, January 24, 1913, "Detroit File," IRO; J. Oppenheimer, Logansport, Ind., to Mr. Siegel, Detroit, Mich., October 28, 1912, IRO.

7. Harry L. Lurie, *General Summary of Survey of Detroit Jewish Community, 1923* (New York, 1923), "History of Jewish Population," 5–8; Henry J. Meyer, "A Study of Detroit Jewry, 1935," in Sophia M. Robison, ed., *Jewish Population Stuides* (New York, 1943), 114; estimated population figures given in *The American Jewish Yearbook from 1900 to 1915.*

8. *Detroit Free Press,* June 18, 1900, 5.

9. *Detroit Free Press,* June 18, 1900, 5; *Jewish American,* November 15, 1901, 4; April 10, 1908, 4.

10. *American Israelite,* May 26, 1882, 378; December 5, 1895, 5; *Jewish American,* August 23, 1907, 4.

11. Sabbath School of Temple Beth El, Detroit, Mich. *Report of the Superintendent, Rabbi Louis Grossman, September 29, 1895* (Detroit, 1895), 7; Miriam H. Hart to David Bressler, April 10, 1912; August 21, 1913, "Detroit File," IRO; Leo M. Franklin, "Always the Jew," sermon, preached on Yom Kippur eve 1914, in Leo M. Franklin, "Sermons," vol. 1, in the Michigan Historical Collections, Ann Arbor, Mich.; *American Israelite,* December 5, 1895, 5; *Jewish American,* March 24, 1905, 4; September 9, 1910, 4.

12. See "Hebrew Ladies' Sewing Society, Minutes, 1882–87," March 15, 1884, 48–49; Ladies' Society for the Support of Hebrew Widows and Orphans, Minutes, 1888–1907," September 19, 1890, 51; "Minutes, United Jewish Charities, 1899–1908," December 4, 1899, 16–17; Anna W. Chapin, "History of the United Jewish Charities of Detroit, 1899–1949," 5, typescript, Jewish Welfare Federation, Detroit, Mich.

13. "Minutes, Ladies' Society for the Support of Hebrew Widows and Orphans," October 5, 1905, 357; October 31, 1888, 8; May 16, 1900,

231; J. L. Levin, Rabbi, to B. Ginsburg, April 10, 1904, in the files of the Jewish Welfare Federation of Detroit; and Miriam H. Hart to David Bressler, April 12, 1911; David Bressler to Miriam H. Hart, April 15, 1911; Miriam H. Hart to David Bressler, January 8, 1912, "Detroit File," IRO; *Jewish American*, December 12, 1902, 4; February 6, 1903, 4.

14. Mr. Michael Greene, private interview, August 5, 1969.

15. *Jewish American*, December 12, 1902, 4; Herman Marcus to Removal Office, April 24, 1906, IRO; David Bressler to Miriam H. Hart, June 13, 1911; Philip Seman to Miriam H. Hart, August 21, 1912, "Detroit File," IRO.

16. "Minutes, Ladies' Society for Support of Hebrew Widows and Orphans," November 15, 1896–December 15, 1898, 168–201; *First Annual Report of the United Jewish Charities of Detroit, Michigan* (Detroit, 1900), 4–5; *Jewish American*, June 17, 1904, 4; October 14, 1904, 7; November 11, 1904, 8; November 1, 1907, 4; *Reform Advocate* (1912), 13.

17. Lurie, *Survey of Detroit Jewish Community*, "Economic Status and Organization," 48.

18. Classes were held in Temple Beth El (see *American Israelite*, October 26, 1893, 2; *American Hebrew*, November 3, 1893, 26; "Temple Beth El Annual Reports, 1874–1950," Report of Louis Selling, 1895, Cong. Beth El Archives, Burton Historical Collection, Detroit Public Library), in the city's public schools (*American Hebrew*, October 15, 1900, 599; United Jewish Charities, *Twelfth Annual Report* [Detroit, 1911], 41; *Reform Advocate* [1912], 13), and in the Hannah Schloss Memorial Building (*Reform Advocate* [1912], 13).

19. *Jewish American*, April 11, 1902, 2, 6; August 21, 1908, 4; *Fourteenth Annual Report of the United Jewish Charities of Detroit, Michigan* (Detroit, 1913), 11; "Beth El School Board Minute Book, 1871–98," November 18, 1894, 190; "Temple Beth El Annual Reports, 1874–1950," Report of Louis Selling, October 5, 1894; *American Israelite*, April 18, 1895, 2.

20. *Detroit Free Press*, April 2, 1911, Pt. 5, 1.

21. *American Israelite*, December 8, 1882, 195; March 2, 1889, 3; October 29, 1891, 3; *Jewish Messenger*, January 6, 1882, 2; Detroit Association of Charities, *Eleventh Annual Report* (Detroit, 1890), 37.

22. *American Israelite*, July 21, 1882, 22; September 1, 1882, 71; Irving L. Katz, *The Beth El Story* (Detroit, 1955), 92.

23. *Jewish Messenger*, September 13, 1882, 2; "Hebrew Ladies' Sewing Society, Minutes 1882–87," August 20, 1882, 12; October 12, 1882, 20; November 22, 1882, 24; March 15, 1884, 48–49; April 20, 1885, 65–66; *Jewish American*, October 9, 1903, 3; *Detroit Free Press*, September 26, 1903, "Burton Scrapbook," 16: 188, Burton Historical Collection, Detroit Public Library.

24. *American Israelite*, October 15, 1891, 5.

25. *American Israelite,* November 23, 1899, 3; "Minutes, United Jewish Charities of Detroit, 1899–1908," November 7, 1899, 1, Jewish Welfare Federation, Detroit, Mich.

26. *Jewish American,* November 1, 1901, 4.

27. "Minutes, United Jewish Charities, 1899–1908," April 21, 1904, 45; May 5, 1904, 46; July 7, 1904, 48–49; *Jewish American,* November 3, 1905, 7; *American Israelite,* March 2, 1899, 3; *Detroit Free Press,* September 26, 1903, "Burton Scrapbook," 16: 188.

28. *Jewish American,* January 9, 1903, 4; April 24, 1903, 4; *American Israelite,* October 1, 1903, 2.

29. *Jewish American,* November 4, 1904, 5–8; November 11, 1904, 7–8; October 27, 1905, 6; *American Hebrew,* May 9, 1913, 44; Detroit Association of Charities, *Twenty-Seventh Annual Report* (Detroit, 1906), 20–21; United Jewish Charities, *Fourteenth Annual Report* (Detroit, 1913), 25.

30. *Jewish American,* September 12, 1902, 6; Blanche J. Hart to David Bressler, January 16, 1911, "Detroit File," IRO; *Tenth Annual Report of the IRO, 1910,* 34; Blanche J. Hart to David Bressler, January 25, 1912; David Bressler to Fred M. Butzel, April 20, 1914; Fred M. Butzel to David Bressler, April 23, 1914; David Bressler to Miriam H. Hart, May 13, 1914; May 14, 1914; May 23, 1911; David Bressler to Blanche J. Hart, January 13, 1913; Miriam H. Hart to David Bressler, January 24, 1913, "Detroit File," IRO.

31. Birdie Pick to David M. Bressler, January 20, 1908; Miriam H. Hart to David Bressler, July 25, 1912; Miriam H. Hart to Philip Seman, November 13, 1912; Cashier (Sara Cohen) to Miriam H. Hart, May 26, 1913; Miriam H. Hart to Philip Seman, September 13, 1913, "Detroit File," IRO.

32. Blanche J. Hart to David Bressler, August 8, 1910; Alice K. Goldsmith to David Bressler, October 31, 1910; Miriam H. Hart to David Bressler, February 14, 1911; January 31, 1912; Blanche J. Hart to David Bressler, August 23, 1912, "Detroit File," IRO.

33. Miriam H. Hart to David Bressler, May 3, 1911; November 2, 1911, "Detroit File," IRO.

34. Birdie Pick to David Bressler, January 8, 1908; Miriam H. Hart to David Bressler, April 26, 1911; May 2, 1911, "Detroit File," IRO.

35. Birdie Pick to David Bressler, January 12, 1908; February 12, 1908; March 17, 1908; Blanche J. Hart to David Bressler, November 22, 1910; Miriam H. Hart to Philip Seman, September 9, 1911; Miriam H. Hart to David Bressler, November 6, 1911; January 8, 1912; December 20, 1912; December 22, 1913; December 24, 1913; December 29, 1913; Blanche J. Hart to David Bressler, December 18, 1914, "Detroit File," IRO.

36. Miriam H. Hart to David Bressler, May 2, 1912; Philip Seman to Miriam H. Hart, May 3, 1912, "Detroit File," IRO.

37. *American Israelite,* July 14, 1882, 10; December 8, 1882, 195;

June 15, 1899, 2. *Jewish American*, October 25, 1901, 4; July 28, 1905, 7; Alice K. Goldsmith to David Bressler, October 6, 1910; Blanche J. Hart to David Bressler, February 5, 1912; Miriam H. Hart to David Bressler, May 2, 1912; Philip Seman to Miriam H. Hart, May 7, 1912; Miriam H. Hart to David Bressler, January 24, 1913, "Detroit File," IRO; "Minutes, Ladies' Society for the Support of Hebrew Widows and Orphans," February 12, 1900, 226; United Jewish Charities. *Twelfth Annual Report* (Detroit, 1911), 9; *Hamagid* (in Hebrew), February 11, 1886, 49.

38. *American Israelite*, March 9, 1899, 2; *Detroit News-Tribune*, June 22, 1902, 4; Hannah Schloss Old Timers, interviews with a number of board members, August 11, 1969; *Jewish American*, January 10, 1907, 7.

39. *Jewish American*, October 28, 1904, 4; November 6, 1908, 4.

40. *American Israelite*, March 9, 1899, 2; March 23, 1899, 2; *Jewish American*, October 7, 1904, 4; June 9, 1905, 4; May 25, 1906, 4; December 21, 1906, 4; October 28, 1908, 4; December 30, 1910, 4.

41. *Detroit Journal*, September 19, 1903, "Burton Scrapbook," 16: 43.

42. *Jewish American*, October 23, 1908, 4.

43. *American Israelite*, September 26, 1901; *Jewish American*, April 11, 1902, 4; May 2, 1902, 2–4; *Hazefirah* (in Hebrew), June 18, 1893, 547.

44. See *Detroit News-Tribune*, September 13, 1896, Pt. 2, 13; *Detroit Journal*, December 21, 1889, 2.

45. *American Israelite*, January 7, 1892, 6; May 16, 1912, 3; *Jewish American*, September 18, 1903, 4; February 3, 1905, 4; December 8, 1905, 5; March 29, 1907, 4; September 9, 1910, 4; December 9, 1910, 4; Franklin, "Always the Jew."

46. "Minutes, United Jewish Charities, 1899–1908," November 7, 1899, 3; *Reform Advocate* (1912), 6–7; *Jewish American*, February 13, 1903, 4; March 29, 1907, 7; April 11, 1902, 4; April 26, 1907, 4; "Cong. Beth El Minutes, 1908–1912," September 21, 1910; March 12, 1911; "Cong. Beth El Minutes, 1912–29," November 3, 1912.

47. *Jewish American*, October 9, 1908, 3; Lurie, *Survey of Detroit Jewish Community*, "Economic Status and Organization," p. 48.

18 Right On With the Young Lords*

José Yglesias

SUDDENLY IN EAST Harlem last summer people began throwing garbage and wrecked furniture into the middle of the streets. Traffic was stopped frequently; midtown businessmen avoiding the clog of the East River Drive found themselves stalled inside stifling cars in an area whose residents looked upon their discomfiture with little sympathy. The police and sanitation workers would clear one intersection and find that two blocks away—east or west, downtown or up—another one was blocked with the kind of debris that in middle-class sections of the city is not allowed to languish on the sidewalks. The Mayor's office got the message and a 24-hour pickup of garbage was begun. For a while El Barrio, that part of Harlem where the first Puerto Rican migrants settled, was cleaner than anyone remembered. With this "garbage riot," the Young Lords first made their presence felt in New York.

Indeed, it was then that they earned the name. Afterward, the Young Lords Organization in Chicago, a Puerto Rican street gang

* Reprinted with permission from José Yglesias, "Right On With the Young Lords," *New York Times Magazine* (June 7, 1970), 32, 84–5, 87, 90–5. © 1970 by The New York Times Company.

that by late 1968 had evolved into a political-action group, gave the El Barrio youths a license to start a New York chapter, and by last September the new affiliate had signed a lease for a storefront on Madison Avenue between 111th Street and 112th, and set up shop.

The Barrio got to know them right away. The rest of New York did not pay attention until in December they occupied a Methodist church in the area. They had negotiated for weeks with the minister for use of the church to conduct a breakfast program, health clinic and day-center. It was not a confrontation that the Lords disingenuously sought: the church was conveniently located in the heart of the Barrio, it was in use only on Sundays, there was no other space that they could afford—"and, anyway, churches are tax-exempt because they are supposed to serve the community," any Lord will tell you.

The minister was adamantly opposed. He was a Cuban exile, and he must have felt that the revolution he had fled was dogging him. The Lords held the church for 10 days and for that period turned it into a center of service for the community. The Cuban minister obtained an injunction that required the Lords to vacate the church or face contempt proceedings. There was much sympathy for the Lords—there were even indications from the Methodist hierarchy that it was not pleased with the unbending position of the local minister—but when they did not leave, the police forcibly removed them.

Felipe Luciano, the chairman of the New York Lords, came out of it with a broken arm, and trials for the group arrested are pending. During late March, when I spent two weeks visiting the Lords, there were still two cops on duty in front of the church every day; it was still open only on Sundays, despite an announcement by the minister in December that it was going to be used for community programs; and the congregation was still small, most of its members Cuban exiles and most of them outside the Barrio.

But the rush thereafter by young Puerto Ricans to join the Lords—who will also accept non-Puerto Rican blacks from the Barrio —was so great that the organization has had to close its rolls temporarily, and take steps to make certain that each applicant understands the kind of commitment that is required of him and to prevent police and F.B.I. agents from infiltrating. (How many Young Lords there are is kept secret.) Membership is not confined to the Barrio; members also come from the Puerto Rican ghettos in the South Bronx, Brooklyn and the Lower East Side. One such, a girl from Brooklyn, getting a rundown from Felipe Luciano in my presence, asked, "Are the pigs still in the church?" Felipe smiled. "They're still there but they're going to have to go away someday," he said. "When the enemy advances you get out of the way. When he withdraws you move in. I didn't say that—Glap did!"

The first "rule of discipline" of the organization reads: "You are a Young Lord 25 hours a day;" and after one sees the Lords sign in and out of their headquarters, getting their daily assignment from the Officer of the Day who sits at the front desk, the statement seems no exaggeration. Those who don't support themselves with part-time or full-time jobs are carried by the organization. Each day the O.D. doles out stipends for breakfast, lunch and dinner; and, as the organization grows, the central committee decides which Lords to put on this supported basis.

Since the church bust, as the Lords refer to the evacuation of the Methodist Church, the Tactical Police Force has several times held mock raids on Madison Avenue between 111th and 112th Street. Traffic is stopped between 110th Street and 113th and between Park and Fifth Avenue, police cars swoop into the area, and police take stances on street corners and tops of buildings. So at least the Lords describe these rehearsals. The Lords have a rule that no one in uniform is allowed to walk into their office without a warrant, and to date the police have not attempted that.

Last Maundy Thursday, one of the two or three days when I wasn't in the Barrio, the Lords responded to a report that narcotics agents were arresting two young men on 111th Street; as is usual in such cases, the agents had taken the two into the hallway of a tenement to search them. The people on the street came to the Lords because the young men, they said, were being beaten, an accusation that when made against the police no one in Harlem ever doubts. When the Lords got there the street was crowded with angry residents and the two agents were being attacked; a passing fire engine had called for police reinforcements and when they arrived the Lords gave the order "to split."

The police headed for the Lords, caught one and issued a warrant for a second three days later. The charges brought against them ranged from felonious assault to incitement to riot—and lend credence to the Lords' contention that the police are out to get them.

On Good Friday, Madison Avenue between 111th and 112th Street was full of people, all of them keeping their cool but all on the lookout. While waiting for a press conference the Lords had called, I saw an unmarked car with five plainclothesmen circling the block; during the course of an hour it came to a halt regularly across from the Lords' headquarters, and its occupants would give us all lingering looks. A bad move. One of the first newspaper people to arrive was a tough grandmotherly reporter from a Spanish-language daily, and Yoruba Guzman, the Lords' minister of information, gave her a hug and a kiss and told her what was happening. She listened to him skeptically, but a few moments later got an opportunity to see the car and the occupants who looked so out of place that far uptown on Madison Avenue. She went away, called the police precinct, and returned with the message that the plainclothesmen were there because an anonymous phone caller had said that a cop was in trouble.

"So you should figure," she concluded, "that you have an informer in the neighborhood."

David Perez, the Lords' minister of defense, a tough, bright 20-year-old, tried to tell her that the police don't need any anonymous calls to do what they were doing and, while he was at it, did his best to "politicalize" her. She was an archetypal reporter, impatient with generalizations. At first she only demurred. When David persisted, she scolded him like a loving Puerto Rican mother. *"No seas tán cabezón que te doy un cocotazo*—don't be so hard-headed or I'll rap you on the noggin!" David liked that, and for a moment politics was forgotten.

It's the Lords' politics, however, that the authorities cannot forget. The Lords are revolutionary nationalists, and the one-sentence preamble to their 13-point program reads, "The Young Lords Organization is a revolutionary political party fighting for the liberation of all oppressed people." When the phone rings in the tiny front office—beyond it are two improvised rooms only Lords may enter—the O. D. always answers, "Free Puerto Rico now!" That is the first point in their program, and there is almost no other that is not an affront to the defenders of the status quo.

. . .

Some of the Lords' other points call for "self-determination for all Latinos," "liberation of all third-world people," "community control of our institutions and land." (Their programmatic point on community control certainly extends the meaning that phrase has had in local New York City politics: "We want control of our communities by the people and programs to guarantee that all institutions serve the needs of the people. People's control of police, health services, churches, schools, housing, transportation and welfare are needed. We want an end to attacks on our land by urban removal, highway destruction, universities and corporations.")

The Lords also demand "freedom for all political prisoners"; they oppose "capitalists and alliances with traitors" and "the American military." They state: "We believe armed self-defense and armed struggle are the only ways to liberation"; and "We want a socialist society." The final salutation of the written program is, "*Hasta la victoria siempre*—always until victory," the phrase Che Guevara used in his farewell letter to Fidel Castro.

. . .

"The people on the street," a phrase the Lords often use, is their equivalent of the liberals' "common man," the Marxists' "working class." A former drug addict, a 20-year-old who had kicked the habit cold only three weeks earlier, sat with me at La Cabaña, a Puerto Rican restaurant across from their offices, explaining how he had gone to the Lords for help and how proud he felt to be a Lord now. I asked him what specific political ideas he had gained from the organization in the short time he was with them. He smiled modestly and then spoke gently so as not to seem to be criticizing me for my shortsightedness. "The people in the street know everything about oppression. We know where it's at. I was just cynical. Defeated. When we get over that . . ." And still smiling he looked over my head as if he could see that day come.

He had watched the Lords' actions in the neighborhood, admired them, hoped if he could kick the habit that they might accept him. On his own he had tried going off dope a couple of times and found that he had no friends except junkies. It was very lonely sitting in his mother's apartment enduring the disapproving presence of his stepfather. Late this February he went to the Lords' office, full of determination, and talked to Felipe Luciano. "I told him I wanted to kick and become a Lord and he rapped to me for a while and then said right on I could stay with two brothers and they would help me." He went home to pack a bag and on the way a couple of junkie friends called to him; they had their own kind of bag and he could have shot up then and there. Should he put off kicking? He went upstairs and packed and returned to the Lords.

He has never been alone since. During the worst of it there were always two Lords in the apartment to help hold him down. Next to him at the restaurant sat Jim, assigned never to leave him by himself. On Maundy Thursday, when the order came to split, they were separated for a while, and at the membership meeting the following night Yoruba publicly criticized Jim.

Without any self-consciousness the former addict spoke of the onerousness of always having to make sure Jim was with him when he stepped out of the office or the apartment, and hoped that there would soon be some trust in him. Yoruba told him that it should be some six months before this could happen, and reminded everyone of the case of one brother who backslid.

But at the restaurant the new Lord had no complaints. "I got a family now," he said, and Jim confirmed it. "We're three of us in the apartment and it's together, man."

"I see my street partner every once in a while," the new Lord said. "He passes me by and he thinks it's beautiful what I'm doing now and hopes he can do it too some-day." For two and a half years the new Lord had never worked; he and his partner got all the money they needed for their habit with holdups and muggings. "I feel a little guilty about it still, you know, 'cause sometimes we stole from brothers. That was bad. It was an escape from reality into a worse reality."

I asked him what he meant by that and he gave me an example of something that happened to him which is not an uncommon occurrence with dope addicts. He was almost killed last summer because some of the other junkies told stories to his pusher. The pusher got mad with him because they made him believe that he (the new Lord) would never pay him off. "I always had, but he comes on me in the street when I had no money. I told him and he stepped back and took out his gun. He shot four times but the gun only went click, click. So I walked toward him and he shot again and this time a bullet came out. I was almost killed. The bullet went through my groin and got to my spine and so they never took it out. It bothers me when the weather changes. A reminder."

One of the most popular cadres in the Lords is a 16-year-old they call Cake. He is light-skinned, small, lithe, with black curling hair and enormous black eyes. In the Lords' purple beret he looks like a young Che Guevara. I had spent a couple of hours outside the Barrio with him on my first day, when he acted as guard for the minister of finance at a speaking engagement at Finch College, and learned that for all his happy, light manner he was shrewd and politically fluent. "You don't know the half about Cake," Juan Gonzalez said about him a few days later. When Cake came to the Lords last fall, he was a street cat with only one interest—fighting; and one political commitment—hatred of whites.

That reputation stayed with Cake and one day in a self-criticism session Yoruba Guzman said to Cake: Sometimes it seems to me you think fighting is all the Lords is about. "You know how we criticize each other," Juan explained to me. "Well, Yoruba got an answer from Cake that almost brought tears to his eyes. No, man, Cake says, I've done so many things since I'm a Lord—I've given free breakfasts to the kids, free clothes to the people and rapped about politics with the cats in the street. I've done so many things I don't care if I die now."

Juan continued, "Cake said another thing that goes for a lot of us. If the pigs vamped on us and wiped out the organization—'cause that's all we got, that storefront—I don't know what I'd do with myself. My life would be over."

When you interview a Lord, he is more likely to talk about another than about himself. Always appreciatively. It is also a rule of discipline that a Lord may not criticize another when not in his presence. Membership meetings on Wednesday nights and political-education classes on Mondays are occasions for that. In their daily dealings with one another they are also strict, calling each other down for attitudes, opinions and actions not consistent with being a Lord. Women Lords don't let what they consider male chauvinist remarks by a brother pass. The Officer of the Day is one guardian of such behavior; he hands out disciplinary corrections for infractions of all kinds and often the O. D. is a woman. A Lord signs in late in the morning and you may find him in the back doing 25 push-ups or, if a girl, running a number of times up and down the block.

The Lords run a breakfast program at Emmaus House (a non-sectarian religious institution on 116th Street devoted to social work), which lends them its kitchen from 7 to 8:30 every school day morning; the Lords not only prepare and serve the breakfasts but also escort the children from their area of Madison Avenue to Emmaus House and then to their school.

For a few months now the Lords have devoted Saturdays to giving tuberculin tests in the Barrio. They are also prodding the health authorities by testing children for lead poisoning in the old tenements that despite new housing projects still dominate the landscape of East Harlem.

They collect clothes and distribute them free to the people of the neighborhood, and word of that has got out of the community—the only non-Puerto Rican whites you see on 111th Street these days are elderly ladies from as far away as Washington Heights bringing bundles of clothes. The Lords have also been getting ready to distribute, also free, several hundred pots, factory seconds donated by a sympathizer. They have also taken the first steps toward establishing, away from their crowded offices, what they call a Guerrilla Clinic to rehabilitate dope addicts, and also an information center on Puerto Rico and Latin America, to find locations for them they sent out searching parties for apartments and storefronts.

Every Monday the Lords tape a half hour show for WBAI, and every day of the week they are out with leaflets or with Y.L.O., the organization's newspaper (published in the Chicago headquarters), or responding to appeals for help from Barrio residents with medical and welfare difficulties. Besides the newspaper sales and donations, the Lords' only source of income is from selling buttons showing an upraised brown arm holding a rifle against a green outline of an island and above them the statement in Spanish, "I Carry Puerto Rico in My Heart."

Although some of the unmarried Lords of the same sex live together, there are no communes. "We don't relate to that," is the way Yoruba puts it, "and we don't get involved in people's private lives unless it interferes with the organization." One top leader was busted from his post in February because of complications in his love life, and it takes very little time for an observer to confirm that for a full-time Lord the organization is his whole life. It *is* one big family.

Not that the Lords encourage members to leave their homes. On the contrary, they like to organize along family lines, to get a whole family involved in one activity or another of the organization. Political-education classes are not to be interrupted, but one night when I sat with the section that met in the back of the storefront, two telephone interruptions were allowed because in each case it was a mother calling a Lord. One call was for Yoruba, the minister of information who is 19, and when he finished, he announced, "That's my mother for you. One day she throws me out of the house because of my politics and now she calls up to find out when I'm going to be on radio!" He is very proud of his father, who lost a job last fall when he swung at another worker who called his son a Commie.

Benny, a 15-year-old who every morning shows up at Emmaus House to cook and serve breakfast before he goes off to junior high school, told me his mother works in the free-clothing drive. "She's for the Lords, too," he said. When he had a moment to relax after all the children had been fed, he lit up a cigarette and the older Lord in charge called him down for it. "I got permission from my mother," Benny said, "but I don't smoke in front of her because I lose respect."

The older Lord enjoyed his response as much as I had, but he insisted, "You can't do anything in front of me that you wouldn't do in front of your mother, so put it out." Benny did.

In all this they are very Latin. If they agree with white revolutionaries on the nature of American imperialism and racism, they do not insist on the generation gap. They honor the mores and traditions of Puerto Ricans. Even about so unequalitarian a tradition as *machismo* they take an unexpected stand; they say it "must be revolutionary, not oppressive." For them, being a *macho*, a real male, means standing up to the Man, a statement they make in the context of arguing for full equality for women. "I don't care if they call us liberals and everything else," said Juan Gonzales. "We're going to be with our people. Like Felipe says, we are going to be the sons and daughters of our fathers and mothers. Except that we're political."

The Lords' ministers and cadres and active sympathizers go out together to distribute leaflets or move through the tenements with the tuberculin tests; their leaders are available to anyone. Felipe Luciano, the chairman, seemed surprised when I commented on it. "Listen, if any Puerto Rican mother on the street doesn't feel free to grab my Afro and say, *Oye, eórtate ese moño*—Hey, why don't you cut down that bush—then there's something wrong with the way I'm acting." They are not going to pick up guns until the Barrio is ready to do the same.

However thought-out this strategy is, its origins, it seems to me, spring from the belated realization by these young people that they are Puerto Ricans. I say belated, although so many are not yet out of their teens and it could be argued that this is properly the time for their ideological coming-of-age. In any case, their identification with Puerto Rico is relatively recent. Most are first-generation mainlanders and had turned away when they were children from their parents' language and ways, as happens with the children of most minority groups. Thus, some of their leaders first became politically conscious through their association with American blacks, and little by little, over the last two years came to sense their own special cultural and political identity.

Many of them are trying now to become fluent in Spanish. At a membership meeting in March the members forced Felipe Luciano to speak entirely in Spanish. "It was beautiful," he said. "The brothers and sisters helped me along, but it was tough going." David Perez, the minister of defense, can go the longest in Spanish because he came from Puerto Rico at age 10. "That's oppression, man," said Yoruba to a Latin American who had asked him what language they should converse in. "We can understand Spanish but . . ." None, however, are trying to practice a pure Castilian or a standard Latin American Spanish. They know that the Spanish of the Barrio has undergone its Norman conquest; it does not bother them that *la carpeta* comes from carpet, *frisar* from freeze. Latin Americans with whom it is a custom to bemoan the corruption of the language in Puerto Rico are going to be surprised by the linguistic liberality of these revolutionary Puerto Rican nationalists.

One of the Lords mulling over this subject pointed out to me that at a street demonstration this year commemorating a nationalist anniversary it was a younger-generation speaker frequently lapsing into American phrases who most aroused the audience. The older nationalist speakers in full command of traditional Spanish rhetoric received only respectful attention. The experience led the Lord to believe that one of the reasons that Pedro Albizu Campos, the nationalist leader responsible for the postwar uprising in Puerto Rico, failed was that he spoke an unreconstructed Spanish. "Don Pedro wasn't talking the language of the people," the Lord concluded. "In the Barrio the language is something we call Spinglish."

The Lords' attitude toward left-wing political jargon is similar. The first time I talked to Felipe Luciano he described to me the personal background of the members of the Lords' central committee. I said, "Then all of you are of working-class background?" He smiled and replied, "Working-class? No, man, we're talking about welfare people." Returning to the Barrio from taping a radio show at WBAI, Yoruba was reading a story on the Lords in Workers World, a Marxist newspaper, and quoted a phrase describing them that amused him—"young workers." He likes to tell what would happen to a Communist using the word *lumpenproletariat* with people in the Barrio—"They'd give him a lump in the face!" In an interview last summer, Cha-Cha Jiminez, head of the Young Lords in Chicago, is quoted as saying: "We're not so politically educated, from books or anything, but we're educated from the streets, from being Puerto Ricans, from being different shades of skin."

They speak, then, the language of the streets, a language in which obscenity plays its part but is seldom nasty. In a political education class they will go from a discussion about a street action (extracting from it tactical lessons) to the Declaration of Independence (drawing a parallel between the 13 colonies and the black colonies in the mother country) without any self-conscious modulation of speech. In this, as in many other things, they are like the Black Panthers, but they have not had much exposure outside the Puerto

Rican communities and consequently there has been little opportunity for respectable whites to express outrage at their language.

True, some of the articles written these days about the "rhetoric of violence" are inspired by its use by young white radicals for whom it is a conscious choice, but the Lords speak the way they do not to shock anyone but because that is simply the way they and their people speak. To "deal" is to be active in a confrontation with the police and "to lay in the cut" is to shy from it, lively variants we should all be able to appreciate, but it may take real knowledge of conditions in the Barrio and the black ghettos to understand that sometimes only a four-letter word carries sufficient descriptive force.

A few minutes after I arrived in the Lords' office the first day, a call came for a speaker at Finch College in the fashionable East Seventies. Of the top leadership only the minister of finance, Juan Ortiz, known as Fi, could be spared. He didn't want to go. "It's one hundred dollars, man!" an education lieutenant said, and Fi, who carries the burden of financing the Lords, was thus reluctantly convinced. I was to find out some days later that he is 15 years old. Cake, the 16-year-old cadre, was assigned to be his bodyguard. The three of us started that journey downtown past the housing projects, the outcroppings of Mount Sinai Hospital, across the frontier of 96th Street into solid affluence; in the weeks to come, making that trip back home alone several times, I was to feel a little, just a little, of what Fi and Cake must experience each time, that shriveling of one's sympathy for the people who do not live in the ghetto, an attrition of empathetic responses that is known as the putdown.

Finch College is quietly rich. It is in good taste. Fi took one look at the lobby and yawned widely. Two or three girls sat on the carpeted stairs chatting, occasionally breaking out in hoots of laughter; in a pitch-black room you would have known those tones came from the kind of girls they were, perfectly preserved replicas of J. D. Salinger heroines. Cake looked mischievously at Fi and said, "Beat me, rape me!" Fi remained impassive. The lady administrator who came out of the office seemed ill at ease because in approaching Fi and Cake, both of whom are black, it was not possible to pretend to inquire who they were: a traditional politeness had to be skipped over.

Fi spoke in a casual meeting room in the basement of one of the buildings, and whether they sat in the neat upright chairs or on the soft rug on the floor or stairs, the girls lounged. Ease was built into their gestures and movements and questions. Fi spoke briefly about the history of the Lords and described some of their activities, and was as true to his own tone as the girls were to theirs. He used phrases like, "When you've been ———— year after year . . . when the ———— is coming down . . ." and the teachers with their demure strings of pearls and the girls with their long, brushed chestnut or blond hair did not blink. It looked as if it were going to be a cushioned confrontation.

But there was evidence, during the question-and-answer period, that Fi managed to break through. "Why do you think that only you are oppressed?" began one girl. "We all are. We are paying the same enormous taxes."

Fi smiled for the first time. "Well, maybe the difference is you can afford it."

On the question of conditions in the Barrio, one girl commented sympathetically, "Have you considered getting out? Living in New York is absurd!" She suggested some place like New Mexico. But Fi didn't have to answer that. "For heaven's sake," called out another girl, who felt disgraced by her schoolmate. "It would be bad for them wherever they went!"

Fi had mentioned that the obligatory use of the pill by welfare mothers—he said it was being required—was part of the genocide of black people. One girl had an objection to this. "But if you're on welfare you don't want another child anyway. You can't afford it." The questions were not hostile nor the girls indifferent; it was just that in an hour the girls would be as intensely interested in something else. This did not discourage Fi; he answered every question, but the level tone of his voice showed his heart wasn't in it.

One young man visiting there asked Fi if the Lords were Marxists and opined that if revolution was what they wanted they would not succeed.

"Why?" Fi asked.

"For one thing, you don't control the money," the young man replied. "You don't have the power."

Fi gave him a serious look. "David Rockefeller's nose will bleed if you punch it. A cop will die if he's shot."

The last question was asked by a girl who had been quiet throughout. She described the present international position of the United States as a kind of historical peak. "Do you not see this as time, work and intelligence?" she ended, inferring the Lords needed all three. Fi took a deep breath and began as if ready to start all over again, "This is a sick society. I am talking about exploitation. This is a society that steals your culture and then sells it back to you . . ."

I forced Cake and Fi to take a taxi back to Harlem. Cake had criticisms of Fi's performance. He felt Fi should have spoken about the 13th point of the Lords' program when asked what kind of system they would want to replace the present one with. Socialism. Fi shook his head. "They're sick, man, they're sick," he said. "That's what I finally had to tell them." He opened the envelope they had handed him and looked at the check for one hundred dollars.

Cake said no more, but Fi continued to think about the talk. After we had crossed 96th Street going uptown, he said, "They don't know anything, they're sick," he said. "I like to talk to my people—I like to rap to blood."

19 From Arson to a Thousand Candles: A Review of Budd Schulberg's From the Ashes: Voices of Watts*

Piri Thomas

"FROM THE ASHES, voices of Watts"—what a beautiful realization of the Negro's cry for dignity, a cry not only from the mind but from the soul. This book is to me as close as the aorta through which my heart pumps blood to all parts of my body. It is a freedom cry, expressed in essays, poetry, short stories—the writings of suppressed people who having no alternative (this I know from my own experience) have been forced, yes, literally forced to react no longer as slaves but as men, with trumpets that blare out loud and clear: "Give us the same liberty that you have claimed for yourselves."

In a brief review it is virtually impossible to salute all those who are heard in this anthology of voices from the ghetto—the Watts Writers' Workshop, writers at Douglass House (named for the great Negro Frederick Douglass)—voices that white Americans would do well to heed. Since 1965 membership in the Watts workshop has grown to more than thirty, and there have been some thirty-five addi-

---

* Reprinted with permission from Piri Thomas, "From Arson to a Thousand Candles," *Saturday Review*, 50 (September 23, 1967), 78. Copyright 1967 Saturday Review, Inc.

tional applicants. Think of the contribution already made by this small group and how much greater America could be if their achievement could be multiplied by the thousands.

A short biographical sketch precedes each writer's selection in the anthology, and at times the drama in his history communicates almost as much to the reader as the composition itself. Although many themes recur, the overall screaming message is that poverty and denial of dignity warp, embitter, and destroy millions of lives. By some lovely miracle these "nitty-gritty" writers have been strong enough and articulate enough to write about not only their near defeat in life, but also their faith in ultimate victory.

The individuality of each is particularly evident in the poetry. Guadalupe de Saavedra, the son of Mexican migratory workers, concludes his poem, "The Shoe Shine":

> Someday you'll know
> But you won't like it
> Because things are going to change.
> So let me say it once more.
>
> I shore tanks yo', boss.

Johnie Scott attended Harvard College one year and then returned to Watts to write:

> You become a man when
> you stop all of those faces
> from coming out of your
> mouth and begin shaping your
> lips to sing the recognizable
> features of your own past,
>
> *and what you know is true.*

Jimmie Sherman's poem "Sammy Lee" conveys the same feeling of indignity that I as a dark-skinned Puerto Rican have known. And Blossom Powe's "Black Phoenix" captures the essence of this remarkable book:

> Of this black kind of Phoenix
> With trembling hands—
> Crying! Brooding! Trying somehow
> To create . . . a new mosaic
> From broken bricks and charcoal faces!

The young Negro poet Alvin A. Saxon, Jr., who frequently uses the pen name of "Ojenke," gives honor to the writing profession. "Some men satisfy their longing for a better world by escapism, some by defeatism, and some by coming to grips and defining these terms of existence responsible for man's conditions. The latter is my job as a writer."

The poem that brought tears to my eyes, and I mean real tears, was by Birdell Chew, a woman over fifty years old, born in Texas and one of the earliest members of the Watts Writers' Workshop. The poem, "A Black Mother's Plea," closes with these poignant words:

Please do not give my son a reason to hate, so he will destroy himself while he is still a boy. Allow him a chance to fill his heart with love for all mankind, for he was conceived by woman from man, same as the Whites.

Harry Dolan has already achieved well-earned recognition as a writer and playwright. His short story, "I Remember Papa," echoes what I, growing up in Spanish Harlem, and many ghetto youngsters heard from the lips of their parents:

"Be careful, boy, there are so many ways to fail, the pitfall sometimes seems to be the easiest way out. Beware of my future, for you must continue, you must live. You must, for in you are all the dreams of my nights, all the ambitions of my days."

At the same time, I really dug the humor blended with the stark reality of the nitty-gritty in Haley Mims's two short stories, "Passing" and "Maggie."

From the Ashes is a monumental work, not of fiction, but in its depiction of the agony and frustration and destruction that have stricken our land. Each of the eighteen writers here represented, along with the others who could not be part of *From the Ashes*, speaks from his or her own heart, yet it is one heart that gives white America another opportunity to listen to the voices of men and women who are determined even unto death that their heritage from America is not to be hunger, pain, sorrow, indignity, and the denial of their full rights as Americans.

A special tribute is due Budd Schulberg for his courage and perseverance in starting the Watts Writers' Workshop and keeping it going. I am sure it will be an inspiration to all such workshops now in existence and yet to be founded all over this country. As Schulberg so eloquently puts it in his introduction:

> His single candle may light a thousand, thousand candles. And the light and warmth of these candles may help redeem and regenerate the core of the ghetto, that decomposed inner city waiting either for a phoenix to rise from the ashes, or for bigger and more terrible fires.

Keep swinging, my brothers and sisters in Watts. Keep wailing! We're gonna reach the mountaintop yet.

Section Five

The Enduring Ghetto

The ghetto has changed its shape even as it has remained a constant in American history. Writing about Puerto Rican migration, Joseph P. Fitzpatrick ("Puerto Ricans in Perspective: The Meaning of Migration to the Mainland," *International Migration Review*, Spring, 1968) declared that it could only be understood "by perceiving it as the continuation of the experience which New York City has always had with newcomers. . . . It is precisely the presence of the stranger that has given New York many of its unique characteristics." More insidious and permanent for nonwhite residents than for their ethnic predecessors, the ghetto is a vital determinant of the future of American cities.

In a 1948 essay entitled "Harlem Is Nowhere," published in *Shadow and Act* (1964), novelist Ralph Ellison compared the ghetto to a distorted nightmare. With "its crimes, its casual violence, its crumbling buildings with littered areaways, its ill-smelling halls and vermin-invaded rooms," the ghetto, in Ellison's words, was like a mugger lurking threateningly in a passageway. The racism that created the ghetto trapped blacks in three ways, he concluded. Racism emasculated its victims with feelings of inferiority; it forced black people to devote most of their energies and imagination to overcoming discrimination rather than engaging in positive activities; and it compounded the black person's ability to cope with the revolutionary pace of change that confronted modern man in general. In spite of this, Ellison held out some possibility of hope. He wrote that

> if Harlem is the scene of the folk-Negro's death agony, it is also the setting of his transcendence. Here it is possible for talented youths to leap through the development of decades in a brief twenty years, while beside them white-haired adults crawl in the feudal darkness of their childhood. Here a former cotton picker develops the sensitive hands of a surgeon, and men whose grandparents still believe in magic prepare optimistically to become atomic scientists.

Ellison concluded that Harlem was a world "so fluid and shifting that often within the mind the real and the unreal merge, and the marvelous beckons from behind the same sordid reality that denies its existence." (*Shadow and Act*, pp. 294–302, © Random House, Inc.)

In the only selection in the concluding section, an official in Chicago's Real Estate Research Corporation, Anthony Downs, suggests alternative remedies for arresting the growth of the ghetto. Downs restricts his discussion to black ghettos, which, he writes, threaten to engulf entire cities and separate them from white suburban enclaves. He argues that the most viable alternative to allowing the United States to degenerate into separate, hostile camps is the dispersal of center-city ghetto residents into the suburbs, where there are increasing job opportunities and better schools. Downs details the mechanics of scatter-site housing, its benefit to all races, and the ultimate necessity of changing urban-suburban population trends. His recommendations are similar to those of President Lyndon B. Johnson's National Advisory Commission on Civil Disorders, to which Downs was a consultant.

Some useful studies on the enduring ghetto and the future of American cities are Milton G. Gordon, "Assimilation in America: Theory and Reality," *Daedalus* (Spring, 1961); Gilbert Osofsky,

"The Enduring Ghetto," *Journal of American History* (September, 1968); Gunnar Myrdal, *An American Dilemma,* 2 vols. (1944); Jane Jacobs, *The Death and Life of Great American Cities* (1961); Robert Weaver, *The Urban Complex: Human Values in Urban Life* (1964); Morton Grodzins, *The Metropolitan Area As a Racial Problem* (1959); Edward C. Banfield, *The Unheavenly City: The Nature and Future of Our Urban Crisis* (1970).

20 Alternative Futures for the American Ghetto*

Anthony Downs

IN THE PAST FEW YEARS, the so-called "ghetto" areas of large American cities have emerged as one of the major focal points of national and local concern. Yet there have been very few attempts to develop a comprehensive, long-run strategy for dealing with the complex forces that have created our explosive ghetto problems.

. . .

. . . Every analysis of ghettos and their problems must avoid two tempting oversimplifications. The first is conceiving of the ghetto population as a single homogeneous group, all of whose members have similar characteristics, attitudes, and desires. Thus, because many ghetto residents are unemployed or "underemployed" in low-paying, transient jobs, it is easy—but false—to think of all ghetto households as plagued by unemployment. Similarly, because some ghetto residents have carried out riots and looting, whites frequently talk as though *all* ghetto dwellers hate whites, are prone to violence, or are

* Reprinted from Anthony Downs, "Alternative Futures for the American Ghetto," by permission of *Daedalus,* Journal of the American Academy of Arts and Sciences, Boston, Mass., vol. 97, Fall 1968, *The Conscience of the City,* pp. 1331, 1334–35, 1345–53, 1357–60, 1362–72, 1376–78.

likely to behave irresponsibly. Yet all careful studies of recent riots show that only a small minority of ghetto residents participated in any way, a majority disapprove of such activity, and most would like to have more contact with whites and more integration.[1]

In reality, each racial ghetto contains a tremendous variety of persons who exhibit widely differing attitudes toward almost every question. Many are very poor, but just as many are not. Many have radical views—especially young people; many others are quite conservative—especially the older people. Many are "on welfare," but many more are steadily employed.

This diversity means that public policy concerning any given ghetto problem cannot be successful if it is aimed at or based upon the attitudes and desires of only one group of persons affected by that problem. For example, take unemployment. Programs providing job training for young people could, if expanded enough, affect a large proportion of ghetto dwellers. But the inability of many adult ghetto men to obtain and keep steady, well-paying jobs is also a critical ghetto problem.[2] Also, many women with children cannot work because no adequate day-care facilities are available. Thus, public policy concerning every ghetto problem must have many complex facets in order to work well.

A second widely prevalent oversimplification of ghetto problems is concentration of remedial action upon a single substandard condition. For instance, improving the deplorable housing conditions in many slums would not in itself eliminate most of the de-humanizing forces which operate there. In fact, no single category of programs can possibly be adequate to cope with the tangled problems that exist in ghettos. Any effective ghetto-improvement strategy must concern itself with at least jobs and employment, education, housing, health, personal safety, crime prevention, and income maintenance for dependent persons. A number of other programs could be added, but I believe these are the most critical.[3]

...

... There are five basic alternative strategies relevant to future development of ghettos. For convenience, each has been assigned a short name to be used throughout the remainder of this article. These strategies can be summarized as follows:

1. *Present Policies:* concentration, segregation, non-enrichment.
2. *Enrichment Only:* concentration, segregation, enrichment.
3. *Integrated Core:* concentration, integration (in the center only), enrichment.

4. *Segregated Dispersal:* dispersal, segregation, enrichment.
5. *Integrated Dispersal:* dispersal, integration, enrichment.

• • •

The Present-Policies Strategy

In order to carry out this strategy, we need merely do nothing more than we do now. Even existing federal programs aimed at aiding cities—such as the Model Cities Program—will continue or accelerate concentration, segregation, and non-enrichment, unless those programs are colossally expanded.

I do not wish to imply that present federal and local efforts in the anti-poverty program, the public housing program, the urban renewal program, health programs, educational programs, and many others are not of significant benefit to residents of ghettos. They are. Nevertheless, as both recent investigations and recent violence have emphasized, existing programs have succeeded neither in stemming the various adverse trends operating in ghetto areas nor in substantially eliminating the deplorable conditions there. Therefore, the strategy of continuing our present policies and our present level of effort is essentially not going to alter current conditions in ghettos.

• • •

The Enrichment-Only Strategy

• • •

The basic idea underlying the enrichment-only strategy (and part of every other strategy involving enrichment) is to develop federally financed programs that would greatly improve the education, housing, incomes, employment and job-training, and social services received by ghetto residents. This would involve vastly expanding the scale of present programs, changing the nature of many of them because they are now ineffective or would be if operated at a much larger scale, and creating incentives for a much greater participation of private capital in ghetto activities. Such incentives could include tax credits for investments made in designated ghetto areas, wage subsidies (connected with on-the-job training but lasting longer than such training so as to induce employers to hire unskilled ghetto residents), rent or ownership supplements for poor families, enabling them to rent or buy housing created by private capital, and others.[4]

It is important to realize that the enrichment-only strategy would end neither racial segregation nor the concentration of non-whites in central cities (and some older adjoining suburbs). It would help many Negroes attain middle-class status and thus make it easier for them to leave the ghetto if they wanted to. Undoubtedly many would. But, by making life in central-city ghettos more attractive without creating any strong pressures for integration or dispersal of the nonwhite population, such a policy would increase the in-migration of nonwhites into central cities. This would speed up the expansion of racially segregated areas in central cities, thereby accelerating the process of "massive transition" of whole neighborhoods from white to nonwhite occupancy.

The Integrated-Core Strategy

This strategy is similar to the enrichment-only strategy because both would attempt to upgrade the quality of life in central-city ghettos through massive federally assisted programs. The integrated-core strategy would also seek, however, to eliminate racial segregation in an ever expanding core of the city by creating a socially, economically, and racially integrated community there. This integrated core would be built up through large-scale urban renewal programs, with the land re-uses including scattered-site public housing, middle-income housing suitable for families with children, and high-quality public services—especially schools.

All of these re-uses would be based upon "managed integration" —that is, deliberate achievement of a racial balance containing a majority of whites but a significant minority of Negroes. Thus, the integrated-core strategy could be carried out only if deliberate racial discrimination aimed at avoiding *de facto* segregation becomes recognized by the Supreme Court as a legitimate tactic for public agencies. In fact, such recognition will probably be a necessity for any strategy involving a significant degree of integration in public schools, public housing, or even private residential areas. This conclusion was recently recognized by the Chicago Board of Education, its staff, and its consultants, who all recommended the use of quotas in schools located in racially changing neighborhoods to promote stable integration.[5]

The integrated-core strategy essentially represents a compromise between an ideal condition and two harsh realities. The ideal condition is development of a fully integrated society in which whites and Negroes live together harmoniously and the race of each individual is not recognized by anyone as a significant factor in any public or private decisions.

The first harsh reality is that the present desire of most whites to dominate their own environment means that integration can only be achieved through deliberate management and through the willingness of some Negroes to share schools and residences as a minority. The second harsh reality is the assumption that it will be impossible to disperse the massive Negro ghettos of major central cities fast enough to prevent many of those cities from eventually becoming predominantly, or even almost exclusively, Negro in population. The development of predominantly Negro central cities, with high proportions of low-income residents, ringed by predominantly white suburbs with much wealthier residents, might lead to a shattering polarization that would split society along both racial and spatial lines.

This strategy seeks to avoid any such polarization by building an integrated core of whites and nonwhites in central cities, including many leaders of both races in politics, business, and civic affairs. Negro leadership will properly assume the dominant position in central-city politics in many major cities after Negroes have become a majority of the municipal electorates there. By that time, integration of leadership within those cities will, it is to be hoped, have become a sufficient reality so that leaders of both races can work together in utilizing the central city's great economic assets, rather than fighting one another for control over them.

Thus, the integrated-core strategy postulates that a significant movement toward racial integration is essential to keep American society from "exploding" as a result of a combined racial-spatial confrontation of central cities vs. suburbs in many large metropolitan areas. It also postulates that development of integration in the suburbs through massive dispersal cannot occur fast enough to avoid such a confrontation. Therefore, integration must be developed on an "inside-out" basis, starting in the core of the central city, rather than in the suburbs.

The Concept of Dispersal
The two dispersal strategies concerning the future of ghettos are both based upon a single key assumption: that the problems of ghettos cannot be solved so long as millions of Negroes, particularly those with low incomes and other significant disadvantages, are required or persuaded to live together in segregated ghetto areas within our central cities. These strategies contend that large numbers of Negroes should be given strong incentives to move voluntarily from central cities into suburban areas, including those in which no Negroes presently reside.

. . .

Clearly, such dispersal would represent a radical change in

existing trends. Not only would it stop the expansion of Negro ghettos in central cities, but it would also inject a significant Negro population into many presently all-white suburban areas. It is true that policies of dispersal would not necessarily have to be at this large a scale. Dispersal aimed not at stopping ghetto growth, but merely at slowing it down somewhat could be carried out at a much lower scale. Yet even such policies would represent a marked departure from past U.S. practice.

Such a sharp break with the past would be necessary for any significant dispersal of Negroes. Merely providing the *opportunity* for Negroes to move out of ghettos would, at least in the short run, not result in many moving. Even adoption of a vigorously enforced nationwide open-occupancy law applying to *all* residences would not greatly speed up the present snail's-pace rate of dispersion. Experience in those states that have open-occupancy ordinances decisively proves this conclusion.

Hence, positive incentives for dispersion would have to be created in order to speed up the rate at which Negroes voluntarily move from central cities and settle in suburban areas. (Certainly no policy involving *involuntary* movement of either whites or Negroes should ever be considered.) Such incentives could include rent supplements, ownership supplements, special school-support bonus payments linked to the education of children moving out from ghettos, and other devices which essentially attach a subsidy to a person. Then, when the person moves, he and the community into which he goes get credit for that subsidy. This creates incentives both for him to move and for the community to accept him gladly. Both of the strategies involving dispersal would thus represent radical changes in existing practices.

Segregated vs. Integrated Dispersal

One of the fundamental purposes of any dispersal strategy is providing Negro Americans with real freedom of choice concerning housing and school accommodations. The experience of other ethnic groups indicates that Negroes would exercise that choice in suburban areas in a combination of two ways. Some individual Negro households would become scattered "randomly" in largely white residential areas. But other Negro households—probably a larger number—would voluntarily cluster together. This would create primarily Negro neighborhoods, or even primarily Negro suburban communities. Such a combination of both *scattering* and *clustering* would occur even if Negro households had absolutely no fears of hostility or antagonism from white neighbors. It is unrealistic to suppose, however, that *all* prejudice against Negro neighbors can be eliminated from presently all-white suburbs in the immediate future. As a result, even if a dispersal strategy is carried out, there will still be some external pressure against Negro newcomers. This will encourage an even higher proportion of in-coming Negro households to cluster together than would do so in the absence of all fears and antagonism. Moreover, public policies to accomplish dispersion might include deliberate creation of some moderate-sized clusters of Negro families, as in scattered-site public housing developments.

Once all-Negro clusters appear in previously all-white suburbs, there is a high probability that they will turn into "ghetto-lets" or "mini-ghettos." The same forces that produced ghettos in central cities are likely to repeat themselves in suburbs, though in a much less pathological form. Those pressures are a rapidly expanding Negro population, the "Law of Cultural Dominance" among whites, and at least some restriction of Negro choice in areas far removed from existing all-Negro neighborhoods. Therefore, once a Negro cluster becomes large enough so that Negro children dominate a local elementary school, the typical phenomenon of white withdrawal from the local residential real-estate market is likely to occur. This has already taken place regarding Jews and gentiles in many suburban areas. Thus, any dispersal strategy that does not explicitly aim at preventing segregation, too, will probably create new segregated neighborhoods in the suburbs.

This new form of *de facto* segregation will, however, have far less damaging effects upon Negroes than existing segregation concentrated in central cities. In the first place, if Negro clusters are deliberately created in almost all parts of the metropolitan area at once, whites will be unable to flee to "completely safe" suburbs without accepting impractically long commuting journeys. This will strongly reduce the white propensity to abandon an area after Negroes begin entering it. Moreover, the presence of some Negroes in all parts of suburbia will also make it far easier for individual Negro families to move into all-white neighborhoods on a scattered basis. Thus, any dispersal policy that really disperses Negroes in the suburbs will immediately create an enormous improvement in the real freedom of residential choice enjoyed by individual Negro families. This will be true even if most of those families actually choose to remain in Negro clusters.

Second, any dispersal strategy would presumably be accompanied by strongly enforced open-occupancy laws applying to all housing. At present, these laws do not lead to scattering, but they would in the climate of a dispersal strategy. Then Negro willingness to move into all-white areas would rise sharply, and white antagonism toward such move-ins would drop.

Third, *de facto* residential segregation need not lead to segregated suburban schools. In relatively small communities, such as most suburbs, it is easy to bus students to achieve stable racial ballance. Thus, the formation of clustered Negro housing would not have to cause the quality-of-education problems that now exist in central-city ghettos. True, if a given suburb became predominantly Negro, its schools might become quite segregated. In that case, school systems in adjoining suburbs might have to merge or at least work out student exchange procedures with the segregated community in order to counteract segregation. This may be difficult to accomplish (though in the climate of a dispersal strategy, it would be at least thinkable). Hence it is possible that some segregated school systems might appear in suburban areas. But Negro families would still have far more opportunities than they do now to move to areas with integrated schools.

A dispersal strategy that did not succeed in initially placing Negro households in almost all parts of the metropolitan area would be more likely to generate "ghetto-lets." Hence, if dispersal tactics call for initially concentrating on dispersion only to a few suburbs, it is quite possible that segregated dispersal would result. This implies that integrated dispersal could be attained in only two ways. Either the initial dispersal strategy must place Negroes in almost all suburban communities, or specific integration-furthering mechanisms —such as school and residential quotas—must be adopted.

...

Can Present Policies Be Sustained?

... The present-policies strategy is the one society has so far chosen. Almost all current public policies tend to further concentration, segregation, and non-enrichment, as mentioned earlier. The few supposedly anti-concentration devices adopted, such as open-occupancy laws, have proved almost totally ineffective. All we have to do to confirm our choice of this strategy is to continue existing policies. In fact, avoiding this strategy will be difficult, because doing so will require major changes in present attitudes as well as in existing resource allocations.

The "Black Power" Case for the
Enrichment-Only Strategy

The enrichment-only strategy is consistent with a current ideology that has come to be called the "Black Power" viewpoint. This viewpoint has been criticized by many, and some of its proponents have misused it to incite violence. Yet it is certainly an intellectually respectable and defensible position containing some persuasive elements.

The "Black Power" argument states that the Negro American population needs to overcome its feelings of powerlessness and lack of self-respect before it can assume its proper role in society. It can do so only by exerting power over the decisions that directly affect its own members. According to this view, a fully integrated society is not really possible until the Negro minority has developed its own internal strength. Therefore, the ideal society in which race itself is not an important factor can only come much later. It could exist only after Negroes had gained power and self-respect by remaining in concentrated areas over which they could assume political and economic control and direction. Hence this view contends that a future in which central cities become primarily Negro and suburbs almost entirely white would be an advantage rather than a disadvantage.

The "Black Power" view has several notable strong points. First, such assumption of local power would be fully consistent with the behavior of previous nationality groups, such as the Irish in New York and Boston. They, too, came up from the bottom of the social and economic ladder, where they had been insulted and discriminated against. And they did it by gaining political and economic control over the areas in which they lived.

Second, it is unquestionably true that one of the two most important factors providing Negroes with all their recent gains in legal rights and actual welfare has been their own forceful presentation of grievances and demands. (The other factor has been high-level prosperity in the economy in general.) Negro-originated marches, demonstrations, protests, and even riots have had immensely more impact in improving their actual power, income, and opportunities than all the "purely voluntary" actions of whites combined—including those of white liberals.

Third, time is on the side of the "Black Power" argument if current population growth and location trends continue. As pointed out earlier, Negroes are likely to become a majority of the electorate in many large American cities within the next fifteen years, unless radically new policies are adopted. By giving Negroes political control over these cities, this trend would provide them with a powerful bargaining position in dealing with the rest of society—a tool they now sorely lack.

Fourth, the "Black Power" viewpoint provides many key ideological supports for Negro self-development. It stresses the need for Negroes to become proud of their color and their history, more conscious of their own strengths. It also focuses their attention on the need for organizing themselves economically and politically. Hence it could provide a focal point for arousing and channeling the largely untapped self-development energies of the Negro American population. One of the greatest difficulties in improving ghettos is discovering effective ways in which the lowest-income and most deprived residents can develop their own capabilities by participating more fully in the decisions and activities that affect them. Such "learning by doing" is, in my opinion, a vital part of the process of bringing deprived people into the main stream of American society. Insofar as "Black Power" proponents could develop such mechanisms, they would immensely benefit American society.

There are, however, also significant flaws in the "Black Power" argument. First, Negroes do not in fact have much power in the U.S. Nor is it clear just how they can obtain power solely through their own efforts, particularly in the near future. "Black Power" advocates constantly talk about "taking what is rightfully theirs" because they are dissatisfied with what "whitey" is willing to turn over to them voluntarily. They also reject the condescension inherent in whites' "giving" Negroes anything, including more power. But what bargaining power can Negroes use to compel whites to yield greater control over the economic and political decisions that affect them?

There are two possible answers. First, they could organize themselves so cohesively that they would become a potent political and economic force through highly disciplined but fully legal action. Examples would be block voting and economic boycotts. So far, nearly all efforts at such internal organization have foundered on the solid rocks of apathy, lack of funds, internal dissension, and disbelief that anything could be accomplished.

Second, Negroes could launch direct action—such as demonstrations and marches—that would morally, economically, or physically threaten the white community. This approach has so far proved to be the most successful. But many Negroes believe it has not improved their situation as fast as is necessary. Hence, there is a tendency to shift the form of threat employed to more and more violent action in order to get faster and more profound results. This tendency need only influence a small minority of Negroes in order to cause a significant escalation of violence. Yet such an escalation might result in massive retaliation by the white community that would worsen the Negroes' position. What is needed is enough of a threat to cause the white community to start changing its own attitudes and allocation of resources in ways far more favorable to Negroes, but not so much of a threat as to cause withdrawal of all white cooperation and sympathy.

This conclusion points up the second flaw in the "Black Power" case: Ultimately, U.S. Negroes cannot solve their own problems in isolation, because they are fully enmeshed in a society dominated by whites. The solution to Negro problems lies as much in the white community as in the Negro community. This is especially true because whites control the economic resources needed to provide Negroes with meaningful equality of opportunity. Hence, any strategy of action by Negro leaders that totally alienates the white community is doomed to failure.

Yet "Black Power" advocates are probably correct in arguing that Negroes must develop an ideology that focuses upon self-determination and therefore has some "anti-white" tinges. They need an "enemy" against which to organize the Negro community. History proves that organization *against* a concrete opponent is far more effective than one *for* some abstract goal. They also need an abrasive ideology that threatens whites enough to open their eyes to the Negroes' plight and their own need to do something significant to improve it. The question is how they can accomplish these goals without going too far and thereby creating violent anti-white hostility among Negroes and equally violent anti-Negro sentiment among whites.

• • •

Can the Enrichment-Only Strategy Create "Separate But Equal" Societies?

The "Black Power" viewpoint essentially argues that racially separate societies in America can provide equal opportunities for all their members if Negroes are able to control their own affairs. Yet there is a great deal of evidence that this argument is false.

Certainly concerning employment, equality of opportunity for Negroes cannot possibly be attained in a segregated labor market. Negroes must be provided with full freedom and equality regarding entry into and advancement within the white-dominated enterprises that are overwhelmingly preponderant in our economy. Only in this way can they have any hope of achieving an occupational equality with whites.

In education, the evidence is far more ambiguous. The recent reports of the Office of Education and the Civil Rights Commission contend that both racial and economic integration are essential to the attainment of educational equality for Negroes.[6] Yet critics of these reports point out that many types of enrichment programs were not tested in the studies conducted by the authors. Unfortunately, most alternative approaches have not yet been tried on a scale large enough to determine whether any of them will work. Yet one conclusion does seem reasonable: Any real improvement in the quality of education in low-income, all-Negro areas will cost a great deal more money than is now being spent there, and perhaps more than is being spent per pupil anywhere.

Thus, society may face a choice between three fundamental alternatives: providing Negroes with good-quality education through massive integration in schools (which would require considerably more spending per pupil than now exists), providing Negroes with good-quality education through large-scale and extremely expensive enrichment programs, or continuing to relegate many Negroes to inferior educations that severely limit their lifetime opportunities. The third alternative is what we are now choosing. Whether or not the second choice—improving schools in all-Negro areas—will really work is not yet known. The enrichment alternative is based upon the as-yet-unproven premise that it will work.

Regarding housing, the enrichment-only strategy could undoubtedly greatly improve the quantity, variety, and environment of decent housing units available to the disadvantaged population of central cities. Nevertheless, it could not in itself provide Negroes of *any* economic level with the same freedom and range of choice as whites with equal incomes have. Clearly, in this field "separate but equal" does not mean *really* equal. Undoubtedly, all-white suburban areas provide a far greater range and variety of housing and environmental settings than can possibly be found in central cities or all-Negro suburbs alone.

Moreover, there is an acute scarcity of vacant land in many of our largest central cities. Therefore, greatly expanding the supply of decent housing for low-income families in those cities at a rapid rate requires creating many new units for them in the suburbs too.

Thus, if society adopts one of the many possible versions of the enrichment-only strategy, it may face the prospect of perpetuating two separate societies—one white and one Negro—similar to those that would develop under the present-policies strategy. If the enrichment programs carried out proved highly effective, then the gap between these two societies in income, education, housing, and other qualities of life would be nowhere near so great as under the present-policies strategy. Hence, the possibility of a potentially catastrophic "confrontation" between these two societies sometime in the next twenty years would be greatly reduced.

Nevertheless, I do not believe it will really be possible to create two separate societies that are truly equal. Therefore, even if the enrichment-only strategy proved extraordinarily successful at improving the lot of disadvantaged central-city residents of all races and colors (which is by no means a certainty), it would still leave a significant gap in opportunity and achievement between the separate white and Negro societies which would continue to emerge over the next twenty years. This gap would remain a powerful source of tension that might lead to violence, for experience proves that men seeking equality are not placated by even very great absolute progress when they perceive that a significant gap remains between themselves and others in society who are no more deserving of success than they. And that would be precisely the situation twenty years from now under the enrichment-only strategy—whether linked to "Black Power" concepts or not.

Why Dispersal Should Be Seriously Considered

As pointed out earlier, either of the two dispersal strategies would require radical changes in current trends and policies concerning the location of Negro population growth. Moreover, it is likely that massive dispersal would at present be opposed by *both* suburban whites and central-city Negroes. Many of the former would object to an influx of Negroes, and many of the latter would prefer to live together in a highly urbanized environment. Why should we even consider a strategy that is not only socially disruptive, but likely to please almost nobody?

In my opinion, there are five reasons why we should give enrichment plus dispersal serious consideration. First, future job-creation is going to be primarily in suburban areas, but the unskilled population is going to be more and more concentrated in central-city ghettos unless some dispersion occurs. Such an increasing divergence between where the workers are and where the jobs are will make it ever more difficult to create anything like full employment in decent jobs for ghetto residents. In contrast, if those residents were to move into suburban areas, they would be exposed to more knowledge of job opportunities and would have to make much shorter trips to reach them. Hence they would have a far better chance of getting decent employment.

Second, the recent U.S. Office of Education and U.S. Civil Rights Commission reports on equality of achievement in education reach a *tentative* conclusion that it is necessary to end the clustering of lower-income Negro students together in segregated schools in order to improve their education significantly.[7] As I understand these reports, they imply that the most significant factor in the quality of education of any student is the atmosphere provided by his home and by his fellow students both in and out of the classroom. When this atmosphere is dominated by members of deprived families, the quality of education is inescapably reduced—at least within the ranges of class size and pupil-teacher ratios that have been tried on a large scale. Therefore, if we are to provide effective educational opportunities for the most deprived groups in our society to improve themselves significantly, we must somehow expose them to members of other social classes in their educational experience. But there are not enough members of the Negro middle class "to go around," so to speak. Hence this means some intermingling of children from the deprived groups with those from not-so-deprived white groups, at least in schools. Because of the difficulties of bussing large numbers of students from the hearts of central cities to suburban areas, it makes sense to accomplish this objective through some residential dispersal. This consideration tends to support the integrated-dispersal strategy to some extent, even though these reports have received significant criticism, as noted above.

Third, development of an adequate housing supply for low-income and middle-income families and provision of true freedom of choice in housing for Negroes of all income levels will require out-movement of large numbers of both groups from central cities to suburbs. I do not believe that such an out-movement will occur "spontaneously" merely as a result of increasing prosperity among Negroes in central cities. Even the recently passed national open-occupancy law is unlikely to generate it. Rather, a program of positive incentives and of actual construction of new housing in suburban areas will be necessary.

Fourth, continued concentration of large numbers of Negroes under relatively impoverished conditions in ghettos may lend to unacceptably high levels of crime and violence in central cities. The outbreak of riots and disorders in mostly nonwhite areas in our central cities in the past few years is unprecedented in American history. As the report of the National Advisory Commission on Civil

Disorders indicates, continuing to concentrate masses of the non-white population in ghettos dominated by poverty and permeated with an atmosphere of deprivation and hopelessness is likely to per-petuate or intensify these disorders. This could lead to the disastrous outcome already discussed in connection with the present-policies strategy.

Fifth, a continuation of ghetto growth will, over the next three or four decades, produce a society more racially segregated than any in our history. We will have older, blighted central cities occu-pied by millions of Negroes, and newer, more modern suburban areas occupied almost solely by whites. Prospects for moving from that situation to a truly integrated society in which race is not a factor in key human decisions are not encouraging. In fact, by that time we will be faced with a fantastically more massive dispersal problem than the present one if we really want to achieve a society integrated in more than just words.

Thus, only the two enrichment-plus-dispersal strategies explic-itly seek to create a single society rather than accepting our present perpetuation of two separate societies: one white and one Negro. Dispersal would involve specific policies and programs at least start-ing us toward reversal of the profoundly divisive trend now so evi-dent in our metropolitan areas. It may seem extraordinarily difficult to begin such a reversal. But however difficult it may be now, it will be vastly more difficult in twenty years if the number of Negroes segregated in central cities is 8 million larger than it is today.

• • •

Some Tactical Mechanisms for Encouraging Dispersal

Any attempt to achieve dispersal must involve specific answers to two basic questions:

What *mechanisms* can be designed to encourage voluntary out-movement of large numbers of Negroes into the suburbs and their peaceful acceptance and welcome by whites there?

What *incentives* can be developed leading particular interest groups in society to press politically for—or at least support—employment of those mechanisms?

Let us consider the mechanisms first. Americans have always used one basic approach to get people to overcome inertia and make voluntarily some socially desirable change. It consists of providing a significant economic or other reward for persons who behave in the desired manner. That reward might be free land (as for homesteaders and railroads in the nineteenth century), or tax reductions (as for homeowners or investors in equipment in the past few years), or direct payments (as for farmers), or services and income supplements tied to participation in specific programs (as for users of the G.I. Bill in education).

In the case of dispersion, I believe the system of rewards used should probably have the following characteristics:[8]

1. Advantages should accrue both to the Negro households moving out from central cities and to the suburban households into whose communities the newcomers move.

2. Whenever possible, these advantages should consist of rewards administered under metropolitan-area-wide organizations specifically set up for such a purpose. These organizations could be quasi-private bodies able to cooperate directly with existing local governments and other geographically limited organizations. Hence they would *not* be metropolitan governments.

3. Advantages to out-moving households might include the following:

> The possibility of sending their children to top-quality schools that receive special grants because of participation in programs involving out-moving children.

> Home-buying or renting financial aids available only to out-moving families or at least with assigned proportions of their total funding available only to such families.

> Top-priority access to special programs concerning employment and on-the-job training in suburban industrial and other firms. In my opinion, such programs might be effectively built around the self-selection principle embodied in the G.I. Bill—that is, eligible persons would be given certificates enabling those firms who hire them to receive special benefits to compensate for their lower productivity or training costs. Such benefits might include tax credits or direct payments. The persons receiving these certificates would then make their own choice of employers among firms participating in such programs. This would preserve maximum individual choice among program participants.

4. Advantages to households already living in the receiving areas might include:

 Special aid to schools receiving children of out-moving Negro families. Such aid should consist of funds linked to the students in such families (as Title I funding under the Elementary and Secondary Education Act is now linked to low-income families). But the per-student amount of aid given should greatly exceed the added direct cost of teaching each out-moving student. Hence the school district concerned would have a positive incentive to accept such students because of the financial "bonuses" they would bring with them. Those bonuses could be used to upgrade the entire receiving school or cut locally borne costs therein.

 "Bonus" community financing to participating suburban local governments. Again, the payments involved should significantly exceed the added costs of servicing in-coming families, so that each participating community would be able to improve other services too.

 Giving higher priority in other federal programs to communities participating in out-movement programs than to those refusing to participate. These related programs could include sewer and water financing, planning aid, and selection as locations for federal installations.

5. Benefits available for out-moving families and receiving areas could be restricted by geographic area to avoid either paying people discriminately by race or wasting funds paying families who would move out anyway. A precedent for giving residents of certain neighborhoods special benefits already exists in the urban renewal and Model Cities programs. Thus, specific ghetto neighborhoods could be designated "origination" areas and largely white suburban communities designated "receiving" areas. Benefits would accrue only to persons moving from the former to the latter or to residents of the latter participating in reception programs.

6. If these programs were part of an integrated-dispersal strategy, they could be linked to quota systems concerning newcomers to each school or community involved. Thus, the special bonus aids would be available only up to a certain fraction of the total school enrollment or residential popu-

lation of a given receiving community. This restriction would be aimed at retaining in the schools or communities concerned the dominance of the groups originally residing there. It is to be hoped that the result would be suburban integration, rather than a shift of massive neighborhood transition from central cities to suburbs.

The above suggestions are highly tentative and exploratory. Yet I hope they at least indicate that practical mechanisms can be created that might achieve a substantial amount of peaceful Negro out-movement—*if* they were adopted in a general atmosphere of social encouragement to dispersal.

. . .

Developing Political Support for Dispersal
The concept of dispersal will remain nothing but an empty theory unless a significant number of Americans decide their best interests lie in politically supporting specific dispersal mechanisms. It is conceivable that such support might result from a massive "change of heart" among white suburbanites. They might view dispersal as a way to "purge themselves" of the kind of "white racism" which the National Advisory Commission on Civil Disorders described. I do not think this will occur. In fact, I believe recent urban violence has tended to make white suburbanites more hostile than ever to the idea of having Negroes live next door to them.

Yet, on the other hand, several specific groups in society are beginning to realize that dispersal might benefit them immensely. The motivation of persons in these groups varies widely, from pure moral guilt to sheer self-interest. But almost all significant social change in the United States has occurred because a wide variety of different types of people with diverse motives have formed a coalition to accomplish something. In my opinion, only through that kind of process will any of the basic strategies I have described (except the present-policies strategy) ever be achieved.

I believe the groups favorable to dispersal now include, or soon will include, the following:

Suburban industrialists. In many metropolitan areas, they are experiencing acute labor shortages, particularly of unskilled workers. They will soon be willing to provide open and powerful political support for the construction of low-income and moderate-income housing for Negro workers and their families in currently all-white suburbs.

Downtown-oriented retailers, bankers, restaurant operators, hotel operators, and other businessmen in our larger cities. In cities where disorders have penetrated into central business districts (such as Milwaukee and Washington), many former patrons have stopped visiting these areas altogether—especially at night. If disorders in these areas get worse, the impact upon both consumer patronage and future capital investment in big-city downtowns could be catastrophic. Those whose enterprises are "locked in" such areas will soon realize they must vigorously support both stronger law enforcement and positive programs aimed at alleviating Negro discontent. At first, these programs will consist primarily of ghetto enrichment, but these groups will soon begin to support dispersal too.

Home builders. They would benefit from any large-scale programs of housing construction. But the delays and difficulties of carrying out such programs within central cities are much greater than they are on vacant suburban land. Hence they will eventually exert at least low-level support for dispersal if it means large-scale subsidy of privately built homes.

White central-city politicians in large cities. As the populations of their cities shift toward Negro majorities, they will be more and more willing to support some dispersal policies, as well as the enrichment programs they now espouse.

Businessmen in general with plants, offices, or other facilities "locked in" large central cities. An increasing number of such persons will realize that they will emerge losers from any major "confrontation" between black-dominated central cities and white-dominated suburbs, as described earlier.

Persons of all types whose consciences influence them to accept the National Advisory Commission's conclusion that dispersal of some kind is the only way to avoid perpetuating two separate societies, with the Negro one forever denied equality.

Since these groups now constitute a small minority of Americans a great many other Americans must change their existing values considerably if large-scale dispersal is ever to occur. Yet the alternatives to such a strategy—especially the one we are now pursuing—could conceivably lead us to equally grave changes in values. For example, if there is an extremely significant increase in violence in Negro ghettos which spills over into all-white areas, the white population might react with harshly repressive measures that would significantly restrict individual freedoms, as noted above. This, too, would call for a basic shift in our values. But it is a shift which I regard with much more alarm than the one required by a dispersal strategy. In fact, in this age of rapid technological change, it is naïve to suppose that there will not in the future be significant alterations in attitudes that we presently take for granted.

. . .

At present, most public discussion and thought about racial and ghetto problems in America suffer from a failure to define or even to consider explicit possible long-range outcomes of public policy. This is one reason why such discussion seems so confused, inchoate, and frustrating. I hope that the ideas set forth in this article can serve as a nucleus for more fruitful public discussion of this crucial topic, for the future of American ghettos will determine to a large extent the future of America itself.

Notes

1. See Raymond J. Murphy and James M. Watson, *The Structure of Discontent,* mimeographed (Los Angeles: University of California at Los Angeles, June 1, 1967).

2. *Report of the National Advisory Commission on Civil Disorders* (Washington, D. C., March 1, 1968), 127.

3. Ibid., Ch. 17.

4. Ibid.

5. See their statements as quoted in the Chicago *Daily News,* August 25, 1967.

6. See James Coleman et al., *Equality of Educational Opportunity* (Washington, D. C., 1966); U. S. Civil Rights Commission, *Racial Isolation in the Public Schools* (Washington, D. C., 1967).

7. Ibid.

8. Many of the programs described in this section have been recommended by the National Advisory Commission on Civil Disorders. See Ch. 17 of its *Report.*